Christian Unity

Richard Baxter

Christian Unity

Richard Baxter

Originally published as

The True Catholic and Catholic Church Described, and Catholic Unity

LEXHAM PRESS

Contents

Part I: The True Catholic and Catholic Church Described

And the vanity of the papists, and all other schismatics, that confine the catholic church to their sect, discovered and shamed

— *The Preface*

Reader,

The tumultuary contentions and distractions about the catholic church, which have been raised by many heretical and schismatical firebrands, have moved me to publish these popular sermons, in order to the satisfaction and settlement of such minds as have been ensnared to a misunderstanding of this article of the Creed. It grieved me to hear so many Christians, that were all baptized into the catholic church, and there received the badge of Christianity and Catholicism, to be doubtfully inquiring which is the true catholic church, and many dividers confining it to their sects: and lastly, the Seekers, (instructed by the Papists) with seeming seriousness questioning whether there be any church and ministry at all? But never any sect did cause my admiration so much as the Papist! That ever so many princes and learned men should so odiously vilify the catholic church, and that under pretence of magnifying it, and appealing to it. They are not contented in their doctrine of transubstantiation, to deny sense and reason, ('Et contra rationem nemo sobrius') and in many writings to speak diminutively and dishonourably of the Holy Scriptures, (too like to infidels: 'Et contra Scripturas nemo Christianus;') but they also cut off themselves (as sectaries) from the universal church, as far as an uncharitable, odious condemning of the far greatest part of the church can do it, and call the church (even that greatest part) by the name of heretics and schismatics; ('Et contra ecclesiam nemo pacificus.') And as confidently and contentiously do they labour to cut off the main body of believers, and to appropriate the catholic church to themselves, and to make their corrupted sect to be the whole, as if the catholic church had been limited to the Roman in the Scripture, or the Creed; or as if they had the consent of Christ himself for the divorcing of his spouse. And the men that call charity the form, and soul, and life of the new creature, do seem to be insensible of the brand of their unhappiness; and that there is no greater uncharitableness to be found on this side hell, than the malicious reproaching, condemning, and unchurching of the far greatest part of the church of Christ; except that of infidels, who condemn the whole. When yon hear them glorifying of their charity, come hither and rub your eyes, and see what Popish charity is.

For the right understanding of this following discourse. I shall only desire the reader to observe, 1. That it is not a particular church, but the universal, that I am here inquiring after. 2. That I do not intend hereby to equalize the several parts of the catholic church, as to purity of doctrine, discipline, or worship. 3. That yet I would have all Christians join themselves in actual particular communion with the purest churches, if they can obtain it, without greater hurt to themselves or others, than the benefits will countervail. And that I do not intend that we must hold local communion with every congregation, which must be owned as a part of the catholic church. It is possible they may require a participation in some sin of all those that they will admit to their communion: and in such cases, (when they exclude us) we can hold but such a general distant communion, which they cannot prohibit. 4. That when I condemn the schism and uncharitableness of the Papists, or any others, I yet condemn not, but commend our exercise of charity to them, as far as I can discern it.

Lastly, be advertised, that whereas in another book, that comes out with this, (called "Catholic Unity,") I have again taken up many of the particulars wherein the godly are united; I think it need not offend the reader, as an unnecessary repetition, that being but the application of the truth which is here asserted. There I labour to convince the ungodly, that concord can be obtained by no other means, and no other terms, than those which I have here shewed the godly are all agreed in.

Reader, If indeed thou love the church of Christ, join with me in thy heartiest daily prayers, and in thy faithful diligent endeavours, for the destroying of divisions, and the repairing of decayed charity, and restoring of catholic principles and affections to all the members of the church.

—Richard Baxter
December 12, 165

— *The True Catholic, and Catholic Church Described*

For as the body is one, and hath many members, and all the members of that one body, being many, are one body: so also is Christ.

—1 Corinthians 12:12

It is a pitiful case with the poor afflicted church of Christ, that almost all the members cry out against division, and yet cause and increase it, while they speak against it. And that all cry up unity, and yet very few do any thing that is very considerable to promote it; but multitudes are destroying unity, while they commend it: and those few that would heal and close the wounds, are not able by the clearest reasons, and most importunate requests, to hold the hands of others from opposing it; and to get leave of the rest to do that work, which they will not do themselves while they extol it. You would think this were rather the description of a bedlam, than of a Christian! to set all on fire, and furiously to rail at all that would quench it, and at the same time to rail as much at incendiaries, and cry out for concord, and against division, and call other men all that is naught, for doing that which they do themselves, and will not be persuaded from! But to the injurious dishonour of Christianty itself it is thus with millions of professed Christians! thus is the church used: the sin and shame is made so public, that no charity can much excuse it, and no shift can cover it from the reproachful observation of those that are without. Alas, our flames do rise so high, that Turks, and Jews, and Heathens stand looking on them, and ask, 'What is the matter that these Christians thus irreconcileably worry one another?' Do we need any proof, when we feel the smart? When we see the blood? When we hear the noise of revilers at home, and see the scornful laughters of those abroad? When almost all Christendom is up in arms? When the churches are so many by-names, and broken into so many odious fractions; and so many volumes fly abroad, containing the reproaches and condemnations of each other? And (which is enough to break an honest heart to think or speak of) that all this hath continued so long a time! And they be not so wise as the passionate, or the drunken, that in time will come to themselves again; and that it hath continued notwithstanding the greatest means that are used for the cure: Mediation prevaileth not: pacificatory endeavours have done almost nothing: nay, sin gets advantage in point of reputation, and dividing is counted a work of zeal, and ministers themselves are the principal leaders of it; yea, and ministers of eminent parts and piety; and piety itself is pretended for this, which is the poison of piety; and pacification is become a suspected or derided work; and the peace-makers are presently suspected of some heresy; and perhaps called dividers for seeking reconcillation. It made my heart ache with grief, the other day, to read over the narrative of the endeavours of one man (Mr. John Dury), to heal the Protestant churches themselves, and to think that so much ado should be necessary to make even the leaders of the Christian flocks to be willing to cease so odious a sin, and come out of so long and doleful a misery; yea, and that all should do so little good, and get from men but a few good words, while they sit still and suffer the flames to consume the deplorable remnant: yea, such havock hath division made, and cut the church into so many pieces, that it is become one of the commonest questions among us, which of these pieces it is that is the Church; one saith, 'We are the catholic church;' and another saith, 'No, but it is we!' and a third contendeth that it is 'only they:' and thus men seem to be at a loss; and when they believe the holy catholic church, they know not what it is, which they say, they believe. Though I dare not presume to hope of much success in any attempts against this distraction, after the frustration of the far greater endeavours of multitudes that have attempted it with far greater advantage, yet I have resolved by the help of Christ to bear witness against the sin of the dividers, and leave my testimoyn on record to posterity, that if it may not excite some others to the work, yet at least it may let them know, that all were not void of desires for peace in this contentious age.

To which purpose I intend, 1. To speak of the unity and concord of the catholic church. 2. Of the unity and concord of Christians in their particular churches, and in their individual state. And the first discourse I shall ground upon this text, which from the similitude of a natural body doth assert, 1. The multiplicity of the members: and 2. The unity of the body or church of Christ, notwithstanding the multiplicity of the members. The members are here said to be many for number, and it is intimated (which after is more fully expressed) that they are divers for office, and use, and gifts. The church here spoken of is the universal church, as it is both in its visible and mystical state: It is not only a particular church that is here meant; nor is it the catholic church only as mystical, or only as visible, but as it containeth professors and believers, the body and soul, which make up the man, having both ordinances and spirit in their possession. That it is the catholic church is apparent: 1. In that it is denominated in the text from Christ himself, "So also is Christ." And the universal church is more fitly denominated from Christ as the Head, than a particular church. It is not easy to find any text of Scripture that calleth Christ the Head of a particular congregation (as we use not to call the king the head of this, or that corporation, but of the commonwealth), though he may be so called, as a head hath respect to the several members: but he is oft called the Head of the catholic church. (Ephes. 1:22; 4:15; Col. 1:18; 2:19; Ephes. 5:23.) The head of such a body is a commoner phrase than the head of the hand or foot. 2. Because it is expressly called "the body of Christ," which title is not given to any particular church, it being but part of the body, verse 27. 3. It is such a church that is here spoken of, to which was given apostles, prophets, teachers, miracles, healings, helps, governments, tongues, &c. verse 28, 8, 9, 10. But all particular churches had not all these; and it is doubtful whether Corinth had all that is here mentioned. 4. It is that church which all are baptized into, Jews and Gentiles, bond and free: but that is only into the universal church. The Spirit doth not baptize, or enter men first or directly into a particular church; no, nor the baptism of water neither always, nor primarily. The scope of the chapter, and of the like discourse of the same apostle, (Ephes. 4,) do shew that it is the catholic church that is here spoken of.

The sense of the text then lyeth in this doctrine.

Doct. The universal church being the body of Christ is but one, and all true Christians are the members of which it doth consist.

Here are two propositions; first, that the catholic church is but one. Secondly, that all Christians are members of it, even all that by the one spirit are baptized into it. These are both so plain in the text, that were not men perverse or very blind, it were superfluous to say any more to prove them. And for the former propositions, that the catholic church is but one, we are all agreed in it. And therefore I will not needlessly trouble you with answering such objections as trouble not the church, which are fetched from the difference of the Jewish church, and the Gentile church, (or strictly catholic) or between the called (the true members) and the elect uncalled; or between the church militant and triumphant.

And as for the second proposition, that the catholic church consisteth of all Christians, as its members, it is plain in this text, and many more. It is all that (heartily say "Jesus is the Lord," (verse 3,) and all that "are baptized by one Spirit into the body," (verse 13,) and all that Paul wrote to, and such as they: and yet some of them were guilty of division, or schism itself, and many errors and crimes, which Paul at large reprehendeth them for. The Galatians were members of this church; (Gal. 3:26-29;) for all their legal conceits and errors, and for all that they dealt with Paul as an enemy for telling them the truth. This church consisteth of all that have the "one Spirit, one faith, one baptism, one God and Father of all, &c." and of all that "have so learned Christ, as to put off the old man, and to be renewed in the spirit of their minds, and put on the new man, which after God is created in righteousness and true holiness." (Ephes. 4:4-6, 20-24.) This church consisteth of all that "Christ is a Saviour of," and that are "subject" unto Christ, and for "whom he gave himself, that he might sanctify and cleanse them by the washing of water by the word." (Ephes. 5:23-26.) It containeth all such as the Romans then were to whom Paul wrote, (Rom. 12:4, 5,) however differing among themselves to the censuring of each other. It containeth in it all "such as shall be saved." (Acts 2:47.) These things are beyond all just dispute.

When I say, that all Christians are members of the catholic church, I must further tell you that men are called Christians, either because they are truly and heartily the disciples of Christ; or else because they seem so to be by their profession. The first are such Christians as are justified and sanctified, and these constitute the mystical body of Christ, or the church as invisible: professors of this inward true Christianity doth constitute the church as visible to men. Professors of some pieces only of Christianity, leaving out or denying any essential part of it, are not professors of Christianity truly, and therefore are no members of the visible church: and therefore we justly exclude the Mahometans.

And whereas it is a great question, Whether heretics are members of the catholic church? The answer is easy: contend not about a word. If by a heretic you mean a man that denieth or leaves out any essential part of Christianity, he is no member of the church: but if you extend the word so far as to apply it to those that deny not, or leave not out any essential part of Christianity, then such heretics are members of the church. It is but the perverseness of men's spirits, exasperated by disputation, that makes the Papists so much oppose our distinction of the fundamentals of religion from the rest: when at other times they confess the thing in other words themselves. By the fundamentals we mean the essentials of the Christian faith, or religion: And do they think indeed that Christianity hath not its essential parts? Sure they dare not deny it, till they say, 'it hath no essence, and so is nothing, which an infidel will not say?' Or do they think that every revealed truth, which we are bound to believe, is essential to our Christianity? Sure they dare not say so, till they either think that no Christian is bound to believe any more than he doth believe, or that he is a Christian that wants an essential part of Christianity, or that Christianity is as many several things, as there be persons that have several degrees of faith or knowledge in all the world. For shame therefore, lay by this senseless cavil, and quarrel not with the light by partial zeal, lest you prove your cause thereby to be darkness. But if you perceive a difficulty (as who doth not, though it be not so great as some would make it) in discerning the essential parts from the integrals, do not therefore deny the unquestionable distinction, but join with us for a more full discovery of the difference.

In a few words, every man that doth heartily believe in God the Father, Son, and Holy Ghost, by a faith that worketh by love, is a true Christian. Or every one that taketh God for his only God, that is his Creator, Lord, Ruler, and felicity, or end, and Jesus Christ for his only Redeemer, that is, God and man; that hath fulfilled all righteousness, and given up himself to death on the cross in sacrifice for our sins, and hath purchased and promised us pardon, and grace, and everlasting life; and hath risen from the dead, ascended into heaven, where he is Lord of the church, and intercessor with the Father, whose laws we must obey, and who will come again at last to raise and judge the world, the righteous to everlasting life, and the rest to everlasting punishment: and that taketh the Holy Ghost for his Sanctifier, and believeth the Scriptures given by his inspiration, and sealed by his work, to be the certain word of God. This man is a true Christian, and a member of the catholic church; which will be manifested when he adjoineth a holy, sober and righteous life, using all known means and duties, especially baptism at first, the Lord's-supper afterward, prayer, confession, praise, meditation, and hearing the word of God, with a desire to know more, that his obedience may be full: living under Christ's ministers, and in communion of saints, denying himself, mortifying the flesh and world, living in charity and justice to man; he that doth this is a true Christian, and shall be saved, and therefore a member of the catholic church as invisible; and he that professeth all this, doth profess himself a true Christian, and if he null not that profession, is a member of the catholic church as visible. These things are plain, and in better days were thought sufficient.

He that hath all that is contained but in the ancient Creed, the Lord's-prayer and Ten Commandments, with baptism and the Lord's-supper, in his head, and heart, and life, is certainly a member of the catholic church. In a word, it is no harder to know who is a member of this church, than it is to know who is a Christian. Tell me but what Christianity is, and I will soon tell you how a Church member may be known.

But because it will tend both to the further clearing of this, and the text itself, I shall next shew you in what respects the members of the church are divers, and then in what respects they are all one, or in what they are united.

And as the text tells you, that the members are many numerically, so they are divers in their respects.

1. They are not of the same age or standing in Christ. Some are babes, and some are young men, and some are fathers, (1 John 2:12–14.) Some are novices, or late converts, and raw Christians, (1 Tim. 3:6,) and some are of longer standing, that have "borne the burden and heat of the day." (Matt. 20:12.)

2. The members are not all of the same degree of strength. Some are of small understanding, that reach little further than the principles of holy doctrine, and have need to be fed with milk, being unskilful in the word of righteousness: Yea, they have need to be taught the very principles again, not as being without a saving knowledge of them (for they are all taught of God, and these laws and principles are written in their hearts); but that they may have a clearer, more distinct and practical knowledge of them, who have but a darker, general, less effectual apprehension. (Heb. 5:11–13; 6:1.) And some being at full age, are fit for "stronger meat," that is harder of digestion. (Heb. 5:14.) Who by reason of use have their senses exercised to discern both good and evil. Some have faith and other graces but as a "grain of mustard-seed," and some are thriven to a greater strength. (Matt. 18:20; 12:31.) Some grow in grace, and are able to resist a temptation, and

do or suffer what they are called to, (2 Pet. 3:18,) being "strengthened with might by the Spirit in the inner man, according to the glorious power of grace," (Ephes. 3:17; Col. 1:11,) being "strong in faith, giving glory to God." (Rom. 4:20.) Having accordingly "strong consolation," (Heb. 6:18.) And some are "weak in the faith," apt to be offended, and their consciences to be wounded, and themselves in greater danger by temptations, whom the stronger must receive, and take heed of offending, and must support them, and bear their infirmities." (Rom. 14:1, 2. 21; 15:1; 1 Cor. 8:7. 10–12; 9:22; 1 Thess. 5:14; Acts 20:35.)

3. Moreover the members have not all the same stature or degree of gifts; nor in all things the same sort of gifts; some excel in knowledge, and some in utterance; some in one sort of knowledge, and some in another; and some are weak in all. But of this the chapter speaks so fully, that I need say no more but refer you thither.

4. The members are not altogether of the same complexion. Though all God's children be like the Father, being holy as he is holy, yet they may be known from one another. Some are naturally more mild, and some more passionate: some of colder and calmer temper, and some so hot, that they seem more zealous in all that they say or do: some of more orderly, exact apprehensions, and some of more confused: some of quick understanding, and some dull. (Heb. 5:11.)

5. The members are not all of the same degree of spiritual health. Some have much quicker and sharper appetites to the bread of life than others have: some are fain to strive with their backward hearts before they can go to secret duties, or hold on in them, and before they can get down the food of their souls: and some go with cheerfulness, and find much sweetness in all that they receive: some are of sounder understandings, and others tainted with many errors and corrupt opinions: as appears in Paul's writings to the Romans, Corinthians, Galatians, and others. Some relish only the food that is wholesome, and some have a mind of novelties, and vain janglings, and contentions, needless disputes, like stomachs that desire coals and ashes, or hurtful things. Some in their conversations maintain their integrity, and walk blamelessly, and without offence. (Luke 1:6; Phil. 2:15.) And some are overcome by temptations, and give offence to others and grievously wound themselves; as David, Lot, Noah, Peter, &c. And being overcome with creature-respects many good men walk not uprightly in some things, nor according to the truth of the Gospel, and others that are good also are led away in a party by the example of their miscarriages, and

the high estimation of their parts and persons, (Gal. 2:11-14.) Some are firm and stedfast in the truth, and some hold it with shaking, and are of looking behind them, and sometimes are declining and going backward, and have need to be called upon to return to their first love, and to strengthen the things that remain: yea, some grow to forsake many excellent truths; and neglect many weighty duties, yea, to oppose these truths and duties, and speak against them, as thinking them to be none. Hence it follows that some live in a holy peace and joy, as health is mostly accompanied with ease; when others live in continual lamentations and complaints; and some in too much stupidity and carelessness; and some with dangerous mixtures of an ungrounded, misguided, deluding peace.

6. Hence also it follows, that the members are not all of the same usefulness and serviceableness to the church and cause of Christ. Some are as pillars to support the rest, (Gal. 2:9; 1 Thess. 5:14,) and some are a trouble to others, and can scarce go any further than they are guided and supported by others. Some lay out themselves in the helping of others: and some are as the sick, that cannot help themselves, but trouble the house with their complaints and necessities, which call for great and continual attendance. Some are fit to be teachers of others, and to be pastors of the flock, and guide the Lord's people in the way of life, and give the children their meat in season, rightly dividing the word of truth. And some are still learning, and never come to much knowledge of the truth, and do no great service to God in their generations: yea, too many weary their teachers and brethren by their frowardness and unfruitfulness: and too many do abundance of wrong to the church, and Gospel, and the world by their offensive miscarriages: yea, too many prove as thorns in our sides, and by some error in their understandings, cherished and used by the too great remnant of pride, self-conceitedness, passion and carnality, are grievous afflicters of the church of Christ, and causes of dissention; one saying I am of Paul, and another I am of Apollos, and another I am of Christ, as if Christ were divided, or else appropriated to them, and Paul or Apollos had been their saviours. (1 Cor. 3:1-5.) Some live so as that the church hath much benefit by their lives, and much loss by their death: and some are such troublers of it, by their weakness and corrupt distempers, that their death is some ease to the places where they lived. And yet all these may be truly godly, and living members of the catholic church.

7. Moreover, the members are not all the same in regard of office. Some are appointed to be pastors, teachers, elders, overseers, to be stewards of

God's mysteries, and to feed the flock, taking heed to them all, as being over them in the Lord, as their rulers in spiritual things. (Ephes. 4:11; Acts 14:23; Tit. 1:5; 1 Cor. 4:1; Acts 20:17. 28; 1 Thess. 5:12; Heb. 13:7. 17.) And some are the flock, commanded to learn of them, to have them in "honour, and highly esteem them for their work sake, and to obey them." (1 Thess. 5:12; Heb. 13:17; 1 Tim. 5:17.) In this chapter saith Paul, "If the whole body were an eye, where were the hearing? If the whole where hearing, where were the smelling? Are all apostles? Are all prophets? Are all teachers?" (1 Cor. 12:17. 29.) As there are diversity of gifts, so also of offices: for God hath designed men to use the gifts they have in such order and manner as may edify the church. All the body is not the bonds, or nerves, and ligaments, by which the parts are joined together. (Eph. 4:16.) All are not "pastors and teachers, given for perfecting of the saints, the work of the ministry, and edifying of the body of Christ." (Ephes. 4:11–13.)

8. Consequently the members have not all the same employment: magistrates must rule by force, and ministers must guide or rule by the light and force of the word of God: all must not administer sacraments: all must not be the overseers of the flock. Masters and parents have their own work, and servants and children have theirs. Nay, difference of understanding may cause a great deal of difference among ministers and people in the manner of God's worship, when yet all worship him acceptably and in sincerity. Some may be too much ceremonious in meats, and drinks, and observation of days. (Rom. 14 and 15.) In gestures, vestures, and other circumstances, sinfully laying much more in these than God would have them: and others may be as rigorous against them: and others more temperate between both. Some may pray and praise God in forms composed by themselves or others, or read them in a book: and some may abhor all this as unlawful; and some may be so wise as to know that it is a matter that God hath left in itself indifferent, and is to be determined according to the suitableness of times and persons. And thus many modal circumstantial differences there may be in the true worshipping of God, by the members of this one universal church.

9. And from what is said already, it follows, that all the members of the church are not all equally to be honoured and loved. Even among the elders, there are some that are worthy of double honour, and some of more than they (1 Tim. 5:17.) Some are of high and excellent gifts and graces; and as more of God doth shine forth in them, so a greater love and honour is due to them. Some are so eminently self-denying, and of public spirits, and

wholly carried to the service of God, and the good of the church, that few others are "like-minded, naturally caring for the people's state, but all do too much seek their own, and too little the things that are Jesus Christ's." (Phil. 2:20, 21.) The body hath some parts that are less honourable, and less comely:" (1 Cor. 12:22-24:) though these also have their honour and comeliness: those that most honour God shall be most honoured; (1 Sam. 2:30; Job 12:26;) and they that will be the "servants of all, shall be the greatest." Luke 22:26; Matt. 23:11.)

10. To conclude, from all this imparity it will follow, that the members will not have an equal degree of glory, as not having an equal preparation and capacity. All are not in Abraham's bosom, as Lazarus was. "To sit on Christ's right hand and left in his kingdom will not be the lot of all, but of those to whom the Father will give it." (Matt. 20:23.) All are not to sit on thrones, in full equality with the apostles. (Luke 20:30.) There are of the first for time of coming in, that shall be last of dignity, and of the last that shall be first. (Matt. 19:30; 20:16.) All shall not be rulers of five cities, but only they that have double five talents. (Matt. 25.) And thus I have shewed you the disparity of the members, wherein they differ.

Secondly. I am now to shew you the unity of them, and of the body which they constitute. The members of the catholic church are united in all these following respects:

1. They have all but one God, the fountain of their being and felicity, and are all related to him as children to one Father, reconciled to them, and adopting them in Jesus Christ. (John 1:12.) "Ye are all the children of God by faith in Christ Jesus." (Gal. 3:26.) "There is one God and Father of all," &c. (Gal. 4:5, 6; Eph. 4:6.)

2. The members of the church have all one Head, the Redeemer, Saviour, Mediator, Jesus Christ. (Ephes. 4:5.) As the commonwealth is denominated from the unity of the sovereign power that heads it; so the church is hence principally denominated one from Christ, who is the Head, the Sovereign, and the Centre of it. And therefore it is called frequently his body, and he the Head of it. (Ephes. 4:15; 1:22; Col. 1:18; 2:19; Ephes. 5:23; Col. 3:15; Rom. 12:4, 5; 1 Cor. 10:17; Ephes. 2:16.) He is the foundation, and the church is the building that is erected upon him, "and other foundation can no man lay." (1 Cor. 3:11, 12.) "From this head the whole body fitly joined together, and compacted by that which every joint supplieth, according to the effectual working of the measure of every part, maketh increase of the body to the edifying of itself in love." (Ephes. 4:16.) All therefore are members of the

catholic church that are members of Christ. He is "the chief corner-stone
that is laid in Zion, elect and precious, and he that believeth on him shall
not be confounded; to whom coming as to a living stone, we also as lively
stones are built up a spiritual house." (1 Pet. 2:4–6.) As this "One died for
all," (2 Cor. 5:14,) because all were dead, so by the righteousness of this One,
the free gift cometh on all to justification of life, and by the obedience of
this One shall many be made righteous." (Rom. 5:18, 19.) "And by one Jesus
Christ we shall reign in life." (Rom. 5:17.) "In him the church of Jews and
Gentiles are made one." (Ephes. 2:14, 15.) "To this one Husband we are all
espoused." (2 Cor. 11:2.) So that we "are all one in Christ Jesus." (Gal. 3:28.)
And "to us there is but one God the Father, of whom are all things, and we
in him; and one Lord Jesus Christ, by whom are all things, and we in him."
(1 Cor. 8:6.)

3. The whole catholic church (strictly taken, as comprehending only the
living members) have only one Holy Ghost dwelling in them, illuminat-
ing, sanctifying and guiding them, and are animated as it were by this one
Spirit. "By this one Spirit we are all baptized into one body, and have been
all made to drink into one Spirit." (1 Cor. 12:13.) And "whoever hath not this
Spirit of Christ, the same is none of his." (Rom. 8:9.) "By this one Spirit we
have all access to the Father." (Ephes. 2:18.) And through this Spirit we are
"one habitation of God." (Ephes. 2:22.) And therefore "he that is joined to
the Lord is called one Spirit." (1 Cor. 6:17.) And it is said of Christ, so may it
be of the Spirit in a sort, "He that sanctifieth, and they that are sanctified
are all one." (Heb. 2:11.) This is the scope of the chapter that my text is in.

4. The church is one as to their principal, ultimate end. The same God
is their end who is their beginning. The same eternal glory with him, is
purchased and prepared for them, and intended by them through their
Christian course. The wicked have a lower end, even flesh and self: but all
the members of Christ are united in the true intention of this end. They are
all the "heirs of life, and partakers of the inheritance of the saints in light,
and have all lain up their treasure in heaven." (Matt. 6:20, 21; Col. 1:12; Gal.
4:7; Rom. 8:17; 1 Pet. 3:7; Tit. 3:7; Gal. 3:29; Heb. 1:14; Ephes. 3:6.) "All that are
risen with Christ, do seek the things that are above," (Col. 3:1,) "and have
their conversation with him in heaven." (Phil. 3:20, 21.)

5. All the members of the catholic Gospel-church have one Gospel to
teach them the knowledge of Christ. (Gal. 1:10, 11.) And one word of promise to be the charter of their inheritance, (1 Tim. 4:8; Heb. 9:15; Gal. 3:22.
29,) and one holy doctrine to be the instrument of their regeneration, and

the "seed of God abiding in them." (1 Pet. 1:23. 25; Luke 8:11.) It is but one that God hath appointed for them; and it is one in the substance that is the instrument of their change.

6. It is one kind of faith, that by this one holy doctrine is wrought upon their souls. Though the degrees be various, yet all believe the same essential points of faith, with a belief of the same nature. There is "one faith;" (Ephes. 4:5;) and in all these essentials the church is of "one mind," (John 17:21; Acts 4:32; 1 Pet. 3:8; 1 Cor. 15:2-4,) though in lesser things there be exceeding great diversity.

7. There is one new disposition, or holy nature wrought by the Spirit of God in every member of the catholic church. This is called their holiness, and the new creature, and the divine nature, and the image of God. (1 Pet. 1:16; 2 Pet. 1:4; John 3:6.) "That which is born of the Spirit, is spirit." (Col. 3:10; 2 Cor. 5:17.)

8. The affections which are predominant in all the members of the church, have one and the same object. Sin is the chiefest thing that all of them hate, and the displeasure of God the chief thing they fear, and God in Christ is the prime object of their love; and they have all the same object of their desires and hopes, even the favour of God, and everlasting life: and they all chiefly rejoice in the same hopes and felicity; as were easy to manifest and prove in the particulars, as to all the essentials of Christianity that are the objects of the will. (Phil. 1:27; 2:3; Ephes. 4:4; Matt. 22:37, 38; Rom. 8:28; 1 Cor. 2:9.) And thus they are all of one heart and soul, as uniting in the same objects.

9. They have also one rule or law to live by, which is the law of faith, of grace, of liberty, of Christ. (Rom. 3:27; 8:2; James 1:25; Gal. 6:2.) And as one law is appointed for them all, so one law in the points of absolute necessity is received by them all; for "it is written in their hearts," and put into "their inward parts." (Jer. 31:32; Heb. 8:10. 10:16.) Though in the other points of the law of Christ there be much diversity in their reception and obedience. All of them are sincerely obedient to what they know, and all of them know that which God hath made of necessity to life.

10. Every member of the church is devoted to God in one and the same covenant. As the covenant on Christ's part is one to them all; so is it one on their part. They all renounce the world, the flesh and the devil, and give up themselves to God the Father, Son, and Holy Ghost. And this being used by God's appointment, to be solemnly done in baptism, therefore baptism is called the principle or foundation. (Heb. 6:1.) And there is said to be one

baptism, (Ephes. 4:5,) and baptism is said to save us; "Not the putting away the filth of the flesh, (that is, not the outward washing,) but the answer of a good conscience to God," (1 Pet. 3:21,) that is, the sincere, internal covenant of the heart, and delivering up ourselves to Christ. So also the fathers, when they (usually) speak of the necessity of baptism, they mean principally our becoming Christians, and entering into the holy covenant, which was done by baptism. Though if any be so weak as to think that this outward baptism is to be delayed, (as Constantine and many of the fathers did,) if in the meantime he make and profess his covenant with Christ, he is to be taken as a Christian and church-member: but as a soldier without colours, or a king not crowned; he is a Christian not orderly admitted, which is his sin.

11. Every member of the catholic church hath the same instrumental founders of his faith under Christ, that is, the prophets and apostles, infallibly inspired by the Holy Ghost. "We are built upon the foundation of the apostles and prophets, Jesus Christ himself being the chief corner stone; in whom all the building fitly framed together groweth unto an holy temple in the Lord." (Ephes. 2:20, 21.) These were the eye-witnesses of the resurrection of Christ, and the ear-witnesses of his holy doctrine, who have delivered it to us as confirmed by the miracles of the Holy Ghost by Christ, and by themselves. And though possibly some ignorant Christian may not well understand his relation to these founders of his faith, yet from them he had it, and is thus related to them: and commonly this is understood and acknowledged by them.

12. Every member of the church is related to all the body, as a member of it: and are "no more strangers and sojourners, but fellow-citizens of the saints, and of the household of God." (Ephes. 2:19.) But this the very term itself doth sufficiently import to you.

13. Every member of the church hath an habitual love to each particular member of the same church. Though mistakes and infirmities may occasion fallings out, even as with Paul and Barnabas, to a parting; and there may be dislikes and bitterness against one another upon misunderstandings, and not discerning God's graces in each other; yet still, as Christians, they are heartily loved by each other; and did they know more of the truth of each other's Christianity, they would love each other more. Every member is united by love to the rest; for this is a lesson that is taught us inwardly of God: "And by this we know that we are translated from death to life." (1 Pet. 1:22; 1 John 3:11. 14. 23; 4:12. 20, 21. 8; 1 Thess. 4:9; John 13:34, 35.)

14. Every member of the church hath a special love to the whole, and desire after the church's welfare and prosperity. Yea, their love to the body exceedeth their love to the particular members, (Psal. 122:2,) and therefore they desire and pray for its safety and increase.

15. Every member of the church hath a special love to the more noble sort of members. As every man is more careful of the heart, the stomach, the lungs, the liver, than of his finger; so are Christians, as Christians, in greatest love to those that have most of Christ in them, and on whom the church's welfare doth most depend, of them are they most solicitous, so far as they understand it. This is true both of men's graces, gifts and offices. He that loveth grace, loveth those most that have most grace. And he that loveth the church, honoureth those in a special manner whom he discerneth best gifted for the benefit of the church, and to employ his gifts most faithfully thereto. And though I will not say but it is possible for some Christians to be converted by a private man, and die before they know a church-officer, and for some weak ones in a temptation to deny and disclaim, or quarrel with their officers; yet so far as any true Christian is acquainted with the necessity or usefulness of the ministry to the church's good, and God's honour, (as ordinarily all know it in some measure; and they that know it not are in some fit of a frensy,) so far they cannot choose but love and honour them. And thus far all Christians join for the ministry: as God's intention was for all their good in giving pastors, teachers and gifts of special service for the church. (Ephes. 4:11–14.)

16. All members have an inward inclination to hold communion with fellow members, so far as they discern them to be members indeed. As fire would to fire, and water would to water, and earth to earth, and every thing to its like; so Christians would have actual communion with Christians, as delighting in each other, and loving Christ in each other, and finding benefit by each other's communion. Though I know that this inclination may be much kept from execution, and communion much hindered, by mistakes about the nature, and manner, and requisites of it, and by infirmities and passions of our own. Brethren may fall out, but there is naturally in them a brotherly love, and when the mistake or passion is over, they will get together again. (Acts 9:32, 33; 2:42. 44; Heb. 10:25; Psal. 16:3.)

17. There is in every true member of the church an inward inclination and propensity to all the instituted means of grace, and a suitableness of spirit to them, which fitteth them to relish them, and highly to value them: and ordinarily this disposition is brought forth into act. The word

of God is engrafted or innaturalized to them. (James 1:21.) It is to them as milk to the new-born babe. (1 Pet. 2:1, 2.) The Lord's-supper is sweet to him, as representing Christ sacrificed, and offering him Christ the food of the soul, and affording him special communion with the saints. "For the cup of blessing which we bless is the communion of the blood of Christ; and the bread which we break is the communion of the body of Christ; for we being many are one bread, and one body; for we are all partakers of that one bread. (1 Cor. 10:16, 17.) The same holy disposition have they to prayer, confession, the praises of God, and all other parts of his service. Though it is too true, that as diseases may put our mouths out of relish to our meat; so temptations may bring some Christians to mistakes about some ordinances, especially as to the manner, and so may make them guilty of too long forbearance of them.

18. So also every member of the church hath in the main the same holy employment and conversation, that is, the service of God, so far as they know his will, is the business of their lives. (Rom. 12:1.) "We are his workmanship, created to good works in Christ Jesus." (Ephes. 2:10, 11.)

19. And every member hath an inward enmity to that which is destructive to itself, or to the body, so far as he knoweth it, that is, 1. To sin in general. 2. To all known sin in particular. And, 3. Specially to divisions, distractions, and diminution of the church. These things their inward disposition is against; and when they are led to them, it is by temptation producing mistakes and passions against the bent of their hearts and lives. They abhor that which is destructive to the body, as such.

20. Lastly. They shall all at the end of their course obtain the same crown of glory, and see and enjoy the same blessed God and glorified Redeemer, and be members of the same celestial Jerusalem, and be employed everlastingly in the same holy love, and joy, and praise, and glorify and please the Lord in all, and centre, and be united perfectly in him. (John 17:21. 23, 24.) "For of him, and through him, and to him are all things, to whom be glory for ever, Amen." (Rom. 11:36.)

And thus I have shewed you in twenty particulars the unity of the saints; though it is not from every one of these that they are called one church, yet all these are inseparable as to possession from the true members, and as to profession from the seeming members that are adult.

Use 1. The truth being thus plain and certain as it is, that the catholic church is one, and consisteth of true Christians, as its real living members, and of all professors of true Christianity, as its visible members, we have here too great occasion of sad lamentation, for the common ignorance of the contenders of the world about this matter, and the great inconsiderateness and abuse of this unquestionable verity. To four sorts of people I shall direct my expostulations. 1. To the Seekers, or whoever else deny the very being of the catholic church. 2. To the blind contending parties of these times, and the offended ignorant people, that are much perplexed among so many pretenders, to know which is the church. 3. To the several sects that would appropriate the church to themselves only. 4. To the Papists, that ask us for a proof of the continued visibility of our church, and where it was before Luther. To these in order: and,

First, For the Seekers; because it is not their persons that I have to speak against, but the errors which they are said to hold, and because they purposely hide their opinions; and because I meet with them of so many minds, I shall therefore deal only with the opinions commonly supposed to be theirs, not determining whether indeed they are theirs, or no: for I care not who maintains them, so I do but effectually confute them. And here are four degrees of this error supposed to be held by the Seekers. 1. Some of them are said to deny the universal mystical church itself. 2. Some are said to deny only the universal visible church, as such. 3. Some yielding both these, deny the universal church as political only. 4. Some only deny the truth of particular churches, as political, that is, the truth of the ministry. Of these in order:

1. Let that man that questioneth the being of the catholic mystical church, and yet pretends to believe in Christ, read but these three or four arguments, and blush.

Argum. 1. If there be no such universal church, then there are no Christians: for what is the church but all the Christians of the world? And I pray inquire better, whether there be any Christians in the world or not? Read the church history, and the books of the infidels, and see whether there have been Christians in the world since the apostles. He that believeth not that there are Christians in the world, when he dwells among them, and daily converseth with them, deserveth to be otherwise disputed with than by argument. He hath only cause to doubt whether there be any Christian magistrate in this part of the world, that such as he are suffered to rave against Christianity.

And certainly he that thinks there are no Christians in the world, is none himself, nor would be thought one.

Argum. 2. If there be no church, there is no Christ: no body, no head: no kingdom, no king: no wife, no husband: no redeemed ones, no Redeemer or Mediator. Though the person of Christ should be the same, yet the office and relation must cease, if the church cease. This is beyond all dispute. And if this be your meaning, that there is no Christ, no Mediator, no Head, or Teacher, or King of the church, speak out, and call yourselves infidels as you are.

Argum. 3. If there be no church or Christians, then there is no salvation: for salvation is promised to none but Christians, or members of Christ. He is the "Saviour of his body." (Ephes. 5:23.) And he that thinks there is none on earth that shall be saved, it seems expecteth no salvation himself: and how much the world is beholden to him for his doctrine, and how ready they will be to receive it, if they be in their wits, is easy to be conjectured.

Argum. 4. If there be no church, there is no pardon of sin, or adoption, nor any fruit of the promise. For the church only are the heirs of promise, pardoned, adopted. (I would heap up plain Scriptures for these things, if I thought it to any purpose.) And he that thinks the promises are ceased, and the pardon of sin and adoption ceased, doth sure think the Gospel and Christianity are ceased, or never were.

2. As to the second opinion, let them that deny the church as visible, consider of the same arguments again, with the necessary addition, and be ashamed.

Argum. 1. If there be no visible church, there are no visible Christians; for Christians are the church: And if there are no visible Christians, then no man can say, that there are any Christians at all: For how do you know it if they are not visible?

Argum. 2. And consequently no man can tell that there is a Christ, the head and king of the church: for who can judge of that which is inevident? And if you know not that there is a church, you cannot know that there is a Christ.

Argum. 3. And thus you must be uncertain of any to be saved, because they are not visible.

Argum. 4. And you must be uncertain of the continuance of the force of the promise, and of pardon, and sanctification.

Argum. 5. Experience and sense itself confutes you. Open your eyes and ears: do you not see Christians in holy exercises? Do you not hear them make profession of their faith? It is a fine world, when we must be fain to dispute whether there be such a people whom we every day converse and talk with! You may better question, whether there be any Turks or Jews in the world! And as well question, whether there be any men in the world! And how should such be disputed with!

3. For the third opinion, which yields an universal visible church, but not a political, it is a gross contradiction.

Argum. Where there is a sovereign, and subjects, and ruler, and such as are under his rule, there is a political body or society. For the 'pars imperans,' and 'pars subdita,' do constitute every commonwealth: and the relations of these two parties, the ruling part, and the ruled part, is the form of the republic. This is undeniable. But here are these two parts: for Christ is the ruling part, and the church or Christians are the ruled part: and therefore you must either deny that there is a Christ to be King, or that there are Christians his subjects; or else you must confess a political church.

But some of this opinion say, 'We confess there is a visible body headed by Christ, who is to us invisible, though visible in the heavens; but this makes not the church to be visibly political, unless 'secundum quod;' but here is no visible universal head.'

Answ. 1. We perceive now whereabout you are, and from whom, and for whom you fetch your arguments. You must have a Pope, it seems, or else no visible political church: We deny that either Pope or. General Council are the visible heads of the church. We maintain that the church is no otherwise visible in its policy, than in these respects. 1. As the body is visible, and their obedience, As 2. The laws are visible by which they are governed. 3. As the inferior officers or ministers are visible. And 4. As Christ the Head is visible in heaven, there is no other visibility of polity to be here expected.

4. The next opinion denieth only, that there are any true particular political churches. Against this I argue thus:

Argum. 1. If there be no particular churches, there is no universal church: for there can be no whole, if there be no parts: and political particular churches are those principal constitutive parts of the universal, which the Scripture mentioneth. But I have proved that there is an universal church, which is the whole: therefore there are particular political churches, which are parts.

Argum. 2. If there be particular Christian societies with overseers, then there are particular political churches: for a church hath but two essential parts; the guiding or ruling part, which is the elders or overseers, and the guided and ruled part, which are the people. Now here are both these: therefore there are particular political churches. That here are Christian

assemblies methinks I should not need to prove, to men that see them day
to day, and plead against them. The only question, therefore, remaining
is, Whether the elders or teachers be true officers or elders, or not? And
in the upshot this is all the question, and you can stick on no other (nor
well on this) without declaring yourselves to be infidels: and this is a question that belongs not to this place, but I purposely refer you to what I have
already published hereupon.

II. My next address is, to them that are so solicitous to know which is
the true church among all the parties in the world that pretend to it. Silly
souls! they are hearkening to that party, and to that party, and turn it may
be to one, and to another, to find the true universal church; I speak not
in contempt, but in compassion: but I must say, you deal much more like
bedlams than Christians, or reasonable men. You run up and down from
room to room to find the house, and ask, is the parlour it? or is the hall it?
or is the kitchen, or the coal-house it? Why, every one is a part of it; and
all the rooms make up the house. You are in the wood, and cannot find it
for trees: But you ask, which of these sort of trees is the wood? Is it the
oak, or the ash, or the elm, or poplar? or is it the hawthorn, or the bramble? Why, it is all together. You are studying which of the members is the
man: Is the hand the man? or is it the foot? or is it the eye? or the heart?
or which is it? Why, it is the whole body and soul, in which all parts and
faculties are comprised. You wisely ask, Which part is the whole? Why,
no part is the whole. Which is the catholic church? Is it the Protestants,
the Calvinists, or the Lutherans, the Papists, the Greeks, the Æthiopians,
or which is it? Why, it is never any one of them, but all together that are
truly Christians. Good Lord! what a pitiful state is the poor church in, when
we must look abroad and see such abundance running up and down the
world, and asking which is the world? Whether this country be the world,
or that country be the world? They are as it were running up and down
England to look for England, and ask, whether this town be England, or
whether it be the other? They are as men running up and down London to
inquire for London, and ask, whether this house be London, or that street
be London? or some other? Thus are they in the midst of the church of
Christ inquiring after the church, and asking, Whether it be this party of
Christians, or whether it be the other? Why, you doating wretches, it is all
Christians in the world of what sort soever, that are truly so, that constitute the catholic church.

Indeed if your question were only, Which is the purest, or soundest, or safest part of the church, then there were some sense in it, and I could quickly give you advice for your resolution; but that is reserved for a following part of the discourse. If you only ask, whether the parlour or the coal-house be the better part or room of the house? or whether the oak or the bramble be the better part of the wood? I should soon give you an answer. So if you ask, Whether the Protestants, or Papists, or Greeks, be the sounder part of the church? I should soon answer you. The same family may have in it both infants and men at age, sound men and sick men; some that have but small distempers, and some that have the plague or leprosy: and yet all are men, and members of the family: and so hath the church of God such members.

'Object. But will you make all sects and heretics in the world to be members of the catholic church?'

Answ. No: there are none members of the church but Christians. If you call any Christians heretics, those are members of the church: but those heretics that are no Christians, are no church-members. If they deny any essential point of Christianity, they are not Christians, but analogically, equivocally, or 'secundum quid.' I tell you, all that are true believers, justified and sanctified, are true living members of the church: and all that profess true faith and holiness, are true members, and no others, at age and use of reason. Your inquiry, therefore, should be, Which are true Christians? And what is true Christianity? And what heresies deny the essentials of Christianity? And then you may soon know who are of the church.

Object. 'Abundance of the errors now common in the world, do subvert the foundation, or destroy the essentials of Christianity.'

Answ. It is not every consequential destroying of the essentials that will prove a man no Christian. For almost every error in the matters of faith and morality doth consequentially subvert the foundation, because of the concatenation of truths together, and their dependance on each other. And so every man on earth should perish if this were inconsistent with Christianity: for all men err in matters revealed and propounded by God in Scripture to their knowledge and belief. He that holdeth fast the essentials of religion by a practical belief, shall be saved by it, though he hold any opinions which consequently subvert the truth, and doth not understand that they do subvert it: for this is the best men's case. But if he so hold the error, as seeing that it overthrows an essential point, and so holdeth not that point which it is against, this man is not a Christian. Every drop of water is contrary to fire, and yet a great fire is not put out by a single drop. Every degree of sickness, or natural decay, hath a contrariety to health and life: and yet every man is not dead that is sick; nor any man, I think: nor is it every sickness that procureth death. The promise is, "He that believeth shall be saved:" and, therefore, as long as he believeth all the essential verities, it is no contrary opinion that can unchristen him, or unchurch him.

'Object. But how shall we know a visible Christian by this, when we know not whether he hold the truth, or not;'

Answ. By men's profession the visibility of their faith is easily discerned. If they say they believe that Christ rose from the dead, I am to take them as believers of it, notwithstanding they should hold some error, that hath a remote opposition to it. But if they directly deny it, I have no reason to think they believe it; and if they will hold two directly contradictory propositions, they are madmen, and to be believed in neither. The Lutherans maintain, That Christ hath a true human nature; and yet some of them say, That it is everywhere. Though this be contrary to the former by consequence; yet I am bound to judge that they take Christ to be true man still, because indeed they do so, not seeing the contradiction.

But if a man by his contradiction in other terms, do manifest that he doth not believe the truth which he professeth to believe, but speaks the words while he denies the sense; this is to deny the matter itself: for it is the sense that is the doctrine: and so he denies himself to be a Christian. For example: If he say, that Christ is risen, and by Christ tell you he meaneth his own spirit; and by rising he meaneth his rising from sin, as the Familists do, and no more: this is to deny the resurrection of Christ.

Object. 'But will you dishonour Christ and his church by taking in all sects and erroneous persons, that held the essentials: What a linseywoolsey garment will this be? What a large and mingled church will you make?'

Answ. The largeness is no dishonour to it: but by over-narrowing it many sects do dishonour it. The corruptions and infirmities are indeed a dishonour to it: but that reflects not at all on Christ, yea, it maketh for his honour, both that he is so exceeding compassionate as to extend his love and mercy so far, and to bear with such distempers, and pardon such miscarriages of his servants: And should your eye be evil because he is good? O how ill doth it beseem that man that needeth exceeding mercy himself, even to save him from damnation, to be opening his mouth against the mercy of Christ to others! Yea, to repine at, and even reproach the mercy that he liveth by, and must save him, if ever he be saved. Why man, hast not thou as much need of tender indulgence and mercy thyself, to keep thee in the church, and in the favour of God, and bring thee to heaven, as Anabaptists, Separatists, Arminians, Lutherans, and many such sects have, to continue them in the number of catholic Christians? If thou have nor their errors, thou hast others, and perhaps as bad, which thou little thinkest of: and if thou have not their errors, hast thou not sins that are as provoking to God as they? Really, speak thy heart man, be thou Papist or Protestant, or what thou wilt, wouldst thou have God less merciful than he is? Or wouldst thou wish him to be so little merciful as to damn all that be not of thy opinion, or to unchristen and unchurch all these that thou speakest against? Or wouldst thou have him to condemn and cast away all men that have as great faults as the errors of these Christians are? And consequently to condemn thyself? Moreover it is Christ's honour to be the healer of such great distempers, and the cure at last shall magnify his skill. In the meantime the church, though black, is yet comely in the eyes of Christ, and of all that see by the light of his Spirit. And our tenderhearted Saviour disdaineth not to be the physician of such an hospital as hath many sorts of diseases in it, and many of them very great. And when pharisees make it his reproach that he thus converseth with publicans and sinners, he takes it as his glory to be the compassionate physician of those that are sick.

I beseech you therefore, poor, peevish, quarrelsome souls, give others leave to live in the same house with you: Do not disown your brethren, and say, they are bastards, because they somewhat differ from you in complexion, in age, in strength, in health, in stature, or any of the points wherein I told you a little before that the members of the church do usually differ in. Shew not yourselves so ignorant or froward as to make a wonder of it, that God should be the Father both of infants, and men at age, of weak and strong, and that the sick and sound should both be in his family. Doth such cruelty beseem the breast of a Christian, as to wish God to cast out all his children from his family that are weak and sick? Do not make it such a matter of wonder, that God's house should have so many rooms in it; and think it not a reproach to it, that the kitchen or the coal-house is a part of the house. Wonder not at it as a strange thing, that all the body is not a hand or eye; and that some parts have less honour and comeliness than the rest. Hath God told you so plainly and fully of these matters, and yet will you not understand, but remain so perverse? I pray hereafter remember better that the catholic church is one, consisting of all true Christians as the members.

III. My next address is to those several sects (I call them not so in reproach, but because they make themselves so), that sinfully appropriate the catholic church to themselves. Thus did the Donatists in Augustine's time, to whom he gives a confutation of very great use to all that are guilty of that sin in our days. But I shall only speak particularly now to these three sects that are most notoriously guilty: 1. The Quakers.[1] 2. Some Anabaptists. And, 3. The Papists.

1. The Quakers are but a few distempered people, risen up within a few years in this corner of the world: and yet they are not ashamed to condemn the most godly Christians, ministers and churches of the world, that are not of their way; as if the church were confined to these few poor, distracted, erroneous persons do not think that they are all of a mind among themselves; some of them plainly deny the very essentials of Christianity. And for these to reproach the church is no wonder: but to appropriate it to themselves that are no members of it, as if Turks or heathens should have persuaded the world that they are the only Christians. In the meantime I thank God that Christianity is in so much esteem, that even the enemies of it do pretend to it: But for those that go under that name, and deny not the fundamentals, let them consider what I said before to the Seekers: If there be no church, there is no Christ: no body, no head: And no church, no Christians; and no justification or salvation. And therefore I would know of them, where was the true church before the other day that the Quakers rose? If there were any, where was it? If there were none, then there was no Christ, no head! I remember what a boy told them lately near us, 'Your church and religion (saith he) cannot be the right, for I can remember since it first begun.' Surely Christ had a church before the Quakers.

2. The rigid Anabaptists do run the same strain, and appropriate the church to their sect alone; and this upon the Popish conceit, that baptism is either necessary to salvation, or else to the being of a member of the church. None but the re-baptized, or those that are baptized at age, are taken by them to be members of the church; (though I know that many of the Anabaptists are more moderate, and make re-baptizing necessary only in point of duty, and 'ad bene esse.' Of these men I would also know, 1. Where was a church that was against infant-baptism, since the days of the apostles, (much less among them) till within these five hundred or six hundred years at most, (perhaps these two hundred or three hundred?)

---

[1] It is necessary to remark, that the people called Quakers and Anabaptists, in the present day, differ very materially from the sects so called in Mr. Baxter's time.

Had Christ a visible church of such in all ages? If so, tell us where it was, and prove it. If not, tell us how Christ could be a king without a kingdom, a head without a body. 2. And can your hearts endure so cruel a doctrine, as to unchurch all the churches of the world, except so few and such as believe you? 3. And would you have men in their wits believe that Christ hath been so many hundred years without a visible church? Or that his church hath had a false constitution, and that now he is constituting his church aright in the end of the world? 4. Your error is so much the greater and more cruel, as your party is the smaller, and more lately sprung up; that ever it can enter into your hearts to imagine that God hath no church in all the world but you. But I shall say no more to you particularly, partly, because you are an impatient generation, that take a confutation for a persecution; and partly, because I shall offend the more sober, by such needless words, to so gross an error; and chiefly because that which I shall speak to the next party, will also be useful to your information.

3. The principal sect that appropriate the church to themselves, is the Papists. And to them I shall more largely open my mind. They make a great noise against all other parties with the name of the Roman Catholic church, and the confident ostentation that it is only they. They make the Pope the visible head of it, and exclude all from the church, besides his subjects; and all that are not of that church they exclude also from salvation, with an 'extra ecclesiam nulla salus.' What shall we say to these things?

1. Surely it must needs be some admirable qualification that must thus advance the church of Rome to be the whole and only catholic church! And what should this be? Is it their extraordinary holiness? I know they talk much of the holiness of their church: but they dare not put it upon that issue, and let us take that for the church which we find to be most holy. On those terms I think we should soon be resolved, by a little observation and experience. However it would not serve their turn, unless they could prove that none are holy at all but they. What then is the ground of this pretended privilege? Why, because they take the bishop of Rome for the universal bishop, and are under his government. And is this it that salvation is confined to?

2. And surely it must be some very heinous matter, that all the rest of the Christian world must be unchurched and damned for; and what is that? Is it for denying any article of the faith? Which is it that we deny? When they would set them against Protestants, they boast that the Greeks are in all things of their mind, except the Pope's supremacy; and therefore this is the

only heresy that might unchurch and damn them. And it is not for ungodliness; for we are ready to join with them in severer censures of ungodliness than we know how to bring them to. The damning crime is, that we
believe not the church of Rome to be the mistress of all the churches, and
the Pope to be their head. And indeed is this a damning sin, and inconsistent with Christianity, or church-membership? I prove the contrary, that
the catholic church is not confined to the Roman, but containeth in it all
that I have mentioned before.

Argum. 1. If many are true Christians that believe not in the Pope, or
Roman church, as the ruler of the rest, then many may be church-members and saved that believe not in them: but the antecedent is certain. For,

1. He that truly believes in God the Father, Son and Holy Ghost, renouncing the flesh, the world, and the devil, is a Christian: but so do many millions that believe not in the Pope or Roman sovereignty.

2. He that hath the sanctifying Spirit of Christ is a Christian: for Christ
giveth it to no other: but so have millions that believe not the Roman sovereignty, as I shall further shew anon.

3. Those that have all that is essential to a Christian, are true Christians:
but so have millions that believe not the Roman sovereignty. For they have
faith, hope, charity, repentance, and sincere obedience, and therefore are
true Christians. If you say, that the belief of the Roman sovereignty is
essential to Christianity, you must well prove it, which yet was never done.

I prove the contrary by many arguments.

1. No Scripture tells us that your sovereignty is a truth, much less of the
essence of Christianity. Therefore it is not so to be believed. What Bellarmin
brings but to prove the truth of it, I have manifested to be utterly imper-
tinent in my book against Popery.

2. If it had been essential to Christianity, and necessary to salvation,
to believe the sovereignty of the church of Rome, the apostles would have
preached it to all the people, whose conversion they endeavoured, and
have established the churches in it: but there is not a word in Scripture,
or any church history, that ever the apostles, or any preachers of those
times, did teach the people any such doctrine: much less that they taught
it all the people. And sure they would not have omitted a point of necessity to salvation.

3. If the sovereignty of the Pope, or of Rome, is of necessity to
Christianity and salvation, then the apostles and pastors of the primitive
church would either have baptized men into the Pope or Roman church,

or at least have instructed their catechumens in it, and required them to profess their belief in the Pope and Roman church. But there is not a word in Scripture, or any church records, intimating that ever such a thing was once done either by orthodox or heretics; that ever any did baptize men into the name of the Pope or Roman church, or did require of them a confession of the Roman sovereignty; no, nor ever taught any church or Christian to obey the church of Rome, as the ruler of other churches. Paul was more certainly an apostle at Rome (a bishop they call him) than Peter, and you may know his practice by 1 Cor. 1:14, 15, "I thank God that I baptized none of you, but Crispus and Gaius, lest any should say that I baptized in my own name." The ancient forms of baptism are recorded in Scripture and church history; but this is never in. He that believed in God the Father, Son, and Holy Ghost, for remission, justification, sanctification, and everlasting life, was baptized as a Christian.

4. If the sovereignty of the Roman church were necessary to Christianity and salvation, we should have had it in some of the creeds of the primitive church, or at least in the exposition of those creeds. But there we have no such thing. For their affirmation, that the word catholic church in the creed, signifieth as much as the Roman catholic church doth signify no more to us, but the dreaming ungrounded confidence of the affirmers.

5. Thousands and millions were saved in the primitive church, without ever believing or confessing the Roman sovereignty: therefore it is not essential to Christianity. No man can prove that one Christian believed Rome to be the mistress of other churches for many hundred years after Christ, much less that all believed it.

6. If it be an article of faith, and so essential to Christianity, that Rome is the mistress of other churches, then either it was so before there was a church at Rome, or else it begun after. Not before: for when there was no church, it could not be the mistress of all churches. Not after: for then Christianity should have altered its specific nature, and become another thing, by the adding of a new essential part. But Christianity is the same thing since there was a church at Rome, as it was for many years before. And the catholic church is the same thing, ft was many years a catholic church before there was any church at Rome at all.

7. If it be necessary to Christianity or salvation to believe that Rome is the mistress and head of the catholic church, then it is as necessary to know who it is that is this head and mistress; whether it be the Pope, or the particular Church of Rome, or the General Council. For else the bare name of

Rome should be the thing of necessity. But if we know not what that name doth signify, it is no more to us than a nonsensical word, which a parrot may utter. But what it is that is this head or sovereignty the Papists themselves are utterly disagreed in. The Council of Constance and Basil defined, That the General Council is the head, above the Pope, and may judge and depose him, as they did divers. The Laterane Council thought otherwise: and Bellarmin saith the aforesaid council, 'judged the judge of the whole world,' and maintained the Pope to be the head and seat of sovereignty. The Italians go one way, and the French another. But if these be true General Councils, then the matter is determined against the Pope: and therefore is an article of faith to be believed on pain of damnation, that the council is above the Pope: and yet it is also an article of faith to be believed on the same penalty, that the Pope is above the General Council; for the Council at the Lateran under Leo X, hath determined it, ccss. 11. So that councils are contrary, and articles of faith are contrary, and he that will be a Papist must believe contradictions. If to evade this any say, that either the Council of Constance, or that at the Lateran, were not true General Councils, or not approved by the Pope: For that of Constance Bellarmin answers after Turrecremata, Campegius, Sanders, &c., that it was a true and approved Council. (Lib. 2. de Concil. cap. 19.) But they say, 'That it determined only that the Council is above the Pope in case of a schism, when the true Pope is not known.' But Bellarmin dare not stand to this answer: for the express words of the Council are, that 'A General Council hath immediate authority from Christ, which all are bound to obey, though of Papal dignity.' Can plainer words be spoke? But Bellarmin's other shift is worse, 'that P. Martin 5. confirmed all that was done in this council, conciliariter; but this (saith he) was not conciliariter.' See what juggling the articles of the Romish faith are liable to, and how clear an interpreter of the Scriptures, and decider of controversies we have, that speaks so enigmatically when he seems to speak most plainly, even in confirming a General Council, that his own cardinals, nor the Council itself, are able to understand him. But perhaps the Council at the Lateran was false, that determineth of the contrary, that the Pope is above councils: no, not in the judgment of Bellarmin and his party. For (Lib. 2. de concil. cap. 17,) lie saith, that 'vix dici potest,' it can scarcely be said that the council was not general. And the Pope was in it, and confirmed it, and the non-reception of it by others he saith is nothing, because decrees of faith are immutable, and the not receiving cannot change them. What a case then are they in that must needs be damned? Whether they believe the Pope to be the supreme, or the Council to be the supreme? One council is against one way, and the other against the other way, and both councils confirmed by undoubted Popes. But yet they have a remedy, and that is, that yet the matter is doubtful: and where is the doubt? Why it is, whether the council defined this as an article of faith, or no? And therefore saith Bellarmin, 'they are not properly heretics that hold the contrary, but cannot be excused from great temerity.' So that you see what certainty the Papists are at in their faith. It cannot be known, nor will any succeeding Popes determine it, when a council hath decided a point, whether or no they intended it as an article of faith. (And yet in the Trent oath they are to swear obedience to all things defined and declared by the sacred canons and œcumenical councils.) One council decrees, that the Pope is highest, another or two decree, that the council is highest, and the Pope must obey them: yea, both these are confirmed by the Pope. The subjects are sworn to obey both contradictories: and yet after this contrary decision, the case is still undecided with them, and for fear of losing half their party, they dare not say that either are properly heretics. (Mark, properly.) 'Yea, (saith Bellarmin, de concil. lib. 2. c. 13,) though afterwards in the Florentine and Lateran Council the question seems to be defined, (having before been contrarily defined at Constance and Basil) yet to this day it remaineth a question among Catholics, because the Council of Florence seems not to define it so expressly: and of the Council of Lateran, which most expressly defined it, some doubt). So that as there is no understanding their councils in their highest degrees, so we have the confession of the Papists themselves, that it is yet undetermined, and no point of faith, which is the sovereign power in the church: and if it be not so much as determined, then much less is it essential to Christianity. And if it be not necessary to know who hath the sovereignty, then it cannot be necessary to know that it is in the church of Rome: For the name of the Church of Rome is nothing but a sound, without the thing that is signified by it: Moreover, the Pope is not the church of Rome; for it was never heard that one man was called a church: and a General Council is not the churches of Rome: for if there be such a thing, it representeth all churches as much as Rome. And therefore which ever be the sovereign, it cannot be the church of Rome. And as for the particular Roman clergy or people, no man that ever I heard of did yet affirm that it was the sovereign ruler of the churches. It is only the Pope and Council that are competitors.

If any say, That it is the Pope and Council only conjunct. I answer, 1. That two that are both fallible, set together, will not make one infallible power. 2. Then the far greatest part of the Papists are erroneous in holding the contrary: for almost all make either the Pope or the Council to be the seat of supremacy and infallibility. 3. Then what is become of the church when these two disagree, as frequently they have done? 4. The Pope and Council agreeing do often contradict a former Pope and Council agreeing. 5. Then the church is without a head, all this while that there is no council in being. See Bellarmin's arguments against this opinion.

8. Another argument to prove that it is not essential to Christianity, to believe the sovereignty of the Pope or church of Rome is this, it is not necessary to salvation to know that there is such a place as Rome in the world, or whether there be one, or two, or ten places of that name, or which of them it is that hath the sovereignty: and therefore it cannot be necessary to believe that it is the catholic or mistress church: Would God lay men's salvation upon the title of a city, many thousand miles from some parts of his church, which they have no knowledge of? Many Papists say, that heathens have sufficient means of salvation that never heard of Christ; and yet will they damn Christians that never heard of the city or Pope of Rome? For about three hundred years after Christ it was the seat of the greatest idolatry, impiety, and persecuting cruelty in the world. And would God all that while so advance that wicked place as to make it essential to Christianity to believe Rome to be the seat of the sovereignty of the church!

9. We have no certainty of faith that Rome shall not be burned, or be possessed by Mahometans, or turn to infidelity: therefore we have no certainty that it shall be any church at all, much less the true ruling or catholic church.

10. If it were necessary to salvation to believe Rome's sovereignty, God would afford the world sufficient evidence of it, and commission preachers to preach it to the world: "For how should they believe without a preacher; and how shall he preach except he be sent?" But no such commissions are proved to be given to any from the Lord.

Having thus backed my first argument, and proved others besides Papists to be Christians, and consequently members of the catholic church, I may proceed to the rest.

Argum. 2. If millions besides Papists have the Spirit of God, and true faith, and charity, and holiness, then are they members of the catholic church. For out of the church is no salvation; but all that have the Holy

Ghost and charity shall be saved, as the Papists confess, if they continue in it. But that many besides Papists have charity and sanctification, we have large experience to persuade us to conclude: For though no man can know the certain truth of another man's profession, or heart; yet as far as men can know by one another, we have ground to be exceeding confident of the sanctity and charity of multitudes among us. I profess if it were but this one thing that hindered me, I could not be a Papist upon any terms; I live among humble, holy, and heavenly people, that live in continual breathings after God, hating a sinful thought, in great mortification, and willingness to know God's will, that they may obey it; and accordingly abundance have ended their lives in peace and joy in the Holy Ghost: None of these were Papists: and now it is impossible for a man to be a Papist, that will not conclude all these to be out of the catholic church, and consequently to be unsanctified and condemned. And if so, I am resolved never to be a Papist. If I cannot be a Papist without condemning a multitude of the holiest persons that ever I could meet with, and shutting my eyes against the admirable lustre of their graces, let them be Papists that will for me.

Argum. 3. The Lord Jesus shed his blood for all Christians as well as Papists, with a special intent to sanctify and save all that are such indeed. Therefore they are members of the catholic church. (Ephes. 5:25-27.)

Argum. 4. All Christians are subject to Christ, though they be not subject to the Pope: therefore they are the church of Christ. (Ephes. 5:24.)

Argum. 5. Those that are loved of the Father, and reconciled to him, are to be taken for members of the church. But all that believe in the Son, and love him, are loved by the Father, and reconciled to him. (John 16:27; Rom. 5:1, 2.)

Argum. 6. All that are justly baptized are visible members of the church: but many are justly baptized that believe not the sovereignty of Rome. Therefore, &c., the minor is evident by the Scripture-direction for baptizing, and examples of it; and millions at this day in the church of God confirm it to us.

Argum. 7. They that have a promise of pardon, and are the adopted sons of God, and heirs of glory, are members of the church (beyond all question): but so are all that believe in Christ, and love God, whether they believe in the Pope or not; as you may see expressly, John 1:12; 3:15, 16. 18; 17:20-22. 24; Mark 16:16; John 3:36; 5:24; 6:35, 40. 47; 7:38; 11:25, 26; 12:46; Rom. 3:22. 26; 4:11, 24; 9:33; 10:9; Gal. 3:22; 2 Thess. 1:10; Heb. 4:3; Acts 5:14; 1 Pet. 2:6; 1 John 5:1. 5. 10; Acts 13:39.

Argum. 8. If they must live in heaven with us, we have reason to take them for members of the church on earth. But all that truly love God, and believe in Christ, shall live in heaven with us, though they never believed in the Pope. Therefore, &c.

Argum. 9. They that are united in all the twenty particulars in the beginning expressed, are certainly members of the catholic church: but so are many that believe not in the Pope. Therefore,

Argum. 10. The Papists' doctrine goes against the certain experience of the sanctified. Some measure of assurance I have myself of the love of God in me; and much more many others have, as I see great reason to believe. Now popery binds me to conclude that I am void of charity, and all saving, special grace, because I believe not in the Pope; that is, to renounce the experience of God's grace in my soul, and unthankfully to deny all these mercies of God. So that as sure as any Protestant can be of charity or saving grace in himself, so sure may he be that popery is false doctrine, and that is enough.

Having spoken thus much to these several sects that would appropriate the catholic church to themselves, I shall once more speak to them altogether. Whether you are Papists, or what sect soever that are guilty of this grievous crime, I beseech you think of these following aggravations of your sin:

1. How evidently is your doctrine against the merciful nature of God, and contrary to that abundant grace which he hath manifested to mankind. Is he love itself; and his mercy over all his works reaching unto the heavens, and unconceivable by sinners? Hath he not thought the blood of his Son too dear for us? And yet can you believe those men that would persuade you that the far greatest part of the Christians of the world are out of the church, and shall be damned, because they believe not in the Pope of Rome, or because they are not rebaptized, or the like, how holy soever they are in other respects? Is this like God; or hath he thus described himself in his word? We are as willing as you to know the truth; and study, and pray, and seek as much after it, and would most gladly find it at any rates: and the more we search; and study, and pray, the more confident we are that your way is wrong: And must we yet be all unchristened that are not of your opinion?

2. How much do you wrong and dishonour the Lord Jesus in many respects! 1. Hath he purchased his church with his own blood; and now dare you presume to rob him of the far greater part of his purchase, because

they be not of your opinion? I would not stand before him with the guilt of such a sin for all the world. 2. Dare you charge so great unmercifulness on Christ, that hath so wonderfully shewed his mercy, and at so dear a rate? After all his blood and sufferings, dare you feign him to say to the world, 'Believe in me, and love me never so much; if you obey not the church of Rome, you cannot be my disciples, or be saved?' Yea, and would he lay our salvation on this, and yet not reveal it to us, but say so much against it? Let him be of these men's minds that can, for I cannot. 3. Moreover, the weaknesses and diseases of the saints do honour the skill of Christ their Physician, that hath undertaken the cure, and in due time will accomplish it. And will you go and turn them all out of his hospital, and say they are none of his patients?

3. Your design is against the very nature of the catholic church, and the communion of saints. The design of Christ in the work of redemption was to gather all into one body, and bring them to God. To break down the partition-wall between Jew and Gentile, and take away the ordinances and ceremonies that occasioned the division, and to unite them all in himself the universal head. (Ephes. 2:13–15.) "That he might reconcile both to God in one body by the cross, having slain the enmity thereby." (verse 16.) To this end, "When he ascended, he gave pastors and teachers, as well as apostles, prophets and evangelists, for the perfecting of the saints, for the work of the ministry, for the edifying of the body of Christ, till we all come in the unity of the faith, and of the knowledge of the Son of God, unto a perfect man, to the measure of the stature of the fulness of Christ,—that we may grow up into him in all things, which is the head, even Christ, from whom the whole body fitly joined together, and compacted by that which every joint supplieth, according to the effectual working in the measure of every part, maketh increase of the body unto the edifying of itself in love." (Ephes. 4:11, 12, 15, 16.) In these several particulars you directly strike at the very nature of the catholic church. 1. The church is but one, and you tear off a member, and call it the whole, and so would make it many, or divide it. It was the design of Christ to unite all the differing parts; and you cross his design, and go about to separate that which he hath conjoined and cemented, even by his precious blood. 2. The church is united and centered in Christ, and knows no other head: and Papists would set up a mortal and incapable man, and have all unity in him as a vicar head: and having not a word for this from Christ, they pervert one text, "The eye cannot say to the hand, &c., or the head to the feet, I have no need of you." (1 Cor. 12:21.)

See here, say they, is a visible head: But, 1. It is visible to any man that will understand, that the term head is used of the natural body's head, by way of similitude: but when the thing assimilate (the mystical body) is mentioned, there is not a word of a head; but the application is of the more honourable or comely parts in general: many such heads there be, that is, more honourable parts, but no Universal Governor, that is it they should prove; they may else as well pretend, that beside the Pope who is the head, there must be one or two universal eyes, and two universal hands, or feet, for the whole church. Thus men abuse themselves, when they will dare to wrest the Scripture to their interests. 2. But if it had spoke of one universal head, must it needs be the Pope, or an earthly man? I must profess that very chapter is so full and plain against popery, that were there no more I could hardly be a Papist. For mark, I pray you, 1. The Lord Jesus himself is expressly named in verse 12. And yet must we seek for another exposition of the word head? "All the members of that body being many, are one body; even so is Christ." It is Christ that the church is united in.

Object. 'But Christ may say to the feet, I have no need of you.'

Answ. For himself he hath no need of any creature: But, 1. For the completing of the body he hath need of the members, which is the thing here mentioned. 2. And to his own glory he hath use for them. He that said of a colt, when he was to ride into Jerusalem, "The Lord hath need of him," may as well be said to have need of his members. 3. If neither prophet, apostle, or teacher, were head of the church, then the Pope is not: for he pretends not to be greater than Peter the apostle. But none of these were the head, as is most plain, "Now ye are the body of Christ, and members in particular; and God hath set some in the church, first apostles, secondarily prophets, thirdly teachers," (verse 27, 28.) So that Christ only is made the head, and apostles are all together numbered with the prime or most honourable members, and no more.

So (Colos. 1:18–20,) "And he is the head of the body, the church:—For it pleased the Father, that in him should all fullness dwell, and having made peace by the blood of his cross, by him to reconcile all things to himself." What a daring vile attempt is it of that man, that would tear the greater half of the members from his body, when it hath cost him so dear to unite them in himself.

4. Moreover, your course is dishonourable to the church and cause of Christ. I know his flock is small; but to narrow it, as you would do, is exceedingly to dishonour it. To make men believe that God hath no more in all the

world but your party, is to raise temptations and hard thoughts of God in the minds of men without any cause.

5. And if such a dividing censure must needs be past, there is none less fit to do it than you, that are commonly forwardest to divide. If most of the Christian world must needs be unchurched, to whose share were it more likely to fall than to you? Quakers I will say nothing to, their folly being so gross. Anabaptists are setting up a new church-entrance in the end of the world: and if they know anything of church history, they must needs know that, comparatively, there are few in heaven that were of their mind on earth. And for the Papists, we have much ado to maintain our charity, in proving them to be a church at all. And the truth is, the question hath some difficulty, whether the church of Rome be a true church or no: to which I give this true and plain answer in brief.

The word church signifieth four things (pertinent to our present purpose.) 1. The universal or catholic church as visible: so the church of Rome is not the church at all. 2. The universal church as invisible: so the church of Rome is not the church. 3. A particular political church of Christ's institution. And 4. A community or mere country or company of Christians, as part of the catholic church. Now as to these two last, the church of Rome signifieth, 1. Either all the Papists formally as such, that is, as united to a pretended universal bishop. And in this formal respect the church of Rome is a false church, and no true church at all of Christ's appointing. 2. By the church of Rome may be meant, the persons that live under the Papal captivity and subjection; not as his subjects formally, but as Christians, and the subjects of Christ: and thus all Christians in the church of Rome are a part of the universal church of Christ: A part, and but a part, as Christians: no part, but the plague of the church, as Papists. This is the plain truth. Your errors are great and numerous; yet we are willing to extend our charity as far as is possible, to take you for brethren: and will you be so froward as to unchurch others, even all the rest of the Christian world, that have need of so much charity to yourselves? You cry out of the heresy of the Jacobites, Georgians, Syrians, Armenians, &c. Some are Nestorians, some are Eutychians, and I know not what: but woe to Rome if worse men, and more erroneous than they, may not be of the church, and saved. Shall I set down the words of one of your own monks that dwelt among them in Judea? It is Bochardus Descript. Terra sanct. 323, 324, 325, 326. "Sunt in Terra promissionis," &c. "There are in the Holy Land (saith he), men of every nation under heaven: and every nation liveth after their own rites:

and to speak the truth, to our great confusion, there are none found in it that are worse, and of more corrupt manners than the Christians:" (he means the Papists.) Page 235, he saith, "Moreover those that we judge to be damned Heretics, Nestorians, Jacobites, Maronites, Georgians, and the like, I found to be for the most part good and simple men, and living sincerely towards God and men, of great abstinence," &c.—And page 324, he tells you, "That the Syrians, Nestorians, Nubians, Jabeans, Chaldeans, Maronites, Ethiopians, and many other nations of Christians there inhabit, and some are Schismatics, not subject to the Pope; and others called Heretics, as the Nestorians, Jacobites," &c. "But (saith he) there are many in these sects exceeding simple (or plain), knowing nothing of heresies, devoted to Christ, macerating the flesh with fastings, and wearing the most simple garments, so that they even far exceed the very religious of the Roman church."

Thus by the testimony of your own eye-witnesses, even these that you cast out for heretics and schismatics, are far beyond even the religious of your church: What then are the reformed churches? Truly sirs, it is intolerable for the parlour to say, 'I am all the house;' but for the chimney, kitchen, or coal-house, it is more intolerable. If your chief servant shall say, 'the rest are no servants,' it is not well: but for the scullion or groom to say so, is worse. If the oak say, 'I am the whole wood,' it is ill; but if the bramble say so, it is worse. If the best of your children should say, that all the rest are bastards, it is not well; but if the most vicious and deformed say so, it is worse.

And as you are unfit for quality to exclude all others, so also for number you are very unfit. As for the Anabaptists, and such inconsiderable parties, that are not past the thousandth part of the church, or perhaps the many thousandth part of it (when yet the whole visible church is supposed to be but the sixth part of the world); I do admire how any Christian can make himself believe that the love and grace of Christ is confined to so narrow a room, and his church so small. I think he that believeth once that Christ hath not one of so many thousands, is next to believing that he hath no church at all, and consequently that there is no Christ at all.

And for the Papists, how deeply also are they guilty in this! As I said, in their greatest height now they are not near one half the Christians in the world: a great part of their church are the poor Americans, whom they drive to baptism, as cattle to the water, (yet not leaving it to their choice so much as to drink when they come thither:) so that their own writers tell us, that multitudes of them know nothing of Christianity but the name, and many forget that too. Awhile ago the Papists were but a small part of the church, before Tenduc, Nubia, and other kingdoms fell away. One of their own bishops, and a legate there resident, speaks upon his own knowledge of the state of the church in the eastern parts, "That in the easterly parts of Asia alone, the Christians exceeded in multitudes both the Greek and Latin churches." (Jacob a Vitriaco Histor. Oriental. cap. 77.) And a most learned writer of their own, (Melch. Canus Loc. Theol. lib. 6. cap. 7, fol. 201,) saith, "Pugnatum est," &c.—"Both the Greeks, and almost all the rest of the bishops of the whole world, did vehemently fight to destroy the privilege of the Roman church: and they had on their side both the arms of emperors, and the greater number of churches, and yet they could never bring it to pass, that the power of this one Roman Pope should be abrogated." You see here by their own most express confession which way the most of the churches went, and that almost all or most of all the bishops of the world were against them, (and so where our church was before Luther:) and yet are these men a competent number to condemn all the rest of the churches of Christ, and appropriate all the catholic church to themselves? O what a world of faction do we live in! I am bitterly censured on one side for believing that any Papists are parts of the catholic church: and, on the other side, we cannot persuade the Papists, that any other are parts of it: and so they will needs be either the whole church, or none of it.

6. This factious course of unchurching all the Christians, saving yourselves, is contrary to the very internal nature of Christianity. Every Christian as a Christian is taught of God to love the brethren, and by this all must know that we are Christ's disciples; and "he that loveth not his brother abideth in death." There is a holy disposition to unity and closure in all Christians. And if you have not this disposition yourselves, you are but hypocrites: if you have it, how dare you sin against it? Though you must not unite with any in their sin, you must unite with all that are Christians in their Christianity.

7. Moreover, your course is contrary to Christian humility, and proclaimeth the most abominable pride of the dividers. That you should call all the rest of the Christian world Schismatics and Heretics, and say, that none are Christians but you: Why, what are you above other men, that you should say, 'Come not near me, I am holier than thou?' Have none in the world, think you, faith, hope, and charity, but you? Can you indeed believe that none shall be saved but you? Alas, that you should not only so much overlook God's graces in your brethren, but also be so insensible of your

own infirmities! Have you so many errors and sins among you, and yet are none of the church but you? Methinks an humble soul should say, 'Alas, I am so bad, that I am more likely to be cast out than they; I am unworthy of the communion of saints!

8. Yea, you trespass against common reason itself. Do you think it reasonable for us to believe, that all those that we see walk uprightly with God and men, earnest in prayer, and study to know the truth; holy, and humble, and heavenly Christians, are yet out of the church, and state of life, because they be not re-baptized with the Anabaptists, or because they believe not in the Pope of Rome, with the Papists? It is hard to imagine that he that pretends to believe such unreasonable things as these, doth well believe Christianity itself.

9. And how could you honour and gratify the devil more, and magnify his kingdom, than by teaching men that most of the churches are his? Will you not be content to let him go away with all the unbelieving world, and all the hypocrites also in the church, but you will proclaim him the king of Christ's inheritance, even of the best and greatest part of his disciples, because they are not of your opinion, or your sect? What, dealing is this for a Christian to be guilty of?

10. Lastly, consider what uncomfortable doctrine it is that you deliver, especially to yourselves? You will not believe that all these sects and differing parties that hold the essentials are members of the catholic church: You scorn at such a church, and say, What a medley church is this! Will Christ entertain men of so many opinions, and of so much corruption? Yea; or else woe to you, and such as you are! Methinks you should rather say, 'Alas, what will become of me, if sinners and erring persons may not be Christians, but must all perish? O what sins have I that are greater than many of their errors! And who is more likely to err than such an ignorant wretch as I!' Take heed lest you cut a shoe too little for your own foot; and lest you shut out so many that you must yourselves go out with the first. I must profess, after long, impartial studies, if I were of the opinion that most of the Christian world are, out of the catholic church, I could not believe that the Papists are in it.

Consider now of these aggravations of your sin: To think and say, 1. That one piece of the church is the whole church: 2. Yea, and a piece that is no greater: 3. That none of the best, nor far from the worst: 4. Nor any of the ancientest, whatever is pretended. 5. And to exclude the greatest part of Christians for such a matter, as not believing in the Pope of Rome: And

6. Lastly, to do all this in pretence of unity, even to cast away the most of the church to unite it. What an unreasonable, unchristian course is this! Dividing spirits may plead what they will, but God will one day shew them their sin in a fouler shape than here I have opened it, though it seem to them but pious zeal.

V. My next address is to the Papists, for answer to their great question, 'Where was your church before Luther? Give us a catalogue of the persons of all ages that were of your church?'

Answ. Of our church! Why, sirs? Do you think we have a catholic church by ourselves? Is there any more universal churches than one? Do you not know where the catholic church was before Luther, and in all ages? Why, there was our church; for we have no other, we know but one. Do you not know where there were any Christians before Luther, or in all ages? Or would you have us give you a catalogue of Christians? Wherever there were true Christians, there was our church. Would you have the world believe that there were no Christians but the subjects of the Pope? Can you believe it yourselves? Doth not your Canus confess, as before cited, that most of the churches and bishops of the whole world were against the privileges of the church of Rome, and had the arms of emperors on their sides? Doth not your Reinerius long ago say, or whoever was the author of that conclusion, "The churches of the Armenians, Ethiopians, and Indians, and the rest which the apostles converted, are not under the church of Rome." (Contr. Waldens. Catal. in Biblioth. Patr. T. 4. Page 773.) What fuller confessions can we desire? Nay, do we not know how small a part of the world did believe your universal sovereignty till almost a thousand years after Christ; and none at all for many hundred years after him, that any credible history tells us of? and yet do you ask us, where was our church?

But you must have us tell you where was a church that had all our opinions? To which I answer, 1. When you have shewed us a catholic church that held all your opinions, we shall quickly tell you of one that held ours. 2. It is not all our opinions that are essential to a Christian, and the catholic church. It is Christianity that makes us Christians and members of the church: It is not inferior truth. That which makes us Christians and catholics, all true Christians in the world have as well as we: And, therefore, we are of the same catholic church. Æthiopians, Syrians, Armenians, Egyptians, Georgians, Jacobites, the many nations of Greeks, Muscovites, and Russians, and all other that are against the Roman sovereignty, are of the same religion and catholic church as we: and so are all among yourselves too that are Christians indeed. The points which we agree in make us all Christians, and church-members: but the points in which we differ from the Papists do make us so much sounder and safer Christians than these, that I would not be one of them for all the world. A sound man is but a man; and so is a man that hath the plague: but yet there is some difference, though not in their manhood.

If, therefore, you will at any time try whether your doctrines or ours be the sounder, we are heartily willing to appeal to antiquity! Spit in his face, and spare not, that will not stand to this motion: That the oldest way of religion shall carry it: and they that are of latest beginning shall be judged to be in the wrong. I abhor that religion that is less than sixteen hundred years of age, and therefore I cannot be a Papist. I confess in the streams of after-ages there have been divisions in the integrals of Christianity, or the points that tend to the soundness of the churches. And in this, I say, let the oldest be the best. But for the essentials of Christianity, and the Church, there never was division among true Christians: for they could not be Christians that wanted any essential part. And, therefore, that one church which contained all the Christians in the world was our church before Luther; and the catalogues of the professors are our church rolls: but we count by thousands, and by countries, and not by names.

But perhaps you will say, 'You cannot be of the same church with the Greeks, or us, or the other parties that you name; for we and they do all renounce you.' I answer, as if it were in your power who shall be no member of Christ and his church by your renouncing him! Your renouncing may prove you no Christians yourselves perhaps, by proving you, in some cases, uncharitable: but it can do nothing to unchurch or unchristen others. If I should say myself, I am no member of the church, that doth not make me none as long as I am a Christian: much less can your saying so. Saith Paul, "If the foot shall say, because I am not the hand, I am not of the body: is it therefore not of the body? and if the ear shall say, because I am not the eye, I am not of the body: is it therefore not of the body?" (1 Cor. 12:15, 16.) The words of a man's mouth make not another to be what he is not, or cease to be what he is. Every one is not a bastard, or a whore, that another in railing passion calleth so. If Christ do but consent we will be members of his body, whether the Pope will or not.

And now, beloved hearers, you have been acquainted from the Word of God of the nature and unity of the catholic church, I beseech you resolve to retain this doctrine, and make use of it for yourselves and others. If any

man ask you what church you are of, tell him, that you are of that particular church where you dwell: but for the catholic church you know but one,
and that you are of. Thrust not yourselves into a corner of the church, and
there stand quarrelling against the rest: make not sectaries of yourselves,
by appropriating Christ, and the church, and salvation to your party: abhor
the very thoughts and name of any universal church of Christ, which is
of narrower extent than Christianity, and containeth fewer than all true
Christians, and is pretended to be confined to a sect. It is not the Papists that
are the catholic church, nor is it the Greeks, no, nor the Protestants, much
less the new prelates alone; but it is all Christians through the world, of
whom the Protestants are the soundest part, but not the whole. Again, consider what a lamentable case it is, that so great a part of the church do seem
to be at a loss about the church, as if they knew not where it is? That they
run up and down the house of God, complaining that they cannot find the
house, and know not which room it is that is the house. But in the house of
God are many rooms and mansions: one for Greeks, and one for Æthiopians,
one for Armenians, and Georgians, and Syrians; one for many that are
called Papists; one for Lutherans and Arminians; one for Anabaptists, and
one for many that are truly guilty of schism and separation from particular churches: there is room for Episcopal, Presbyterians, Independents and
Erastians: there is room for Augustinians, called Jansenists, and room for
Calvinists: but yet no room for any but Christians and catholics. Alas, that
after so many warnings in plainest words of Scripture, and the history of
so many ages, so many Christians should yet be so carnal, as to be saying, I
am of Paul, and I am of Apollos, and I of Cephas, that is, Peter: Yea, that after
Cephas is here named as a party, the Papists should be so wilfully blind as
still to make him the head of a party! That one is for Rome, and another for
Constantinople, and another for Alexandria! When that Augustine hath so
long ago decided this point against the Donatists, and told them which is
the catholic church, even that which begun at Jerusalem, and is extended
over the world wherever there be Christians: alas, that still men are so
stupid in their divisions, as to be crying out, 'Here is Christ, and there is
Christ: here is the church, and there is the church: we are the church, and
you are none of it:' When the body of Christ and its unity is so frequently
and plainly described in the Scripture. I know that none are members of
the church that deny any essential point of Christianity: but I know that
many other mistaken parties are. Consider what an uncharitable, dangerous thing it is to give Christ's spouse a bill of divorce, or cast his children

out of his family. And in the name of God take heed whilst you live, 1. That you never confine the church to a sect or party. 2. Nor ever cast out the least true Christians, seeing Christ will never cast them out.

But because this disease hath miserably tormented us for so many ages, and because we see so many sick of it at this day, distractedly looking for the catholic church in this or that party, and thinking that all others are shut out, I shall here tell you what are the causes of this distraction, and in the discovery of the causes you may see the remedies. And withal I shall shew you the hindrances of the concord and peace of the church, while so many seem to be all for peace! For it may seem a wonderful thing to hear almost all men cry up the church's peace and concord, and yet that it flieth further from us, when it is in our power to be possessors of it, if we were but truly and generally willing, as we pretend to be, and think that we are.

1. Some men understand not the nature of the union and concord of the church, nor how much is to be expected in this life, and therefore looking for more than is to be looked for, they think we have no unity, because we have not that which they ignorantly expect: and thereupon finding greater unity in this or that sect among themselves than they find in the whole body, they presently conclude that that sect is the church: they see a great many differing parties, and hear them condemning one another, and therefore they foolishly think that all these cannot possibly be of the true church: and then they hear the Papists boast of their unity, as having one head, and one judge of controversies, and one expounder of Scripture, and being all of one belief, and therefore they think that the Papists are the true church.

But consider before you run past your understandings of these two things: First, There is no perfect concord to be expected upon earth: this is the glory that is proper to the life to come. You may easily see this if you were but considerate. For, 1. There can be no perfect concord, but where there is perfect light and knowledge: for while we are ignorant, we shall unavoidably err and differ. What do we quarrel about but matter of opinion? One thinks this is the right, and another thinks that is the right: And if we had all so much knowledge as to resolve all these doubts, do you think we should not be sooner agreed? Doubtless our disagreements are much for want of knowledge; we quarrel in the dark: if such a light would come among us, as would shew us all the truth, it would soon make us friends. But this is not to be expected in this life: even Paul saith, that here we know but in part; we understand as children; and think and speak as children; and is it any wonder to have children fall out? "But when that which is perfect is come, then that which is in part shall be done away: Now we see through a glass darkly; but then face to face: Now we know in part; but then we shall know even as we are known." (1 Cor. 13:9-12.) And therefore we find even Paul and Barnabas so far disagreed as to part asunder, because they had not both so much knowledge as to know whether Mark should be taken with them or not. In heaven only we shall know perfectly: and therefore in heaven only we shall be united, and agree perfectly.

2. And we can never be perfect in union and agreement among ourselves till we are perfect in union and agreement with Christ. For we cannot regularly be nearer to each other than we are to our Centre: for it is the Centre only in which we must unite. It is not possible to be more nearly united among ourselves by a Christian union than we are to Christ: and therefore seeing it is only in heaven that we are perfectly united to Christ, and at agreement with him, it is only in heaven that we must be perfectly united among ourselves. You marvel that we so much differ from one another, but you forget how much we all differ yet from Jesus Christ; and that this is the difference that must be first made up before we do any good of the rest.

3. Moreover, we can never be perfectly united and agreed till we are perfectly holy, and every grace be perfect in us: for holiness is that new nature in which we must be one; and every grace hath a hand in our accord. When we are perfect in love, and perfect in humility, and meekness, and patience, and perfect in self-denial, and all other graces, then, and never till then, shall we be perfect in our union and agreement among ourselves: while there is the least sin in the soul it will hinder our full agreement with God and men. It is sin that woundeth both the soul and the church, and makes all the debate and divisions among us; and when all sin is gone, then all differences will be done, and never till then. What an ignorant thing then is it of you to wonder so much at our many differences, and yet not to wonder at our sinfulness, and unholiness, and difference with Christ, in whom we must agree. Well, remember hereafter, that unity and concord is here to be expected but according to the proportion of our holiness, and therefore so much sin and ignorance as remains, no wonder if so much division remain.

The second thing which I desire you to remember is this: That in all the essential matters of Christianity there is as true a union among all the differing sorts of Christians, as there is among the Papists; or any one sect: even in all the Twenty points of union, which I named at the beginning. And this is the union that is most to be esteemed; or at least, this is enough to make us of one Christ. As the great essential points of faith are of far greater moment and excellency than our several controverted by-opinions, so is a union in these great essential points more excellent than an union in smaller matters: though both together is best of all, if joined with the truth.

To these let me add also a third consideration; that it is no wonder to find the Papists as a sect agreed among themselves; for so are other sects as well as they: yea, let me add more, that I know not of any one sect in the world that differ so much among themselves as the Papists do. The Greeks are kept from so much difference by their want of learning, which keeps them from meddling so much with niceties, and running into so many controversies as the Papists do. The like may be said of the Ethiopians, Armenians, and many more. The Protestants differ not in half, nor a quarter so many points as the Papists do. Nay, the very Anabaptists themselves do not differ among themselves in the tenth part so many points as the Papists. If the many hundred differences among their commentators, schoolmen, casuists, and other writers, were collected and presented to your view, I much doubt whether there be any one sect on the face of the earth that hath the twentieth part so many differences among themselves as the Papists have. Though they think they salve all by saying that they differ not in articles of faith, yet their differences are never the fewer for that. And others may say more in that than they can do.

Well! remember this advice: expect not a heavenly perfection of unity and concord till you come to heaven.

2. Another cause of our distractions and hindrance of concord is, that very few men have peaceable spirits, even when they are extolling peace. A peaceable spirit must have these qualifications, which most men want. 1. He must be united to Christ, the head and centre of union, and have a sanctified nature, and value God's honour above all things else, that so his desires of peace may flow from a right principle, and may proceed upon right grounds, and to right ends; and he may seek a holy peace: And, alas, how few such spirits have we!

2. A peaceable spirit must be a public spirit, highly esteeming the welfare of the whole body, above any interest of his own, or of any sect or party. The great grace of self-denial is of necessity herein. No man hath a Christian, peaceable spirit, that doth not most highly value the peace and prosperity of the universal church, so far as to submit to losses or sufferings himself for the obtaining of it; and that had not rather his party suffered than the whole. But, alas, how rare is a public spirit in any eminency!

how private and selfish are the most! The good of the church can no further be endeavoured, with too many, than self will give leave, and than their party will give leave: these must be made the masters of the consultation.

3. A peaceable spirit must be a charitable spirit; loving all the saints as saints; and that with a pure heart, and fervently: this would put by the matter of contentions: this would provoke men to healing endeavours; and it would put the best construction on men's opinions, words and actions, that they can bear: "Charity suffereth long, and is kind: Charity envieth not: Charity vaunteth not itself, is not puffed up, doth not behave itself unseemly, seeking not her own; is not easily provoked, thinketh no evil; rejoiceth not in iniquity, but rejoiceth in the truth; beareth all things; believeth all things; hopeth all things; endureth all things." (1 Cor. 13:4-7.) O what an effectual healer is charity! what a tender hand will it bear to any distressed member! much more to the whole church. What causeth our distractions more than want of charity; what else makes men look so scornfully, and speak so disgracefully of every sort of Christians, but themselves? And to endeavour to make others as odious as they can; and to make mere verbal differences seem real, and small ones seem exceeding great; and to find out a heresy or a blasphemy in the smallest error, and perhaps in a harmless word: All is blasphemy with some men, or error at least, which they do not understand. Alas, we have real heresies and blasphemies enough among Arians, Socinians, Ranters, Quakers, Seekers, Libertines, Familists, and many others; let us reject these that are to be rejected, and spare not; but we need not feign heresies and blasphemies where they are not, as if we wanted matter for our indignation.

4. A peaceable spirit must be in some measure meek and patient, with a humble consciousness of its own frailties and offences: but, alas, what passionate, rash and turbulent spirits do abound in the poor divided church! Such as are made of gunpowder, and speak fire and sword; that will do no right, nor bear any wrong; that will speak well of few but their own party, and yet cannot endure to be ill spoken of themselves; that are possessed with the "wisdom which is from beneath, which is earthly, sensual and devilish," and are strangers to the heavenly "wisdom, which is first pure, and then peaceable; gentle, and easy to be entreated." (James 3:15, 17.) Even preachers of peace are some of them become the fervent agents of the divider, and go up and down with destroying rage, and make their tongues the bellows of hell, resisting the peaceable endeavours of their brethren.

5. A peaceable spirit must have a high esteem of peace, and be zealous for it, and industrious to obtain it. Only against ungodliness and unpeaceableness must he be unpeaceable. Many have a good wish and a good word for peace, as hypocrites have for godliness, but this will not serve the turn. He that is not for us is against us, and he that gathereth not with us scattereth abroad. The wicked and unpeaceable are zealous and industrious against peace; and those that are for peace are cold and indifferent for the greater part; and the zealous and industrious are so few, that their voices cannot be heard in the contentious crowd. The unpeaceable are commonly the loudest, and are actuated by a fervent zeal, which nature agreeth with, and Satan cherisheth and excites: such will, even as the Quakers, go up and down from one assembly to another, and in the marketplaces, and other places of concourse, revile, and rail, and reproach the ministry, and speak as earnestly as if they were the agents of Christ And others are busy in secret, that will not incur the disgrace of such visible impiety. And when the enemies of unity and peace are many, and hot, and loud, and the friends of unity and peace are either few, or cold, and dull, and silent, what is likely to be the issue but even the mischiefs which we feel? Forsooth, some dare not be fervent for peace, lest they be censured for their fervour to be unpeaceable: these shew how much they love the praise of men, and stick yet in the power of self. There is need of zeal for peace, as well as for other parts of holiness. All the resistance that the enemies of hell and earth can make will be made against it: and will be carried on against all by sleepy wishes, and sitting still! I am sure this agrees not with the precepts of the Spirit. "Follow peace with all men." (Heb. 12:14.) "If it be possible, as much as in you lieth live peaceably with all men." (Rom. 12:18.) It is a sorry surgeon, or physician, that will think it enough to wish well to their patient; the house of God will be neither built nor repaired without zeal, and industry, and patience in the work. If men's hearts were set upon the church's peace, and they did but feel the disjointing of her members, the breaking of her bones, and the smart of her wounds, as sensibly as they feel the like in their own bodies; and if ministers and other Christians, were as sensible of the evil of divisions as they are of drunkenness, and whoredom, and such other sins; and if we were all awakened to quench the flames of the church, as earnestly as we would do the fire in our houses, and would preach for peace, and pray for peace, and plead, and labour, and suffer for peace, then some good might be done on it against the rage and multitude of dividers.

3. One of the greatest hindrances of concord and peace, is the setting up of a false centre, and building peace on grounds that will never bear it. Christian unity is no where centered but in Christ the head, and no way maintained but by the means which he hath ordained to that end. But the miserable world will not discern or take up with this. The Papists are of two churches; for they have two heads, or sovereigns, which specify the society. One of the Popish churches make the Pope the head and centre, and all the church must unite in him, or it can be no church! The other Popish church do make a general council the head, and the Pope only the subordinate sovereign in the vacancy. And these think to have the whole church to unite upon these terms. But it will never be. As Divine faith will have no formal object but Divine veracity, so neither can Christian unity have any universal proper centre but Christ. As at the building; of Babel, when men would unite for their future security in their own devices, it brought them to utter confusion, which the world groaneth under to this day; so when men will build a Babel of their own invention, for the preventing of the inundation of heresies, they are upon the most dreadful work of confusion. The church is taught by the Scripture, and the Holy Ghost within them, to take up nowhere short of God; to call no man on earth the father or master of our faith, nor to trust in man, and make flesh our arm. Man is too dark and too weak a creature to be the head or centre of the church-deluded Papists! You think you befriend the church's unity, when you hang it by a hair, and build it on the sand, and found it on mere weakness: could you prove that ever God had promised abilities and gifts to the Pope of Rome, proportionable to such a work, we should most gladly look out to him for the exercise of those abilities. God setteth none on work but he furnisheth them with a suitableness for it. Have all Popes or councils prophetical and apostolical inspirations and directions? What! those that have been censured, and some of them deposed, for blasphemy, heresy, sodomy, adultery, murder, simony, and such works of darkness! The Spirit useth not to dwell in such persons, nor light to have communion with such darkness. Nay, if all Popes were holy, yea, as holy as Peter, they were too weak to bear up with the unity of the church. It is Christ, and not Peter, that is called the rock, on which the church is built, against which the gates of hell shall not prevail. This rock is Christ. (1 Cor. 10:4.) The church is the spouse of Christ, and must not be made a harlot, by being wedded to the Pope, or any other. Nothing hath more hindered the fuller union of the church than this idol, self-exalting head, and false centre of union.

And if any would unite the church in kings, in councils, in any human devices, they will but divide it.

4. And the same course take they that must needs build our union on insufficient, subordinate means. Some must have confessions in words of their own, to which all that will be accounted Christians must subscribe; or at least, that would have communion with them. Though we would subscribe to the whole Scripture, or any confession drawn up in its phrase and matter, yet this will not serve for union and communion. They tell us, heretics will subscribe to the Scripture: and I tell them, that heretics may subscribe also to their confessions, and force a sense of their own upon them: and that God never left them to make better confessions, and fitter to discover heresies, than Scripture doth afford. But if heretics will subscribe to the Scriptures, or confessions taken wholly out of them, they should be no heretics in our account till they discover that they maintain some heresy against the sense of the Scripture, or confession which they subscribed to; and then they are to be censured by the churches accordingly; not for want of subscribing to a sufficient confession, but for abusing and contradicting the confession which they did subscribe; and so to be corrected for it as a crime against a sufficient law and rule; and we must not think to prevent it by making a better law or rule, which shall tie them more strict, and which they cannot break. It is a strange rule, which can necessitate the subject to observe it, and which cannot be violated. And it is a wild head that must have new laws and rules made, because he sees that malefactors can break these! The law is sufficient to its own part, which is to be the rule of duty, and of judgment. It tells men sufficiently what they must believe and do; but if they will not do it, it judgeth them as offenders. You will never form a confession, or make a law that cannot be misinterpreted and broken. The Papists have set up whole volumes of councils and decrees for the rule forsooth, because the Scripture is dark, and all heretics plead Scripture. And what have they done by it, but cause more darkness, and set the world and their own doctors too in greater contentions, so that now councils cross councils, and they can neither agree which be true approved councils, and which not; nor when they intend a decree to be an article of faith, and when not; no, nor what sense to take their words in, and how to reconcile them. And thus men lose themselves, and abuse the church, because God's word will not serve their turn as a rule for us to unite upon. This is the one rule that God hath left, and men will needs blame this as insufficient, and mend God's works by the

devices of their addle brains, and then complain of divisions, when they have made them! One company of bishops must needs make a company of canon laws for the church, and all must be schismatics that will not be ruled by them: another company that are of another mind make contrary canons, and those must be obeyed, or else we are schismatics. They must make us our sermons, and call them Homilies, and make us our prayers, and call them a Liturgy: and the fruit of their brains must be the rule of all others, or else they are schismatics. So wise and holy are they above all their brethren, that none must publicly speak to God in any words but what they put into their mouths. (Read Dr. Heylin's Discourse of Cant. 5. 5. against ministers praying in the church in any other words but what is in the common-prayer-book.) So they do also by their vestures, and gestures, and other ceremonies: Nothing hath more divided the church than the proud impositions of men, that think so highly of their own words and forms, and ceremonious devices, that no man shall have communion with Christ and the church in any other way. Never will the church unite on such terms. The rule that all must agree in must be made by one that is above all, and whose authority is acknowledged by all. Experience might tell these men, that they are building but a Babel, and dividing the church. In the Lord's-supper, where they have limited us to a gesture, we are all in pieces. In singing psalms, where they left us free, we have no dissention. In the places where garments and other ceremonies are not imposed, God's worship is performed without contention, and with as little uncomeliness as with them. Proud quarrelsome men, that must needs be lording it over the church, and turning legislators, may set all on fire for the promoting of their ways, and rail at all that will not be under their yoke: but when they have all done, they will find they are but busily dividing the church, and their canons are but fiery engines to batter its unity and peace. A thousand years experience and more, might have taught us this to our cost. Never will the church have full unity, till the Scripture-sufficiency be more generally acknowledged. You complain of many opinions and ways, and many you will still have, till the one rule, the Scripture, be the standard of our religion. As men that divide and separate from us, do use to accuse the ministers, and then be every man a teacher to himself; so they use to accuse the Scriptures, and, as the Papists, call them dark, and dangerous, and insufficient: and then every sect must make us a new rule, when they have disparaged that which Christ hath given us. Then one makes the Pope a rule by his decretals, and another a council, and another the bishops, canons or articles, and another his own suggestions and impulses. Stick close to this one Bible, and let nothing come into your faith or religion but what comes thence; and when controversies arise, try them by this; and if you cannot do it yourselves, then take the help of ministers or synods, and use them not as masters, but as helpers of your faith; not to make you another rule, but to help you to understand this only rule, and thus may you come to be of one religion, but never otherwise.

5. To these I may add the damnable sin of pride and selfishness, touched at before. All men would have peace: but most would have it on their own terms; yea, and most parties would be the very centre of the churches. If all the world will come over to them, they will be at peace with them, otherwise not. If we will all swear allegiance to the Pope, and turn to them, we shall have concord with the Papists. If we will all renounce Presbyterian ordination, and submit to Episcopacy, with all their canons, forms and ceremonies, we shall have concord with the rigid of that party. If we will all be for an office of unordained elders, that have no power to meddle with preaching or sacraments, we shall have peace with the more rigid sort of that way. If we will causelessly separate, and make the major vote of the people to be church-governors, we may have peace with men of that way. And if we will be re-baptized, we may have peace with the Anabaptists. But can all the catholic church unite upon these private, narrow terms? Every man would be the Pope or the general council himself: or rather every one would be the God of the world; that all men may receive the law at his mouth, and his name may be honoured, and his kingdom may be setup, and his will may be done throughout the world: this is the nature of self-idolizing pride. And hence it is that the church hath as many dividers, as unsanctified men; because every unsanctified man is thus made an idol by his pride, and knows no further end but self. Is there never a man of you that hears me this day, that would not have all the town, and country, and world to be of one mind? I think there is not one but wisheth it. But what mind must it be? It must be of your mind! Or else it will not satisfy you! And alas you are so many, and of so many minds among yourselves, that this way will never unite the world! One must have all of his mind, and another must have all of his mind, when no man well agrees with another, and yet none will be brought to another's mind. But God is one, and his mind is certainly right and good: and the Spirit is one, and the Scripture indited by it is one; and if you would come to that as the only rule, you might be of one religion, and mind, and way: but till then you do

but labour in vain. But you will say still, that every sect pretendeth to the Scripture, and there is so many expositions of it, that we see no hopes that this way should unite us: To this I next answer.

6. It is the bane of unity when men must make every inferior opinion the seat of unity, and will not unite in the essentials of Christianity, endeavouring in love to accord as well as they can in the rest. Though the truth of the whole Scripture, that is known to be holy Scripture must be acknowledged; yet the understanding of the meaning of the whole Scripture is not of necessity to salvation, or church unity: otherwise woe to every one of us! For there is no man on earth that hath the perfect understanding of all the holy Scriptures. And yet all that is in it propounded to be believed is 'de fide' matter of faith, and it is our duty to believe it, and understand it, and our sin that we do not; but not a sin that proves us graceless, or unjustified. I wonder the Papists have not venial errors in matter of faith, as well as venial sins against moral precepts! But all that is 'de fide,' must with some of them be fundamental or essential to Christianity. The Scripture is a full and beautiful body, which hath its flesh, and skin, and a multitude of nerves, and veins, and arteries, as well as the head, the heart, and stomach, and other natural parts; without which parts, that are the seat or chief instruments of the animal, vital and natural spirits, the body were no body. All in the Scripture is true and useful, but all is not essential to Christianity. And in the essentials all Christians do agree; and if you would know how such should behave themselves to one another, hear the Holy Ghost himself, (Phil. 3:12-16,) "Not as though I had already attained, or were already perfect; but I follow after, if that I may apprehend that for which also I am apprehended of Christ Jesus: Brethren, I count not myself to have apprehended, but this one thing I do, forgetting those things which are behind, and reaching forth to those things that are before, I press towards the mark for the prize of the high calling of God in Christ Jesus. Let us therefore as many as be perfect be thus minded; and if in any thing ye be otherwise minded, God shall reveal even this unto you: Nevertheless, whereto we have already attained, let us walk by the same rule, let us mind the same thing." So 1 Cor. 3:11-15. "Other foundation can no man lay, than that is laid, which is Jesus Christ. Now if any man build on this foundation gold, silver, precious stones, wood, hay, stubble, every man's work shall be made manifest: for the day shall declare it, because it shall be revealed by fire, and the fire shall try every man's work of what sort it is. If any man's work abide which he hath built thereupon, he shall receive a reward: If any man's work

shall be burnt, he shall suffer loss; but he himself shall be saved, yet so as by fire." Errors may bring heavy judgments in this life, and out of this fire the erroneous may escape, and not fall into the eternal fire; for thus will God "sit as a refiner, and purifier of silver, and will purify the sons of Levi, and purge them as gold and silver, that they may offer to the Lord an offering in righteousness." (Mal. 3:2, 3.) Dislike every error, and escape as many as you can; but think not that every error must dissolve our unity, or that every truth is necessary to our unity.

And where you say that all sorts do plead the Scriptures, I answer, 1. That all sorts of Christians in the essentials do rightly understand the Scripture. 2. And for the rest, their very pleading that, shews that all sorts are convinced that it is the rule of truth, even where they do not understand it. 3. And this is no proof of the insufficiency of Scripture, but of the imperfection of men's understandings; and instead of seeking for another rule, you should labour for a better understanding of this, and use the help of ministers thereto. The law of the land is the rule of the subjects' actions, and tenures; and yet what controversies are about it, even among the wisest lawyers! and one pleadeth it for one cause, and another saith that the law is for the contrary cause! Yea, one judge differs from another. What then! must we cast away the law? Let us know where to have a better first! But rather, men should labour to know it better, and meddle not contentiously with the niceties of it without need. And thus we must do about the law of God. Agree in the essentials, and learn the rest as well as we can.

7. Another great impediment to our concord is, abundance of dividing, unpeaceable principles, that be grown into credit, or entertained in the world: and if such principles meet with the most peaceable disposition, they will make the man become unpeaceable. For the best men that are will think they must obey God; and therefore when they mistake his will, they will think they will do well when they are sinning against him. There are too few in the world of a peaceable principle: Some lay all peace, as is said, on the opinions of their own parties; and some lay it on a multitude of such low opinions, and such doubtful things, that they might know can never be the matter of universal consent: Some think they must not silence any thing which they conceive to be a truth, for the peace of the church, or the promoting of greater undoubted truths. Some think they ought to reproach and disgrace all that are not of their mind; and some think they ought to destroy them, or cast them out, and think this a part of their faithfulness to the truth of Christ, and that this is but to help him

against his enemies. And there is no more desperate principle of division and persecution than this uncharitableness, which makes the children of God, and the members of Christ, to seem his enemies, and then use them as his enemies: To dress them in a false attire, as they did Christ, and then smite him: To put them in the shape of schismatics, or heretics, or devils, as the Papists do when they burn them, and then use them accordingly. Many more unpeaceable principles I might recite; and if it were not too tedious, I think it would be useful.

8. Another hindrance of unity and peace is, a carnal zeal in matters of religion, which is frequently mistaken for the true zeal of the saints. When men are confident that their opinions are the truth, and overvalue them as to the necessity, because they are their own, though they observe not the reason, they presently think they must be hot against all the gainsayers of their opinions; and herein they place the most, or at least too much of their religion.

There is not one of many that hath this zeal, but thinks it is of God, and is part of their holiness. When as it is often from the devil and the flesh, even when the doctrine is true which they contend for. You may know it from true zeal by these following marks. 1. It is more for controversies and speculations than for practical holiness. 2. It is selfish, and kindled by an overvaluing their own conceits or ways. 3. It is private, and would promote a lower truth to the loss of a greater, or a doubtful point to the loss of undoubted truth; or a single truth to the loss or hindrance of the body of common truth; and it is hotter for a party than for the catholic church, and will promote the interest of an opinion or party, to the wrong of the common interest of the church. 4. It is blind, and carries men to sinful means; as resisting authority, order, or ordinances, or the like. 5. It is unmerciful and unpeaceable, and little sensible of the case of others, or smart of the divided church. Many are calling for fire from heaven for the cause of Christ, that little "know what spirit they are of." (Luke 9:55.) O how true is this of many, that think they excel in knowledge or zeal, and are but defending the truth against erroneous adversaries! But "who is the wise man, and endowed with knowledge among you? Let him shew out of a good conversation his works with meekness of wisdom: But if ye have bitter envying and strife in your hearts, glory not, and lie not against the truth: This wisdom descendeth not from above, but is earthly, sensual, devilish: for where envying and strife is, there is confusion, and every evil work: But the wisdom that is from above, is first pure, then peaceable, gentle, and easy to be entreated, full of mercy and good fruits, without partiality, and without hypocrisy. And the fruit of righteousness is sown in peace of them that make peace." (James 3:13 to the end.) But of this I have formerly spoken at large in many sermons on these words of James. Dividing zeal is a grievous distracter of the church's peace.

6. Another hindrance is, that of the many that are for peace and unity, there are few that have any great skill to promote it, and those few that have skill, want opportunity or interest, and are cried down by the opposers. There is a great deal of skill necessary to discern and manifest the true state of controversies, and to prove verbal quarrels to be but verbal, and to take off the false visors which ignorance and passion puts on them, to aggravate the differences that are debated. There is much wisdom necessary for the securing of truth, while we treat for peace, and the maintaining peace, while we defend the truth. Alas, how few escape one of the extremes in most differences themselves, and, therefore, are unfit reconcilers of others. Few are possessors of that blessed light that doth shew the error of both extremes, and must be the means of our concord, if ever we agree! Few know that truth between contrary errors in which both must meet. How much skill also is necessary to deal with touchy, froward spirits, and to handle both nettles and thorns that must be dealt with. And how few men of wisdom and peace are much regarded by the firebrands of the churches! And how few of them have language, and health, and maintenance, and authority, and a skilful activity to set others on work, which are almost needful for this healing design? And what abundance of private wishes have been buried by the most skilful men for want of opportunities! And how many private writings cast by, that have that in them that deserved public entertainment, and might have been very fit instruments for this healing work.

10. And the various carnal interests of the world, are an exceeding hindrance to the church's peace. The interest of one prince lieth for one party; and another is for another party: one prince thinks it for his interest to unite, and another thinks it for his interest to divide, or secretly to cherish and continue divisions. The ministry also have too oft a carnal interest, which lieth usually in siding with the prince; and the great carnal interest of the Roman clergy lieth sticking close to the Pope. The people hereupon are commonly in such distractions and disturbances, by wars, or secular cares and wants, that motions of peace can scarcely be heard, or attended to; but the noise of guns, drums, and lamentations, and reproaching of

enemies, drowneth all. And when the crossing of secular interests hath made them one another's enemies, they will hardly treat as friends for unity in religion, or the healing of the church.

11. And it is no small hindrance that the princes of the earth are commonly so bad, as either to be strangers to the true interest of Christ and his church, or else to prefer their own before it. It is they that have the greatest interests and opportunities, and might do most for unity if they would. And withal they think that nobody should meddle without their leave; and commonly when they do nothing themselves, they will not suffer the ministers to do it that are their subjects. How easy were it with the Christian princes and states, if they had so much wit and grace to agree together, to bring the churches in their dominions to much agreement. But alas, highest places have greatest temptations, and therefore too oft the worst men: so that they that should do it, and might do it, have no heart to it. And the princes are very rare that prefer Christ's interest before their own; and have truly learned the lesson of denying themselves, and forsaking all they have for him. The great work of converting the heathen world should be promoted by them; but how little is there done in it by any princes!

12. Moreover, the multitude are everywhere almost averse to holy unity and peace: Their dispositions are against it: their principles are against it: their parts unfit for it: and yet how to do it without them will be hard. For 1. They have all of them almost conceits of their own fitness; and think all matters in religion should be regulated by them. They detest that a few should overtop them, and do the work while they stand by; and they grow to a hatred of those few, because they are counted wiser and better than they; yea, they naturally hate the godly, and the practical truths of God: and yet the greater vote must carry it, or else the swarm will be about your ears: When it is a hundred to one, but a hundred for one in most places of the world, are in the wrong, if not bitter enemies to the right. And in the best parts of the world, it is a wonder if the greater part be not the worse. Or if in a corner or two it should be better, what is that to all the Christian world? 2. At least if they will not be passively peaceable, how little can we do, when it is they that must, in part, consent, and it is they that have the strength to resist.

13. And even among the godly the peacemakers are far the smaller number, I mean as to the healing of our common divisions. For the younger sort of Christians, in age, or grace, or gifts, are the greatest number: and these also are of the most active, hot dispositions, and will be forwardest in

all agitations, and will not stand by. And alas, how few of them have meekness, prudence, and charity, answerable to their heat and activity! They
will lead their leaders; and their way must carry it, or else all are censured
and trod down by them: and how ordinarily is their way unpeaceable and
confusive! And how seldom doth it end according to their expectations,
for the churches' good. But for the wise and judicious, experienced, sober,
peaceable men, alas, how few are they; till they grow aged few attain to
this. And yet nothing will be done for the peace and welfare of the church
but by the conduct and direction of these few experienced, judicious, moderate men. None else can do it: and yet few other will suffer them to do it.
And thus we see here in these nations, that even religious men have been
the hinderers of our peace.

14. And withal, the devil, who is the great enemy of peace and unity, is
still watching to cast in some bone of contention, and to make use of the
opinions and passions of all, both good and bad, for the accomplishing of
his ends. And alas, his subtlety overreacheth not only the ignorant people,
but the most learned divines, and prudent princes. They shall not manage
their affairs of state so carefully, but he will engage them against Christ
and the peace of the church, before they are aware: He will do his utmost
to make the interest of Christ and the prince, of the church and the commonwealth, to seem to stand at an enmity to each other, and make princes
walk in a jealousy of Christ, and his Gospel, and ministers, lest they should
encroach upon their honour and greatness: and too oft he engageth them
in flat opposition, till this stone fall upon them, and grind them to powder.

And the ministers of the Gospel shall scarcely manage their work so
wisely, but he will cast in some wildfire, and find some occasion to make
a dissention by. Either the subtlety of men too wise and learned, in their
own eyes, shall start some dividing, fruitless controversies; or the zeal of
men that are orthodox over much, shall rise up unpeaceably against all dissenters: or he will entangle the godly in some dangerous errors; or he will
seek to make men lay snares for their brethren, by needless impositions,
under pretence of order, and decency, and unity, and authority: or some
passionate words shall kindle the fire. There are many unsound hypocrites
among the godly ministers; and there is too much pride and passion in the
best, and Satan knows how to make use of all: What saith he to the proud,
Shall such a one be preferred before thee? Shall he bear away the applause?
Shall he eclipse and stand in the way of thy reputation? Did he not speak
dishonourably of thee; or carry himself disregardfully towards thee? Did

he not disgrace thee by such an opposition or dispute? A hundred temptations hath Satan at hand to kindle dissention, even among the ministers of Christ: and where he meets with proud hearts he seldom misseth of his purpose. If the disciples were striving which should be the greatest, and if Paul and Barnabas fall out to a parting, no wonder if pride and dissention be yet found among the most renowned men. Though it is a sad case that it should be so, when we daily preach humility to our people, and know, that except conversion make us like little children, we can in no wise enter into the kingdom of God. (Matt. 18:3.)

How hard a task hath a peaceable minister to keep one congregation of Christians in peace. But differences will be rising, and one will be provoking another by injuries, or hard words, and few can bear, and forbear, and forgive: Yea, a master of a family finds it hard to keep one small family in peace. Yea, two persons will find somewhat to do to keep peace, especially if they have much trading, or dealing with each other, or any crossing in matters of commodity. Yea, husband and wife, that are as one flesh, have much ado to avoid dissentions. No wonder then if the enemy of peace can disturb the church of Christ.

15. Another cause of divisions is, living among, and hearkening to schismatical persons that are still blowing the coals. It is a dangerous case, especially to young, unexperienced Christians, to fall among those that make it their religion to vilify others as enemies of Christ: When they hear one sect only extolled, and all others spoken of as ignorant, or carnal, or enemies to the church, it is two to one but this imprinteth a schismatical disposition in the hearers' minds. Conversing only with one party doth usually occasion great uncharitableness towards all others, and sear the conscience, so that it grows insensible of revilings, and opprobrious speeches, against those that differ from them.

16. And the unity of the church is exceedingly hindered by an unworthy privacy and retiredness of most Christians that live like the snail in a shell, and look but little abroad into the world. Some know not the state of the world, or of the church, nor much care to know it; but think it is with all the world as it is with us in England: when as if they knew the fewness of Christians, the huge numbers of infidels, the corruptions of other churches, in comparison of ours, it would surely set them lamenting, and praying that the kingdom of Christ might come. Yea, many ministers are of so base a privacy of spirit, that they look little further than their own parishes, and think if all be well there, all is well everywhere;

and seldom inquire how it goes with the church in the rest of the world: nor will scarcely be brought to associate and keep correspondence with their brethren, for the union and communion of the several churches and the common good: far unlike the temper of Paul and the other apostles and servants of Christ in those days. They have not a care of all the churches. They long not to hear of their welfare. They would think it much to travail and labour for it the thousandth part so much as they. They cannot say, "who is weak, and I am not weak," &c.

17. Yea, some are drawn from the church's unity and peace by misunderstanding those texts of Scripture that call for separation from the world, and that speak of the fewness of those that shall be saved. I have heard of one that turned Separatist upon this conceit, because he thought that, seeing the flock of Christ is little, the Protestants were too many to be it: at last the separated church grew so big, that he thought, surely this is not the little flock, and so turned to the Anabaptists: at last the Anabaptists' church so increased, that he thought, surely this is too big to be the little flock; and so went seeking about for the least, as thinking that must needs be in the right. Alas, what low thoughts have such of the church of God! Yea, and of the love and gracious nature of God, and of the great design of Christ in the work of redemption! But the main cause of the delusion of these poor souls is, because they know not the state of the world abroad. If they did but know that it is the sixth part of the world that are baptized common Christians, and not past a sixth or seventh part of that sixth part that are common Protestants, but all the rest are Papists, and Greeks, and many sorts of more ignorant, unreformed Christians; and among the Protestants, no country for godliness is like to England; they would not go about to pen up the church into a narrower room. To believe that Christ died, and made so much ado for so small a part of the world, as comes not to one of forty, or fifty, or an hundred thousand, is next to flat infidelity itself; which thinks he died for none at all.

And for the command, "Come out from among them, and be ye separate," it is pity that any Christian should need be told, that it speaks only to the church to come out of the heathen, infidel world, (such as are Jews, and Mahometans, and heathens;) but there is never a word in all the Bible that bids you 'Come out of the church, and be ye separate!' Wonderful! that God should be so abused by misunderstanding Christians! Because he commands men to come out of the infidel world into the church, they plead it as if he commanded them to come out of the church into a separated sect.

The church is the house of Christ; forsake it not, while he stays in it: forsake it not, for he hath promised never to forsake it. Particular churches indeed he may cast off, but never the universal. Dwell therefore where he dwells.

18. Another hindrance of peace is, that so many Christians as they have carnal dispositions, so they are still looking at carnal means. The endeavours of the ministry they account as nothing; but they are still looking what the Magistrate will do: and till he force them they will not stir, and till he do it they think there is nothing done: such base thoughts have some, even ministers, of their own callings. And hence it is that such men are always on the stronger side, and of the king's religion; or else are seeking carnal advantages to carry on their cause. So the Jesuits are more busy to get the princes of the world engaged for them, and the arms of the nations employed for their ends, than we are to treat of unity and peace: And every party, instead of seeking peace, is seeking to get highest, that they may be able to force all others to their will: and we can never get any peaceable debates upon equal terms, because the several parties do seldom stand on equal terms: but still one is up, and another is down: and he that is in the saddle will not light to treat of peace, nor hearken to any equal motions, but must have his will, and nothing less will serve the turn: and when he is down, and the other party is up, the case is the same. Still he that is lowest is most reasonable and peaceable, (except some impious, implacable spirits:) but the party that is highest will not be brought to reason. And thus the peace of the church is hindered, to our grief and shame.

19. Another great hindrance of unity and concord is the great weaknesses and miscarriages of the professors of godliness, partly because of hypocrites among them, and partly because they are sanctified but in part. Among others, by these several ways, they do disturb our peace.

1. By an ignorant quarrelling with their teachers, thinking themselves fit to correct their guides before they are considerably grounded in the catechism.

2. By entertaining false opinions, and making a disturbance for them.

3. By the great diversity of opinions among themselves, by which they become a scorn or stumbling-block to many about them.

4. By the uncharitable bitterness of their spirits, in rash censures and contendings.

5. By their scandalous lives, and falls, disgracing their profession, and hardening and alienating the minds of others.

And, 6. By their imprudent and intemperate dealing with others; using proud or provoking language, or carriage that more savoureth of contempt than of compassion. And thus the children of the church do divide it. Especially by their childish fallings out with one another, and hearkening to malicious, contentious hypocrites, that would lead them to despise their guides, and break them into shreads among themselves. (Rom. 16:17.)

20. Lastly, The greatest hindrance of our unity is, the ungodliness of the most that profess themselves Christians, whereby they become incapable matter for our truest, nearest union, and yet think that we must be united to them all: when they will not join with us in the vitals of Christianity, but stick in the bark, and take up with the name, yet do they think that we must join with them, and be of their communion and opinions in all external things, and if we differ from them they think we are schismatics. Men lay the church's unity too much in mere speculations, which they call the Articles of faith, and too little in practicals, and holiness of life, whereas there is no article of faith, but is for practice; and as truly as the understanding and will are both essential to the soul; so truly the sanctity of understanding and will are both essential to a Christian: And as the holiness of the heart is as essential as faith to a real Christian, or member of the church regenerate; so the profession of holiness is as essential as the profession of faith to make a man a member of the church visible or congregate. And therefore as we can have no inward union and communion with any but the truly sanctified, so can we have no visible church-union or communion but with those that profess to be truly sanctified. It is a shameful thing to hear every drunkard and scorner at godliness to rail at the many divisions in the church, and to call for unity and concord, when it is he, and such as he, that hinder it, that will not be united to Christ himself, nor join with us in the only centre of union, nor in the greatest and most necessary things, without which all Christian union is impossible. But because I take this to be a necessary point, I shall handle it, God willing, more fully by itself.

To conclude all, let me exhort all Christians to drink in this truth into their judgments and affections. If you are Christians indeed, you are catholics. And if so, you must have, 1. Catholic principles, And, 2. Affections. I beseech you look to both these well.

And as you keep the great catholic principle, which is the subject of our discourse, viz. to know what a true catholic is, and which is the catholic church, that so you may not do as the Papists, that take up a sect under the abused name of Catholicism, and plead against the catholic church for that sect under the name of the catholic church; so also you must know and keep close to the true catholic rule; and not do as the Papists, that have honoured a private and crooked rule by that name, to the church's trouble, and their own delusion: and also you must keep close to the true catholic governor of the church, and judge of controversies, and turn not aside with Papists and others, to an usurper, or a private judge. In these three your Catholicism must much consist. The first, what the catholic church is, and what a true catholic, I have said as much to as I conceive necessary. The other two I shall say a little more to, viz. the catholic rule, and the catholic judge, and then of the fourth and last, which is, the catholic spirit or affections.

1. We are all agreed that the will of God revealed, must be, and is, the catholic rule of faith and life. But we are not all agreed which is this revelation of the will of God. That the book of the creatures and the principles of nature do reveal much natural-moral verity and duty we are agreed: but the doubt is of supernatural revelation. And of this we are agreed, that 'whatsoever is certainly delivered to the church by prophet or apostle, or any person infallibly proving a Divine inspiration or command to deliver what he speaks, must be received as from God. And whatever is so revealed concerning faith or duty, by way of imposition, is our rule: and if revealed to all, it is the rule to all.' We are agreed also, that the holy Scriptures containing those books which the Reformed churches take for the canon, are a Divine, infallible revelation concerning faith and duty. And therefore we are all agreed that the holy Scriptures are the rule. But whether they be the whole rule we are not agreed. The Reformed churches say, that the sign is but to make known the doctrine signified: and that while the inspired apostles were themselves alive, their own voices were the sign, and instead of a written word to all that heard them, and more. But knowing that they must die, and that the word of persons not infallibly inspired, is no rule of faith, and how hardly things not written are preserved from alteration and deprivation, therefore they left their doctrine in writing, for the easier and surer, and more universal communication and preservation. And that universal, infallible tradition hath delivered us down both this Scripture, and also (by itself) the sum of Christianity, in the creed and baptismal covenant, and in the hearts of the faithful from age to age. So that we make very high account of tradition, as bringing us in one hand the essentials of Christianity, and in the other the whole body of sacred doctrine in the Scriptures, containing all these essentials, and more. And this is the rule

of our faith and life: Yet we confess, that if any could prove a certain delivery of any more from the apostles to the church, we are ready to receive it, which way ever it be delivered. But the Papists add, that partly tradition, and partly the canons and decrees of the church, are to be received as the rule as well as Scripture, and that much is revealed by verbal tradition to that end, which is not in Scripture, which is with equal pious affection and reverence to be received; and that the church, which is the keeper of this tradition, is only the Roman church, or all that believe in the Pope of Rome, as the universal head or sovereign of the church.

Now the question is, 'Whether theirs or ours be the catholic rule?'

And here the wickedness of factious disputers hath done the church a world of wrong on both sides. Some are so mad in their contentions, that they care not what they say scarcely, so they do but cry down one another. The Papists cannot cry up their tradition, but they must speak so reproachfully, impiously, foolishly, of the Scriptures, as if they were stark infidels. To omit others, the reading of Rushworth's Dialogues, and White's Additions and Defence, is a notable bait to tice men to infidelity, and those dialogues contain the very same arguments which the new apostate infidels use. And on the other side, many to say as much as they can against the Papists, do so cry down traditions, that they ('tantum non') disable themselves to make good the Scripture itself. O perverseness! O doleful fruits of contentions! Whereas a true catholic should be glad of any light from heaven whatsoever: and must know, that God in great mercy to his church hath by these two hands delivered us his will: not some part in Scripture, and the rest by unwritten traditions, as say the Papists; but some part by such tradition, and all by Scripture, and that Scripture by tradition. So that God hath given us two strings to one bow: and the Papists will have two bows also; and others will have but one string.

Well; 1. I prove that the Scripture is the catholic rule.

That is the catholic rule of faith, which the whole church in all ages and places hath received as the rule: But such is the Scripture. Papists and Protestants, Greeks and Armenians, Abassines and all Christians, confess that the canonical Scriptures are the revelation of the will of God: so that this must be catholic, which the catholic church receiveth.

2. And I prove that the Papists' rule is a sectarian, crooked rule, and not catholic. 1. That is not the catholic rule of faith which the catholic church did never receive: But such is the popish rule of Roman tradition: Therefore if you take it in the general, viz. the traditions of the Roman church to be

received by her peculiar authority. (1.) The Reformed churches now disown it. (2.) The Greeks and other Eastern and Southern churches now disown it. (3.) The primitive church did never own it: so that all the church was once a stranger to their rule, and the most of it is an adversary to it at this day. And can that be the catholic rule which most of the catholic church disclaims? The Eastern and Southern churches think that the Roman traditions are of no more authority than their own; nay, of far less, and much of them false. 2. If you look to their additions of the apocryphal books, to the canon of the Scriptures, the ancient catholic church was against them; as Dr. Reignolds, and newly Dr. Cosin at large, and through every age hath shewed. 3. If you come to particulars: the very essence of the Roman Catholicism and church, and the universal headship still of their Pope, which are the master points of their tradition, are denied and detested by the far greater part of the catholic church on earth to this day. And is this a catholic rule which the catholic church denieth? A great stir the Papists make about catholic tradition, and the judgment of the catholic church. But what good would this do them if we were as much for tradition as they? When the most of the catholic church condemneth them and their traditions, or own them not, even in the principal points essential to their religion?

And what have they to say to this? Nothing but what any thief may say of a true man when he hath cut his purse, even to call him thief first! Forsooth, most that are called Christians, by far, are all heretics, and therefore none of the catholic church; and therefore their votes are no impeachment to the papal claim. And how prove you that? 'Why the Pope saith so, and so do his faction.' Why, but he is a party! How know we that he saith true? Why, here you must leave them: 'He saith that he saith true; therefore he saith true: He saith that the most of the church are not of the church, but heretics, and that none but his subjects are of the church, therefore it is true.' And so he must be the judge in his own cause, and be believed by the catholic church on his own authority. Read but the third section of Rushworth's Second Heathenish Dialogues, and see what a silly shift the self-conceited disputant is at in answering this objection, 'All Christians agree in the acceptation of the Scripture, and far fewer in divers points of doctrine: for the churches of the Roman communion are no such extraordinary part of Christendom, compared to all the rest. Answ. For the extent of the churches I cannot certainly tell you the truth, because I fear many are called Christians, who have little either in their belief or lives to verify that name: But you know in witnesses the quality is to be respected, as well

and more than the quantity: so that those countries in which Christianity
is vigorous, are to be preferred before a greater extent of such where little
remains more than the name. Suppose, in a suit at law, one party had seven
legitimate witnesses, the other as many, and besides them twenty knights
of the post, (known perjured knaves,) would you cast the cause for this
wicked rabble?' Thus Rushworth.

And is this all? And is this a catholic cause or rule? You see now from
their most violent subtle disputers, that they dare not stand to the major
vote. They cannot deny but the Papists are the far smaller number: And
most must not carry it! How then? Why we must be judged by the best, and
not by the most. Content: And I must solemnly profess, that if my salvation
lay upon it, and I were to go to-morrow, either to heaven or hell, according
to my choice of the holier party to trust my faith upon, I should make as
little doubt whether the Reformed or the Roman professors be more holy,
(as far as ever I was able to discern,) as I should do whether the Latin or the
Greek church be the more learned. If godliness and honesty of witnesses
must carry it, I must live and die where I am. But especially when the
Papists are worsted at both, and have neither the greater part, nor the more
honest, (of which I am quite past doubt, as I am whether England be better
and greater than the Orcades,) where then is their catholic faith and rule?

As for all the heathenish cavils of Rushworth against the certainty of
Scripture, because of the language, the translations, and such blind, malignant exceptions, I shall answer them, if God will, in a more fit place.

2. Having spoken of the catholic rule, let me next advise you to keep
close to the Catholic Governor and Judge. And who is that? Even Jesus Christ
himself, and none but he. Why, but is there not a visible head and catholic
judge of controversies on earth? To deny this seems an intolerable absur-
dity to a Papist: Then every man may believe what he list, or what his own
fancy leads him to? Answ. 1. And if the Pope can cure heresy or infidelity,
why doth he suffer most of the world to be infidels, and most of professed
Christians to be, in his judgment, heretics? And if he can decide all controversies, why suffers he so many hundreds to be undecided among his
followers. And it seems by the late determination of the Five Jansenian
Articles, that neither he nor his subjects know when he hath decided a
controversy, and when not. He said he condemned five points of the doctrine of Jansenius: the Jesuits say so too: the Jansenists say, It is not so,
they are none of his doctrines, nor to be found in him in word or sense. 2.
The catholic judge doth not contradict the catholic rule; but the Pope and

his Council doth. 3. The catholic Judge contradicteth not himself, but so do Popes and Councils. 4. That is not the catholic judge whom most of the catholic church disowneth, and never did own: but most of them never owned the Pope. But of all this I entreat the unsatisfied reader to peruse what I have written in the Second and Third Disputation against Popery.

Object. 'But what! Will you have no visible judge of controversies?' Answ. Yes: but not over all the catholic church. Quest. 'But who then shall be judge?' Answ. The case is plain, if men were but impartial. Discerning is one thing, teaching is another, and deciding or determining is another. A discerning judgment, as far as they are able, belongs to all: A directing or teaching judgment occasionally and 'ex charitate' belongs to all that are able; and publicly and ordinarily, 'ex officio,' it belongs to all pastors and teachers. Neither of these is the judgment now inquired after, but the third. If a man know not the articles of faith, the teachers of the church are to instruct him. But if a man deny the articles of faith, the same teachers of the church are to endeavour to convince him of his error, and better inform him: and thus far judicial decisive power is unnecessary. But if he will not be convinced, but still deny the articles of the faith, then comes in the judicial decisive power in order to his punishment. The articles of faith are to be discerned, and judged by, but not judged themselves any otherwise than to be taught: but it is the heretic or offender that is to be judged. And the judgment being in order to execution, there is a twofold judgment, as there is a twofold execution. 1. If the question be, Who shall be taken for a heretic, in order to the corporal punishment or forcible coercion of him by the sword, here the magistrate only is the judge: and it is, 1. A vile usurpation in the Pope to take this power out of his hands. 2. And it is an intolerable abuse of magistrates! It makes them but like hangmen, or mere executioners, when the Pope and his clergy must be the judges of heresies, and the magistrate must but execute their judgment: What if the church or Pope judge a catholic to be a heretic, must the magistrate therefore burn an innocent member of Christ? They confess themselves that the Pope may err in matter of fact, and judge a man to be a heretic that is none: and if he could not err, yet surely his clergy may: Yea, they confess a General Council may, and say, they did err in condemning Pope Honorius of heresy. And must kings, and judges, and all magistrates, hang and burn all innocent people that the Popish clergy shall falsely judge heretics? Will it justify them before God to say, The Pope or bishops bid us burn them? No, I had rather be a dog, than be a king upon these conditions. 3. And indeed it is impossible for the Pope himself to be judge of all men through the world that are guilty of heresy. For he is many hundred or thousand miles off: and there must be a present judge that shall hear the cause and witnesses; and there must be many thousand of these judges to the whole world: and can the Pope or Council then serve alone? If every heretic in England escape till a Pope or Council have the hearing or judging of him, he will not fear.

Object. 'But the Pope and Council are to judge what is heresy, and what not, though not to judge all particular causes; and then the bishops must judge the causes.'

Answ. God hath told us already in his word, which are the articles of our faith, and the universal church hath delivered us all the essential articles in creeds, professions, and the baptismal covenant! And therefore here is no work for a judge, but for a teacher. The pastors of the church must teach us 'ex officio,' with authority, which are the articles of faith; but they have no power to judge an article to be no article, nor to make any new article: and to judge an article to be an article, any man may do by judgment of discerning, and any teachers by a judgment of direction. If moreover you would have no article of faith to be believed to be such, but on the word or credit of the Pope or Council, and so resolve our faith into them, I have fully confuted this in my Third Dispute against Popery! The word of God must be believed, whether men know the mind of the Pope and Council, or not: but this is the highest arrogancy of the Papal sect, that they must not have God's own laws believed, or received by any, but upon their word and credit: and so we must know that they are authorized hereto, and infallible, before we know the articles of our faith; and so we must believe in Christ's vicar before we can believe in Christ? This is the ground of the Papal cause. Well, I think I may take it for granted by this time, that with reasonable, impartial, considerate men the case is plain, that it is magistrates, and not the Pope, that are judges who is to be corporally punished for heresy! And if every bishop must do it, then, 1. They must prove every bishop infallible; and, 2. Then they have not one catholic judge of faith but many.

And what if we had granted them a power in the Pope or Council to judge of God's law, and what is an article of faith, and what is heresy? Yet this will be far from restraining heresies, as long as there is no judge of the particular case: And if we have as many judges of the cause and person as there be bishops, then we have not one catholic judge of persons and causes; and if we must have fallible bishops, yea, and Popes, to judge of the person and fact, then we have but fallible restrainers of heresy.

2. The second sort of judgment is in order to church punishments. When the question is not, Who shall be punished by the sword? But Who shall be avoided by the church as a heretic? Here it is the church that is to judge; even that church that must avoid or reject them from communion. And therefore as communion is of narrower or wider extension, so must excommunication, and judging of heretics be. If the question be only, whether this man be to be avoided as a heretic by this particular church where he liveth? That church must judge. If the question be, Whether he be to be avoided as a heretic by all the churches of the country or nation, it is all these churches that must judge. For who should judge but those that must practise, and answer for their practice? And how can the Pope or Council be able to judge persons and causes that they know not; and to judge so many millions throughout the world? If you could prove that the whole catholic church were bound to take notice of this individual heretic, and were capable of actual communion, and avoiding communion with him, and of congregating to judge him, then I should consent that all Christendom should meet to excommunicate a heretic, if they had no better work the while to do. But the case is plain, that the church that must execute, must judge: the church that must avoid the communion of the heretic, must judge him to be avoided: and I think the Pope and General Councils will not undertake all this work.

You have nothing therefore to say, but to recur to the former way in your objection, viz. That it is the work of Pope and General Councils to judge what is faith and heresies, and the work of provincial synods or bishops to judge the offenders by their canons.

Answ. That is plainly; the Pope and Council must make the law, and the bishops judge by it. But, 1. God hath made the church's law already: we know but this one Lawgiver to the church, to constitute articles of faith and spiritual duty. And is this all that you make such a noise about, when you say, Who shall be judge of faith, and heresy, and controversy? That is, Who shall make laws against them, to tell us which is faith, and which is heresy? Why God hath done this already in the Scripture. 2. And this will not answer your own expectations in resolving your doubt: For if the Pope's legislation be all his judging of controversies, there will be never the fewer controversies or heresies in the world: for there is no law that hath a virtue sufficient to compel all the subjects to obey it. If God's law cannot do it, neither can the Pope's.

Object. 'But every heretic pleadeth Scripture, and saith, it is for him; and shall there be no judge to put an end to all these controversies about the sense of Scripture?'

Answ. 1. If there be any absolute judge of the sense of Scripture, his work is to give the world a decisive commentary upon it: which no Pope or Council hath done. 2. And he should actually decide all the controversies afoot, which the Pope dare not attempt; but leaves hundreds undecided among themselves, and more than ever were among the Protestants. 3. It is the work of a teacher, and not a catholic judge, to acquaint men with the meaning of the law. 4. For all their malignant accusation of the Scriptures, they do as plainly deliver us the articles of Christian faith, and the necessary Christian duties, as any Pope or Council hath done. And if all the work for a Pope or Council be to teach God how to speak or mend his word, and make sense of it, when God hath made it but nonsense, in their presumptuous judgments, then we can well spare such a judge as this. 5. There is as much contention among yourselves about the meaning of the canons of Councils, and the Pope's decretals: and who must be judge of all these controversies? Even the late Council of Trent is pleaded by one party for one side, and another for the contrary: yea, even by the particular divines that were members of the Council: and yet no deciding judge steps up, but let the contenders worry one another, and there is no end of their disputes.

So that the case is as plain as can be desired, 1. That constituting by a law or universal rule, to determine what shall be taken for faith, and what for heresy, this God hath done, who is the only Universal Lawgiver, and we need no Pope for it. 2. To judge who is to be corporally punished as a heretic belongs to the magistrate in his own jurisdiction, and not to the Pope or bishops: (as hath been made good in all ages against them, since they claimed it, as the many tractates of Goldastus' collection manifests.) 3. To judge who shall be cast out of the communion of the church as a heretic, and avoided, belongs to the church that hath communion with him, and that is to avoid him; and to all other churches, so far as they are naturally capable of communion and non-communion with him, and of the cognizance of the case, and bound to take notice of it. So that all human judgment is but limited, and 'ad hoc,' the judgment being but in order to the execution. 4. And therefore the absolute final judgment is only that of Christ himself, to whom we must make our appeals, and from whom there is no appeal: And this is the true decision of this question, that makes so loud a noise,' Who shall be judge of controversies in faith, and of heresies?'

And thus you see that Scripture is the catholic rule, and Christ the catholic judge, and the magistrate the judge 'ad hoc,' who shall be corporally punished, and the pastors and church where communion or avoiding the party is a duty, are judges 'ad hoc,' whether he be to be avoided. And this is the next catholic principle.

Before I come to speak of the last, (which is, catholic affections) I shall briefly name some principles contrary to the catholic principles, which I would warn you to avoid: and I shall not stand upon them, but touch them.

1. It is a private and not-catholic principle, to hold that we are not baptized into the catholic church, but into a particular church only. As the case of the eunuch, (Acts 8,) and the baptismal institution shew.

It is a private principle, contrary to Catholicism, to hold that an authorized minister of Christ, is only a minister in that church which is his special charge, and where we confess he is bound to exercise his ordinary labours, and that he may not preach, baptize, administer the Lord's-supper, yea, and rule 'pro tempore,' as a minister in another church to which he is called. As physicians must first have a general licence, upon exploration and approbation, to practise physic when they are called, and afterward may have a special call and engagement to a particular hospital or city as their charge, and so do practise occasionally upon a particular call abroad, but ordinarily at home, as to their special charge, but to both as physicians; so is it with a pastor in the church of Christ.

3. It is a private and uncatholic principle, that a minister is so bound to that one congregation which is his special charge, as that he must prefer them and their service before the more public service of the churches, and must neglect opportunities of doing apparently much greater good, for fear of neglecting them. All our obligations are strongest to our ultimate end, and next to that which is next that end, and so more to the public than to any particulars as such.

4. And it is a private uncatholic principle, that a minister should more fear or avoid the offending or hurting of his own particular flock, than the offending and hurt of the catholic church, or of many particular churches, where the interest of Christ and the Gospel is greater, we are more obliged to God, and the catholic church, than we can be to any man or particular church. A physician of an hospital, 'cæteris paribus,' must prefer his own charge before any others, and rather neglect a stranger's life than theirs: but he should rather neglect one of his own charge, than a prince, or many

considerable persons abroad, or all his own charge, than persons, or cities, or countries of far more public use and interest.

5. It is a private uncatholic principle, that ministers may satisfy their consciences if they stay at home, and only look after their own congregations, and never go to the assemblies of the ministers, where more public affairs of the churches are transacted, nor by preaching abroad where necessity requireth it, be helpful to other places.

6. And it is an uncatholic principle, to hold that the assemblies and associations of pastors, and concatenation of churches by them, is a needless thing; or that they are not to be ordinary, and fixed, for a certain settled way of the communion of churches and brethren, but only occasional and seldom; and that it is indifferent whether we be there.

7. And it is an uncatholic dividing principle to hold, that when the churches agree upon a circumstance of worship as convenient, any particular persons shall walk singularly, and refuse to consent to that agreement, unless it be against the word of God.

8. It is not according to catholic principles, for any man of another church to make light of the reproofs, advice or teaching, of any faithful minister of Christ, because they are not members of his charge.

9. Nor is it a catholic principle for a minister to hold, that a fit person of another church may not have communion with him and his charge, and partake of the ordinances among them, when they are for a time cast into their neighbourhood, and give sufficient testimony of their fitness.

10. It is a dividing uncatholic principle, to think that for every disorder, or gross sin, that (against our wills) is connived at in the church, we must therefore withdraw from the communion of that church, before sufficient means and patience have been used with them, and before the church do own the sin.

11. It is a dividing uncatholic principle, to hold that we must necessarily require the profession of more than the essentials of Christianity in order to the baptizing of any into the church, or that profession is no satisfactory evidence, (though there be no proof on the contrary to invalidate it,) unless there be some other discovery of the truth of grace. To deny the catholic qualification of visible members is not catholic.

12. It is a dividing, and not a catholic principle, that we must needs preach, profess, or declare every thing that we take to be a truth, though to the apparent hazard of the church, and hindrance of the great essential truths; and that no truth must be silenced for the church's peace, and the

advantage of the more necessary truths. And that we may not hold communion with those that agree not with us in some integrals of the Christian faith, though they agree in the essentials, and forfeit not the communion of the church by wicked lives.

Too many more such principles might be named, but I only warn you briefly of these few.

3. The last part of my advice is, that you labour to preserve a catholic spirit and affections. And a catholic spirit consisteth, 1. In a catholic love. 2. A catholic compassion. 3. A catholic care. And 4. A catholic endeavour to be serviceable to all.

I. A catholic love consisteth in these particulars, 1. That you love a Christian as a Christian, for the sake of Christ, and not for by-respects only: Not chiefly because he is rich, or honourable, or of eminent place, or parts, or personage, or because he loveth you, or any such lower respects; though these may have their parts in subserviency to the main; but the chief reason of your love must be, because he is a member of Christ, and beareth his image, and is serviceable to the glory of God, and one that is likely lo join with you in his everlasting praises.

2. That your love may be catholic, it must be a love to all that are Christians, as far as you can discern them, and have opportunity to observe them. Though he should differ from you in many points of religion, yet if he hold the essentials, and manifest the grace of God in his life, you must love him with the special love of a Christian. Though he have fallen out with you, or wronged you by word or deed, or have a low esteem of you, and slight you, whether deservedly or in a mistake, yet if he manifest the image of God, by his holy profession and conversation, you must afford him this special Christian love. Though he be a very weak Christian of parts, or graces, and subject to passions and infirmities, (consistent with grace) and his profession reach not to that height as may make him eminent, nor his life to that degree of diligence as may make you confident of his sincerity, yet if he have a profession of true faith, and repentance, and holiness, seemingly serious, and not invalidated or disproved by a contrary profession or practice, you must allow him the special love of a Christian. He that loveth a Christian as a Christian, must needs love all Christians that he discerneth to be such: and he must not by uncharitableness hinder that discerning.

3. And catholic love will be somewhat suitable to the excellency of the object, which is a member of Christ. He that loveth a Christian truly, doth

love him above gold, and silver, and worldly things; and therefore can part with his substance to relieve him, and venture his life for him, when God and his honour do require it. And therefore it is that Christ will not at the last day barely ask, Whether we have loved him in his members? but whether our love were such as could carry us to clothe, and feed, and visit, and relieve them to our power.

4. Lastly, catholic love must be diversified in the degree according to the apparent degree of men's graces and serviceableness to God, He that loveth men as Christians and godly, will love those best where he seeth most Christianity and godliness, and those least where he seeth least of it.

There is, 1. A common love of men as men; and this you owe to all, even to an enemy; and this may consist with a dislike or hatred of them as wicked, and God's enemies. 2. There is a love to men for some lovely, natural, or acquired parts; as wit, learning, eloquence, gentleness, a loving nature, and the like: and this is proper to them that are the qualified objects of it; you owe it not to all, and yet you may allow it to those that are no saints. But this is not the catholic love which I speak of. 3. There is the before-described love to a Christian, as a Christian; and this is the catholic love which is due to all that seem Christians. 4. There is a special degree of this love, which you owe to stronger and more excellent Christians, and to those whose profession and conversation doth put you into a more confident persuasion of their sincerity, than you have of many or most common professors. And this special degree is not due to all Christians. As we have but very small and doubtful persuasions of some men's sincerity, and more confident persuasions of others; so our love must be greater to one than to another, even where a special Christian love is due to them all. 5. There is a special suitableness in the spirits of but few, even of those that are stronger Christians, whereby they are fitted to be your bosom friends. And this extraordinary love of a bosom friend, such as was between David and Jonathan, and should be between husbands and wives, is not due to all, no, not all that all are strong Christians.

For natural love to parents, and children, and other natural relations; and for grateful love to benefactors, I shall say nothing to them, as not pertaining to our business; nor yet of the heavenly degree of love which is proper to glory. But I have shewed you what that special Christian love is which is truly catholic; and that it must be to all, and to all with a high degree; but not to all with an equal degree, but must be much diversified by their degrees of grace.

The love which is called, "The fulfilling of the law," containeth all the sorts beforementioned; but the love which is the new commandment of the Gospel, is this special endearedness of Christians to one another in their new relation, even, 1. As they believe in the Messiah as come, in whom they are all fellow-members and brethren. And 2. As they are disposed and elevated to this love, by a special measure of sanctification by the Spirit, proper to Gospel times.

This is the love to the brethren, by which we may know that we are translated from death to life, and so that we are true catholic Christians. (1 John 3:14.) "He that hath not this love abideth in death. By this it is that all men must know us to be Christ's disciples, that is, catholic Christians. (1 John 13:33.) If Christ have more skill in knowing his own sheep and sheep-mark than the Papists have, then this is a better mark of a catholic than believing in the Pope, as the universal sovereign of the church: even loving one another as Christians, for Christ's sake, and that "with a pure heart fervently." (1 Pet. 1:22.) "Not in word and tongue, but in deed and in truth," so as to part with worldly goods for our brethren's relief. (1 John 3:17, 18; Matt. 25:34. 40.

Reader, thou art a blessed man if thou hast this charitable catholic spirit, that thou canst love all Christians, as far as thou canst discern them, with a special Christian love. When others hate and reproach all those that are not of their sect, or at least have no special Christian love for them, let them be dear to thy heart, and amiable, because of the image and interest of thy Lord, even when thou art called to disown and rebuke (yea, or chasten, if a governor) their errors and imperfections. This lesson is written in the very heart of a true catholic; for "they are all taught of God to love one another." (1 Thess. 4:9.) Those, therefore, that malign all dissenters, and malice those that are not of their party, do carry about with them the brand of sectaries, how much soever they may seem to detest them. Those that deny the essentials of Christianity are not the objects of Christian love, but of common love only; but whatever infirmities are consistent with Christianity are insufficient to excuse us from this special love.

And here let me mind you of one other principle, which is notoriously uncatholic, while it pretendeth to be most catholic, and is here most fitly to be mentioned, as being the bane of catholic, Christian love; and that is the doctrine of many Papists, and some few Protestants, that make the necessary qualification of a church-member to be (the reality, 'coram Deo,' and the profession, 'coram Ecclesia,' of) a kind of dogmatical faith, which is short of justifying faith. From whence it followeth, that visible church-members, as such, are not to be taken by us for true living members of the body of Christ; but that esteem is due only to some few that manifest their holiness by an extraordinary profession, or fuller discovery: and consequently, that we are not bound to love any as living members of Christ, but such eminent professors: and so the special catholic love, which is the new commandment, and the badge of a disciple, is turned into a common love specifically different from it, and answerable to the common not-justifying faith: and the special catholic love is reserved as another thing for some few of the visible church: whereas indeed we may say of all that are duly visible members, by profession of a saving faith, not nulled, that as it is the same faith with that of the holiest saints which they profess, so it is the same specific love that is due to the holiest saint that they must be loved with: a great difference there must be in degree, but none in kind. We love none of them as infallibly known to be true living Christians, but all of them as probably such by profession; but with very different degrees, because of the different degrees of probability.

And let me add another principle, that tendeth to corrupt this catholic love, and that is theirs that would have the church lie common; and men that profess not saving faith, or that null that profession by a wicked, impenitent course of life, to be permitted in the church, and discipline laid aside, and so the common and unclean to be numbered with the visible saints. And so when the permitted members are such as by right are no members, nor so much as seeming saints, they cannot be the objects of catholic love. Destroy the object and you destroy the art.

II. The second catholic affection in compassion towards a Christian as a Christian in his sufferings. A sensibleness of their sufferings, as if we suffered with them, "And whether one member suffer, all the members suffer with it, or one member be honoured, all the members rejoice with it." (Heb. 13:3; 1 Cor. 12:26.) "Rejoice with them that do rejoice, and weep with them that weep: Be of the same mind one towards another." (Rom. 12:15, 16.) "Who is weak, and I am not weak? Who is offended, and I burn not?" (2 Cor. 11:29.) A true catholic is grieved to see his brother's calamity, and especially to hear of the dangers, and losses, and sufferings of the churches: be they never so distant from him, it is near to his heart, for their interest is his own.

He that feels nothing but his own afflictions, and can make a small matter of the losses and sufferings of the church, perhaps under pretence of trusting God, so that if all be but well with himself, is certainly no catholic or Christian. And he that little feels the losses of the church, if his own sect or party do but gain or increase by it, doth shew that he hath more of a sectary than of a Christian. Catholic compassion (to which I adjoin also catholic rejoicing) do prove a true catholic.

III. Another catholic affection is a special care of the common Christian state and cause, and of the case of all our brethren that are known to us. I mean not that care which belongs to God only, and which we are forbidden to use, even for ourselves; but, 1. An estimation of the interest of the church and brethren as their own, and 2. An ordinate solicitousness about their welfare, containing an earnest desire of it, and a care to use the means that should obtain it. A catholic spirit is busily careful about the church's and brethren's welfare as well as his own. "That there should be no schism in the body, but that the members should have the same care one for another." (1 Cor. 12:25.) Timothy naturally cared for the state of the churches: Such a care by grace he had of the churches, as he had by nature of himself; proceeding from so deep a love, as was a kind of new nature to him. (Phil. 2:20.) "That our care for you in the sight of God might appear to you." (2 Cor. 7:12.) Titus had an earnest care for the Corinthians. (2 Cor. 8:16.) Every pastor must have a care of his church, (1 Tim. 3:5,) but not stop there; but with Paul, "have a care of all the churches," (2 Cor. 11:28,) though not an apostolical charge of them like his. Carelessness of the church and brethren is not catholic.

IV. Lastly, A true catholic spirit must appear in catholic endeavours, for the good of all the members of the church. 1. It is contrary to a base, covetous, selfish spirit, which causeth men to mind and seek only their own, and not the things of Jesus Christ, and of their brethren: and will not allow men to part with any more than some inconsiderable pittance out of their superfluity, for their brethren's relief, or the church's service. "But whoso hath this world's goods, and seeth his brother have need, and shutteth up his bowels of compassion from him, how dwelleth the love of God in him?" (1 John 3:17.) He that cannot pinch himself, and deny himself even in his daily bread for the church and brethren, when God requireth it, is not a true catholic Christian.

2. And it is contrary much more to a spirit of malignity, by which men envy the good of others, or of those that are not of their party; and yet more to persecution, when men would tread down and destroy their brethren, and the inheritance of the Lord, in a selfish, devilish zeal.

3. But yet it is not contrary to a charitable, moderate correction of offenders, which tendeth either to their own or the church's good, and is necessary to the restraint of iniquity, and the preserving of others from the infection of error; and therefore the sword of the magistrate and the discipline of the church must both be employed in the cause of God; and this is so far from being contrary to the endeavours of a catholic spirit, that it is a necessary part of it. Correction first, proceedeth from love, and secondly, tendeth to good, and thirdly, is not used but in necessity; and this differeth from persecution, as the whipping of a child, from the malignant hurting of the innocent.

Quest. 'But how can the endeavours of a private Christian be extended to the catholic church?'

Answ. 1. His daily and earnest prayers to God may be extended to the whole, and must be. He is not of a catholic spirit that is not disposed to fervent prayers for the universal church of Christ. 2. And his actual assistance must reach as far as he can extend it; and then he that doth good to a part of the church, may well be said to do good to the catholic church in that part.

Quest. 'But what good is it that we should do?'

Answ. Besides that of prayer before-mentioned, 1. Maintain catholic truths and principles; earnestly contend for the catholic faith; and resist dividing, uncatholic principles and errors. 2. Maintain catholic affections in others to your power, and labour to draw them from privateness of spirit, and selfish or dividing affections. 3. Endeavour the actual healing of breaches among all catholics as soon as you perceive them. To that end, 1. Acquaint yourselves with healing truths; and labour to be as skilful in the work of pacifying and agreeing men, as most are in the work of dividing and disagreeing. Know it to be a part of your catholic work to be peace-makers; and therefore study how to do it as a workman that needeth not be ashamed. I think most divines themselves in the world do study differences a hundred hours, for one hour that ever they study the healing of differences; and that is a shameful disproportion. 2. Do not bend all your wits to find what more may be said against others, and to make the differences as wide as you can, but study as hard to find out men's agreements, and to reduce the differences to as narrow a compass as is possible. 3. And to that end, be sure that you see the true state of the controversy, and distinguish all that is merely verbal, from that which is material; and that which is but about methods, and modes, and circumstances, from that which is about substantial truths; and that which is about the inferior truths, though weighty, from that which is about the essentials of Christianity. 4. Be as industrious for peace among others as if you smarted by it yourself; seek it, and beg it, and follow it, and take no nay. Make it the work of your lives. When once God hath so awakened the hearts of his servants to see the beauty, and feel so much of the necessity of unity and peace in the church, as shall make them generally more zealous, and diligent, and unwearied in seeking them, than dividers are in seeking to destroy them, then may we expect a healing, and strength, and glory to the catholic church: but wishing will not serve the turn, nor will we much thank wishers for it if we be healed.

Lastly. Lay the unity of the church upon nothing but what is essential to the church. Seek after as much truth, and purity, and perfection as you can: but not as necessary to the essence of the church, or any member of it; nor to denominate and specify your faith and religion by. Tolerate no error or sin, so far as not to seek the healing of it: but tolerate all error and sin, consisting with Christian faith and charity, so far as not to unchristian and unchurch men for them. Own no man's errors, or sins, but own every man that owneth Christ, and whom Christ will own, notwithstanding those errors and infirmities that he is guilty of. Bear with those that Christ will bear with; especially learn the master-duty of self-denial: for it is self that is the greatest enemy to Catholicism. Self-conceitedness, and self-love, and self-willedness, and selfish interests, are the things that divide, and would make as many religions in the world as selfs. Even among many accounted orthodox, pride and selfishness causeth them so far to overvalue their own judgments, as to expect that all should be conformable to them, and bow to their arguments which have no strength, if not to their sayings and wills without their arguments; and to disdain, and passionately censure and reproach all that dissent and gainsay them. And thus every man, so far as he is proud and selfish, would be the Pope or centre of the catholic church. And therefore it is observable that Christ hath told us, "That except we be converted, and become as little children, we cannot enter into his kingdom." (Matt. 18:3.) "And if we deny not ourselves we cannot be his disciples." (Luke 9:23.) But of this I have spoken in another treatise.

And thus I have plainly from the word of God declared to you the true nature of Catholicism, and which is the catholic church, and who a catholic. I hope it may do somewhat to cure the frensy of the world, that makes men cry, Here is the church, and there is the church. That makes one sect say, We are the church, and another say, We are the church. I hope it may

do somewhat to the confounding of the arrogancy and presumption of all
sects, especially the sect of Papists, that being but a piece of the church,
and that none of the best, dare pretend to be the whole, and restrain the
name of Catholics or Christians to themselves! And I hope it may do somewhat to awake the servants of Christ to more catholic considerations, and
principles, and affections, and endeavours, that those that have lived too
much to themselves, and too much to their own parties, as if the church
had been confined to their narrow provinces, may hereafter look more
abroad into the world, and remember the extent of the kingdom of Christ,
and not think so dishonourably of it as they have done. I hope also it may
help to abate the censoriousness and presumption of those that would rob
Christ of the greatest part of his inheritance, and deliver it up to Satan,
his enemy. And I hope it may somewhat disgrace the dividing principles
and practices of these times, and turn soldiers into surgeons, wounding
into healing, and excite in some a stronger desire for unity and peace, and
cause them to extend their care and charity further than they have done.
However, this here described, is the catholic church which God will own.
This is it that is built on Christ the Rock, which the gates of hell shall not
prevail against. Here is the safe standing, from whence you may look with
boldness, thankfulness, and compassion, upon the many sects, and furi-
ous contentions of the world; and lament their giddiness, without being
brought yourselves to a loss about the truth of your church or faith: and
may see the folly of them that are puzzled to find out the true catholic
church and religion. And here you may see the admirable privilege of a
truly regenerate, sanctified person, that is most certainly a member of the
true catholic church, whoever deny it. To conclude, you may hence see that
it is not as Romanists, Greeks, Armenians, Abassines, Jacobines, Lutherans,
Calvinists, Arminians, &c., that men are saved, but as catholic Christians,
aspiring to the highest perfection.

Part II: Catholic Unity

Or, the Only Way to Bring Us All to Be of One Religion

To be read by such as are offended at the differences in religion, and are willing to do their part to heal them

— *Preface*

To all those in the several Parishes of these Nations, that
complain of the Disagreements in Matters of Religion.

Men and Brethren,

As in the midst of all the impiety and dishonesty of the world, it is some
comfort to us, that yet the names of piety and honesty are still in credit,
and ungodliness and dishonesty are terms of disgrace; so that those that
will be ungodly and dishonest, are fain to use the mask and veil of better
names, to hide their wickedness; so also it is some comfort to us, in the
midst of the uncharitableness and discords of this age, that yet the names
of Love and Concord sound so well, and are honoured by those that are
farthest from the things: for thus we seem agreed in the main cause, and
have this advantage in our debates, that whatever shall be proved to be
against love, and unity, and peace, we are all of us obliged by our professions to disown. I may suppose that all that read these words, will speak
against the uncharitableness, and contentions, and divisions of the present times as well as I. Doth it grieve my soul to hear professed Christians
so censoriously condemning, and passionately reviling one another,
while they are proudly justifying themselves? I suppose you will say, it
grieves you also. Do I mourn in secret, to see so many divisions and sub-
divisions, and church set up against church, and pastors against pastors,
in the same parishes; and each party labouring to disgrace the other and
their way, that they may promote their own? I suppose you will say, you
do so too. Do I lament it as the nation's shame, that in religion men are of
so many minds, and manage their differences so unpeaceably, that it is
become the stumbling-block to the ungodly, the grief of our friends, and
the derision of our enemies? I know you will say, that this also is your

lamentation. And is it not a wonder indeed, that such a misery should be continued, which all men are against; and which cannot be continued but by our wilful choice? Is it not strange that we are so long without so great a blessing as Unity and Peace, while all men say they love it and desire it; and while we may have it if we will? But the cause is evident; while men love unity, they hate the holiness in which we must unite: while they love peace, they hate the necessary means by which it must be obtained and maintained: the way of peace they have not known; or knowing it, they do abhor it. As well as they love unity and peace, they love the causes of discord and division much better. The drunkard, and whoremonger, and worlding say they love the salvation of their souls: but yet while they love and keep their sins, they will miss of the salvation which they say they love. And so while men love their ungodliness and dividing ways, we are little the better for their love of peace. If men love health, and yet love poison, and hate both medicine and wholesome food, they may miss of health, notwithstanding they love it.

Where know you a parish in England, that hath no disagreements in matters of religion? In this parish where I live, we have not several congregations, nor are we divided into such parties as in many other places; but we have here the great division; some are for heaven, and some for earth; some love a holy, diligent life, and others hate it; some pray in their families, and teach them the word and fear of God, and others do not; some spend the Lord's-day in holy exercises, and others spend much of it in idleness and vanity; some take the service of God for their delight, and others are weary of it, and live in ignorance, because they will not be at the pains to learn: some make it the principal care and business of their lives to prepare for death, and make sure of everlasting life; and others will venture their souls on the wrath of God, and cheat themselves by their own presumption, rather than be at this sweet and necessary labour to be saved. Some hate sin, and make it their daily work to root out the relics of it from their hearts and lives; and others love it and will not leave it, but hate those that reprove them, and endeavour their salvation.

And as long as this great division is unhealed, what other means can bring us to any happy unity? It would make a man's heart bleed to consider of the folly of the ungodly rout, that think it would be a happy union, if we could all agree to read one form of prayer, while some love, and others hate the holiness which they pray for: and if we could all agree to use the sign of the cross in baptism, while one half either understand not the baptismal covenant, or wilfully violate it, and neglect, or hate, and scorn that mortified holy life, which by that solemn vow and covenant they are engaged to. They are solicitous to bring us all to unity in the gesture of receiving the sacrament of the Lord's-supper, while some take Christ and life, and others take their own damnation. When they should first agree in being all the faithful servants of one Master, they make a great matter of it, that the servants of Christ and of the devil may use the same bodily posture in that worship where their hearts are as different as Spirit and flesh. Poor people think that it is the want of uniformity in certain ceremonies of man's invention, that is the cause of our great divisions and distractions; when, alas! it is the want of unity in matters of greater consequence, even of faith, and love, and holiness, as I have here shewed. If once we were all children of one Father, and living members of one Christ, and all renewed by one sanctifying Spirit, and aimed at one end, and walked by one rule, (the word of God,) and had that special love to one another which Christ hath made the mark of his disciples, this were an agreement to be rejoiced in indeed, which would hold us together in the most comfortable relations, and assure us that we shall live together with Christ in everlasting blessedness. But, alas! if our agreement be no better, than to sit together in the same seats, and say the same words, and use the same gestures and ceremonies, our hearts will be still distant from each other, our natures will be contrary, and the malignity of ungodly hearts will be breaking out on all occasions. And as now you hear men scorning at the practice of that religion which themselves profess, so if God prevent it not, you may shortly see another war take off their restraint and let them loose, and then they will seek the blood of those that now they seem to be agreed with. At furthest we are sure, that very shortly we shall be separated as far as heaven and hell, if there be not now a nearer agreement than in words and outward shows and ceremonies.

It being then past doubt, that there is no happy, lasting unity, but in the Spirit and a holy life, what hindereth us from so safe, so sweet, so pure a peace? Why might not all our parishes agree on such necessary, honourable and reasonable terms? Why is there in most places, but here and there a person, or a family, that will yield to the terms of an everlasting peace, and live as men that believe they have a God to serve and please, and immortal souls to save or lose? Is not God willing that "all should be saved, and come to the knowledge of the truth;" (1 Tim. 2:4;) and that all should agree in so safe a path? Why then doth he invite all, and tender them his saving mercy, and send his messengers to command and importune them to this holy concord? He would take them all into the bond of his covenant: how often would Christ have gathered all the children of Jerusalem to him, as the hen gathereth her chickens under her wings; but it was they that would not. (Matt. 23:37.) He would have the Gospel preached to every creature, (Matt. 16:15, 16,) and would have the kingdoms of the world become the kingdoms of the Lord and of his Christ.

What then is the cause of this sad division in our parishes? Are ministers unwilling that their people should all agree in holiness? No, it would be the greatest favour you could do them, and the greatest joy that you could bring to their hearts: they would be gladder to see such a blessed unity, than if you gave them all that you have in the world. O how a poor minister would boast and glory of such a parish! He would bless the day that ever he came among them; and that ever he was called to the ministry; and that ever he was born into the world for their sakes. How easy would all his studies and labours be, if they were but sweetened with such success! How easily could he bear his scorns and threatenings, and abuses, and persecution from others, if he saw but such a holy unity among his people to encourage him! So far are your teachers from excluding you from this happiness, that it is the end of their studies, and preaching, and prayers, yea, and of their lives, to bring you to partake of it. And glad would they be to preach to you, and exhort you, in hunger and thirst, in cold and nakedness, in all the contempt and derision of the world, if thereby they could but bring their parishes to agree in a life of faith and holiness.

And surely our difference is not because the godly will not admit you to join with them in the ways of God; for they cannot hinder you if they would; and they would not if they could. It is their joy to see the house of God filled with guests that have on the wedding garment.

We must conclude therefore, that it is the ungodly that are the wilful and obstinate dividers. They might be united to Christ, and reconciled to God, and they will not. They might be admitted into the communion of saints, and into the household of God, and partake of the privileges of his children; and they will not. They have leave to read, and pray, and meditate, and walk with God in a heavenly conversation, as well as any of their neighbours; but they will not. It is themselves that are the refusers, and continue the division, to the displeasing of God, and the grief of their friends, and the gratifying of Satan, and the perdition of their own immortal souls. We might all be united, and our divisions be healed, and God much honoured, and ministers and good Christians be exceedingly comforted, and the church and commonwealth be delivered and highly honoured, and themselves be saved from everlasting misery, if we could but get the hearty consent of these foolish, obstinate, ungodly men.

What say you, wretched souls, can you deny it? How long have your Teachers been labouring in vain, to bring you to the hearty love of God, and heaven, and serious holiness! How long have they been persuading you to set up reading, and catechising, and constant fervent prayer in your families, and yet it is undone! How long have they in vain been persuading the worldling from his worldliness, and the proud person to humility, and the sensual beast from his tippling, and gluttony, and other fleshly pleasures!

And besides this, most of the disorders and divisions in the churches are caused by ungodly men. I will instance in a few particulars.

1. When we ask any godly, diligent ministers, either in London, or the country, why they do not unanimously catechise, instruct and confer with all the inhabitants of their parishes, man by man, to help them to try their spiritual state, and to prepare in health for death and judgment? they usually answer us, that, alas! their people will not consent, but many would revile them if they should attempt it.

2. When we ask them why they do not set up the practice of discipline, which they so unanimously plead for; and why they do not call their people to confirmation, or open profession of faith and holiness in order thereto? they tell us, that their people will not endure it; but many will rather set themselves against the ministry, and strengthen the enemy that now endangereth the church's safety, or turn to any licentious sect, than they will thus submit to the undoubted ordinances of Christ, which the churches are so commonly agreed in as a duty.

3. We have an ancient, too-imperfect version of the Psalms, which we sing in the congregations; and in the judgment of all divines that ever I spoke with about it, (of what side soever,) it is our duty to use a better version, and not to perform so excellent a part of the public worship, so lamely, and with so many blemishes. And if you ask the ministers why they do not unanimously agree on a reformed, corrected version, most of them will tell you, that their people will not bear it, but proudly and turbulently reproach them, as if they were changing the word of God.

4. In many places the sacrament of baptism is more often used in private houses, than in the public assemblies; and if we ask the reason of so great a disorder, the ministers will tell us that it is the unruliness and

wilfulness of the people, that proudly set themselves above their guides, and instead of obeying them, must rule them, and have their humours and conceits fulfilled, even in the holy things of God, or else they will revile the pastors, and make divisions in the church: and this is done by them that in other cases do seem sufficiently to reverence the place of public assembly as the house of God, and that speak against private meetings, though but for prayer, repeating sermons, or singing to the praise of God, while yet themselves are wilfully bent for such private meetings as are set up in opposition to the public, and that for the administration of so great an ordinance as the sacrament of baptism, and in cases where there is no necessity of privacy: And who knows not that our sacramental covenant with God, and engagement to a Christian life, and reception into a Christian state and privileges, is fitter to be done with the most honourable solemnity, than in a conventicle, in a private house?

Too many more such instances I could give you, which shew who they be that are the enemies of our unity; even those that cry out against divisions while they cause them, and cry up unity, concord and obedience, while they destroy them.

And shall we thus continue a division that doth prognosticate our everlasting division? Is there no remedy for so great a misery, when yet our poor ungodly neighbours may heal it if they will? What if the ministers of the several parishes should appoint one day of public conference with all the people of their parishes together, and desire all that are fit to speak, to debate the case, and give their reasons, why they concur not in their hearts and lives with the holy diligent servants of the Lord? And let them hear the reasons why the godly dare not, and cannot come over to their negligent ungodly course? And so try who it is long of among them, that they are not of one mind and way? What if the ministers then urged it on them, to agree all before they parted, to unite on the terms which God will own, and all unanimously to take that course that shall be found most agreeable to his word; and whoever doth bring the fullest proof that his course is best, in reason, the rest should promise to join with him? What if we call the people together, and bespeak them as Elijah did, (1 Kings 18:21,) "How long halt ye between two opinions? If the Lord be God, follow him: but if Baal, then follow him." If a careless, ungodly, worldly, fleshly life be best, and most please God, and will comfort you most at death and judgment, then hold on in the way that you are in, and never purpose hereafter to repent of it, but let us all become as sensual as you. But if it be only the life of faith and holiness, and seeking first the kingdom and righteousness of God, that God, and Scripture, and reason will justify, and that will comfort the soul in the hour of extremity, and that you shall wish a thousand times you had followed, in everlasting misery, when wishing is too late, if now you continue to neglect it; doth not common reason then require, that we all now agree to go that way which all will desire to be found in at the last?

One would think, if a minister should treat thus with his parishioners, and urge such a motion as this upon them, they should not have the hearts or faces to deny, or delay such a necessary agreement and engagement that would make their parish and their souls so happy, and which nothing but the devil and the befooled, corrupted minds of sinners hath any thing to say against! And yet it is likely we should either have such an answer as Elijah had, even silence, ("The people answered him not a word." ver. 21,) or else some plausible promise, while we have them in a good mood, which would quickly be broken and come to nothing. For indeed they are all engaged already by their baptismal covenant and profession of Christianity, to the very same thing; and yet we see how little they regard it.

But yet because it is our duty to use the means for the salvation and concord of our people, and wait on God by prayer for the success, I have here shewed you the only way to both. Read it impartially, and then be yourselves the judges, on whom the blame of our greatest and most dangerous divisions will be laid; and for shame, either give over complaining that men are of so many minds, and profess yourselves the enemies of unity and peace; or else give over your damning, and dividing course, and yield to the Spirit of Christ, that would unite you to his body, and walk in communion with his saints: And let not these warnings be hereafter a witness against yon to your confusion, which are intended for your salvation, and the healing of our discords, by

An unworthy Servant of Jesus Christ, for the calling and edifying of his members,

—Richard Baxter
December 10, 1659

Catholic Unity

Endeavouring to keep the unity of the Spirit in the bond of peace.

—Ephesians 4:3

It seems that unity and felicity are near kin, in that the world is so like affected to them both. As our felicity is in God, and we lost it by falling from God, so our unity is in God, and we lost it by departing from this Centre of unity. And as all men have still a natural desire after felicity in general; but God who is their felicity, they neither know nor desire, so have we still a natural desire after unity in itself considered; but God who is our unity, is little known or desired by the most. And as nature can perceive the evil of misery which is contrary to felicity, and cry out against it, and yet doth cherish the certain causes of it, and will not be persuaded to let them go; so nature can perceive the evil of division, which is contrary to unity, and cry out against it, and yet will not forbear the causes of division. And therefore as we say of felicity, Nature by philosophy seeks it; Divinity findeth it, and Religion possesseth it: so we may say of true unity; Philosophy or nature seeks it, Divinity findeth it, and Religion or holiness possesseth it. And as most of the world do miss of felicity, for all their high esteem of it, and fall into misery, for all their hatred of it, because they love not the object and way of felicity, and hate not the matter and way of misery. Even so most of the world do miss of unity, for all their high esteem of unity, and fall into miserable distractions and divisions for all their hatred of divisions, because they love not the centre and way of unity, and hate not the occasion and causes of division. And as the very reason why the most are shut out of happiness, is their own wilful refusing of the true matter and means of happiness, and no one could undo them but themselves, for all that they are loath to be undone:

even so the very reason why the world attaineth not to unity, is their own wilful refusing of the true centre and means of unity; and it is themselves that are the wilful causes of their own divisions, even when they cry out against divisions. And as there is no way to happiness, but by turning to God from whom we fell, that in him we may be happy; and no way to God but by Jesus Christ as the Saviour, and the Holy Ghost as the Sanctifier; so there is no way to true unity, but by turning to God that we may be one in him; and no way to him, but being united to Christ, and being quickened by that one most Holy Spirit that animateth his members. And yet as poor souls do weary themselves in vain, in seeking felicity in their own ways and devices; so they do deceive themselves in seeking unity in ways that are quite destructive to unity. One thinks that we must be united in the Pope, and another in a General Council; another saith, we shall never have unity till the magistrate force us all one way; and yet they would not be forced from their own way. Another turns atheist, or infidel, or impious, by observing the divisions that be among Christians, and saith, 'It is this Scripture, and religion, and Christ, that hath set the world together by the ears; and we shall never have unity till we all live according to nature, and cast off the needless cares and fears of another life:' And thus the miserable, deluded world are groping in the dark after unity and felicity, while both are at hand, and they wickedly reject them; and many of them become so mad, as to run away from God, from Christ, from the Spirit, as if He were the cause of misery and division, who is the only Centre of felicity and unity. And thus as it is but few that arrive at happiness for all their desire of it, so it is but few that attain to unity; to such a unity as is worth the attaining to.

I dare presume to take it for granted, that all you that hear me this day, would fain have divisions taken away, and have unity, and concord, and peace through the world. What say you? would you not have us all of one mind, and of one religion? And would you not fain have an agreement, if it might be, through all the world? I am confident you would. But you little think that it is you, and such as you, that are the hinderers of it. All the question is, What mind that is that all should be one in? And what religion that is that all men should agree in? Every man would have all men of one mind, and one religion; but then it must be of his mind, and of his religion; and so we are never the nearer an agreement.

Well! what would you give now to be certainly told the only way to unity and agreement? There is but one way; when you have sought about as long as you will, you must come to that one way, or you will be never the nearer it. What would you give to know undoubtedly, which is that one way! O that the world were but willing to know it, and to follow it when they know it. Well! I dare promise you from the information of the Holy Ghost, here given us in this text, that now I have read to you, to tell you the only way to true unity; and blessed is he that learneth it, and walketh in it.

This text is a precept containing the work required of us, with its double object; the one the means to the other. The next verse is an exposition of this. As the natural man hath one body, and one soul, which constitute it a man, so the church which is the mystical body of Christ, is one body, consisting of many members united by one Spirit. Every commonwealth or political body, hath, 1. Its constituent causes that give it its being and its unity; and, 2. Its administration and preserving causes, as laws, execution, obedience, &c., that exercise and preserve, and perfect its being. The constitutive cause is the sovereign and the subject conjoined in their relation. So is it with the church, which is a political body, but of a transcendent kind of policy. The constitutive causes of the church, are Christ and the members united in one Spirit: and this is the final part of the duty here required, "to keep the unity of the Spirit." The preserving cause is the peaceable behaviour of the members: and this is the mediate duty here required "in the bond of peace." Our own endeavours are hereto required; because as every natural body must be eating and drinking, and fit exercise and usage be a cause of its own preservation, and not forbear these under pretence of trusting the all-sufficiency of God; and as every political body, must by government and arms, in case of need, preserve themselves under God; so must the body of Christ, the church, be diligent in using their best endeavours to preserve the being and wellbeing of the whole. So that you see here are two causes of the church's unity expressed: 1. The principal constitutive cause, in which our unity consisteth; and that is, "the Spirit." 2. The preserving cause, by which our unity is cherished, and that is "peace," which therefore is called "the bond" of it. The fifth and sixth verses do open this unity of Spirit in its parts, effects, and ends. "There is one hope of our calling," that is, one heaven or life eternal, which is the end of our Christianity and church constitution. "There is one Lord," Jesus Christ; one head, one Saviour, one sovereign Redeemer, to whom by this Spirit the members are all united. "There is one faith," both one sum of holy doctrine, which all that will be saved must believe which was used to be professed by the adult at baptism, and one internal saving faith, which this Spirit causeth in our spirits, and useth it as a means of our union with Christ, in whom we do believe. "There is one baptism," or solemn covenanting with God the Father, Son and Holy Ghost; and the same promise there to be made by all. And "there is one God the Father of all," from whom we fell, and to whom we must be recovered, and who is the end of all, and to whom Christ and all these means are the way. So that all these are implied in, and conjunct with the "unity of the Spirit."

The sense of the text then briefly is this: As all the living true members of Christ and the church, have one Spirit, and so one faith, by which they are all united to Christ the head, and so to the Father in and by him; which union in one Spirit is your very life, and it that constituteth you true members of Christ and his church; so it must be your care and great endeavour to preserve this Spirit in you, and this vital unity, which by this Spirit you have with Christ and one another: and the way to preserve it, is by the bond of peace among yourselves.' It is here evident then, that all the members of Christ and his body, have one Spirit, and in that is their union. All the question is, What Spirit this is? And that is left past all doubt in the chapter; for though the common gifts of the Spirit are sometimes called by that name, yet these are no farther meant in the text than as appurtenances or additions to greater gifts. As godliness hath the promise of the common mercies of this life, as well as of the special mercies of the life to come; but yet with great difference, the latter being absolutely promised, and the former but limited, so far as God sees best for us: even so the Spirit gave to the members of the church both sanctifying grace, and common gifts; but with great difference; giving sanctification to all, and only the members of Christ; but giving common gifts also to some others, and to them but with limitation, for sort, and season, and measure, and continuance, as God shall see good. It is then the same Holy Ghost as our Sanctifier, into whose name we are baptized, as well as into the name of the Father and Son, and in whom we all profess to believe, that is here meant in my text. And it is only the sanctified that are the people united to Christ, and to one another. This is proved expressly by that which followeth. It is those that have the "one hope, one Lord, one faith, one baptism, one God the Father." (ver. 6, 7.) It is the saints and body of Christ that are to be perfected by the ministry (ver. 12.) It is those that must come in the unity of faith, and knowledge of the Son of God to a perfect man, to the measure of the stature of the fulness of Christ; and that grow up in all things in Christ the head: It is the body that is united to him, and compacted in love, and edifieth itself in love. (ver. 13. 15, 16.) It is those that have so learned Christ, as to put off the old man that is corrupt, and are renewed in the spirit of their minds, and put on the new man, which after God is created in righteousness and true holiness." (ver. 20–24.) If therefore any words be plain, it is plain that it is true saints only that are here spoken of, that have the "unity of Spirit," which they must preserve in the "bond of peace." And therefore I shall make this observation the ground of my discourse.

Doct. 'The true unity of the catholic church of Christ consisteth in this, that they have all one sanctifying Spirit within them.'

By the Holy Ghost within them they are all united to Christ and to one another: by this one Spirit they are all made saints, or a holy people, having one heaven for the matter of their hopes, one Christ their head, one sum of Christian doctrine, which they believe, containing all the essentials of Christian faith; and one living principle of faith to believe it; one solemn covenant with Christ: and one God the Father, their end and all.

It is only the sanctified that have true Christian unity; and it is unholiness or ungodliness that is the cause of the miserable divisions of the world. Now, sirs, you see the only way to unity: even to have one sanctifying Spirit within us, and be all a holy people, and there is no way but this. Now you see the principal cause of division; even unholiness, and refusing the Spirit of grace.

In handling this point, I. I shall give you some propositions that are necessary for the fuller understanding of it. II. I shall demonstrate the point to you by a fuller evidence of reason. III. I shall make application of it.

I. Prop. 1. Though it be only the sanctified that have the true union of members with Christ and the body; yet all that make profession of sanctification, and null not that profession: have an extrinsic, analogical union in profession: as the wooden or dead leg is united to the body, and the dead branch to the vine. And so even hypocrites must not only dwell among us, but be of the same visible church with us, as the chaff and tares are of the same corn field. And as long as they seem saints we must value them and use them as saints, and love them, and have communion with them as saints: not as conceiving them certainly to be such, but probably, and by that human faith, by which we are bound to believe their profession; not as we believe God, who is infallible, but as men that are fallible; and this in several degrees, according to the several degrees of their credibility, and the probability of their profession. So that you must not after this mistake me, as if I tied our external church-communion only to true saints; for then we must have communion with none; because being not able to search the hearts, we know not what professors are sincere. But yet even this external church-communion belongs only to them that make profession of love and holiness, as well as of belief; and no lower profession must serve the turn.

Prop. 2. There is a common unity of human nature that we have with all men, and a common peace, that as much as in us lieth we must hold with all. (Rom. 12:18.) But this is nothing to the unity in question, which belongeth to our happiness. The devils have a unity of nature, and some order and accord in evil; for if "Satan be divided, how can his kingdom stand?" (Matt. 12:26.)

Prop. 3. The unity of the saints in the spirit of holiness, consisteth in this life with much imperfection and discord, according to the imperfection of their holiness. But as grace is the seed of glory, and the beginning of eternal life, for all its weakness, and the sins that accompany it, (John 17:3,) so the unity of the Spirit of holiness is the seed and beginning of the perfect unity in heaven, for all the differences and discord that here accompany it.

II. Having shewed you the only bond of unity, I come now by fuller evidence, to convince you of the truth of what is said, and even to force it into your understandings, if you will but use your reason, and believe the word of God. It is unholiness and ungodliness that causeth our discord; and it is the spirit of holiness that is the uniting principle; and there is no true Christian unity to be had with ungodly men: never think of unity by any other way than sanctification: You are as on the other side of the river, and cannot be united to the servants of Christ till the Spirit convert you, and pass you over. You are dead men, and unfit to be united to the living; and it is the "Spirit that quickeneth," and this life must be our union. You madly rail against division, and yet stand at a distance from Christ and his church, and maintain the greatest division in the world. Believe it, you do but doat and dream, if you think to have true Christian unity on any other terms, than by the sanctifying Spirit of Christ. And this I shall now evince as followeth.

1. You know surely that there can be no Christian unity, but in God as your Father, and the centre of unity: All the true members of the catholic church must say "Our Father," and be as his children united in him. If you will have unity without the favour of God, it must be the unity of rebels, and such a concord as is in hell: the family of God do all unite in him. As all the kingdom is united in one king, so is all the church in God. Can you think it possible to have unity as long as you will not unite in God? Well

then, there is nothing plainer in the Scripture, than that all men by nature are departed from God, and none are united to him but those that are regenerate and made new creatures; not a man is his child by grace, and in his favour, but only those that are sanctified by his Spirit. (John 3:3–5; Matt. 18:3; 2 Cor. 5:17; Heb. 12:14.) So that there is no true unity without sanctification, because there is no reconcillation with God, nor unity with him, without it.

2. There can be no true Christian unity but in Christ the Redeemer and Head of the Church: For how can the members be united but in the head? Or the scholars but in their teacher? Or the subjects but in their sovereign? You know there is no Christian unity but in Christ. Well then, What unity can we have with those that are not in Christ? The unsanctified have indeed the name of Christians; but what is that to the nature? Some branches not bearing fruit are said to be in him the Vine, by outward profession: but they are dead and withered, and must be cut off and cast away for the fire; and so are unfit for communion with the Vine. (John 15.) "He that is in Christ is a new creature: old things are passed away; behold, all things are become new." (2 Cor. 5:17.) "If any man have not the Spirit of Christ, (which is this sanctifying Spirit) the same is none of his." I pray you mark the plainness of these passages. All you that are unconverted and unsanctified are out of Christ, and none of his, though you may talk and boast of him as long as you will. And, therefore you cannot have unity with Christians till you will first have unity with Christ himself. Till you are ingrafted into him, you are not ingrafted into the catholic church, but only seem to be what you are not.

3. The dead cannot be united to the living: Who will be married to a dead corpse? Or would be tied to it, and carry it about? It is life that must unite us. The unsanctified are dead in sin, (Ephes. 2:5,) and the Spirit is given to quicken the dead, that they may be fit for converse. What union can there be between a block and a man; or a beast that hath but a sensitive life, and a man that hath a rational soul? So what union between the sensual world and the sanctified believer? If you could have unity without the Sanctifying Spirit, why are you then baptized into the name of the Holy Ghost as your sanctifier? To have a unity of being is common to us with the devils; for they are God's creatures, and so are we. To have a union of specific being is common to us with all the damned, for they are men as well as we; and common to the devils among themselves. But it must be a unity in the Spirit of holiness that must prove us happy, and afford us comfort.

4. There is no possibility of having unity with those that have not the same ultimate principal end. But the sanctified and the unsanctified have not the same end, nay, have contrary ends. If one of you will go to York, and the other to London, how can you possibly go one way? This is the great difference that sets the world and the sanctified by the ears: You serve mammon, and they serve God: you have one portion, and they another: your portion is in this life. (Psalm 17:14.) Here you have your good things, (Luke 16:25,) and here you lay up your treasure. (Matt. 6:19, 21.) Your belly is your god, and you mind earthly things. (Philip. 3:18.) But it is the Lord that is the portion of the saints. (Psal. 16:5.) They lay up a treasure in heaven, (Matt. 6:20,) and there they have their conversations. (Philip. 3:20.) Being risen with Christ, they seek the things that are above, where Christ sitteth at the right hand of God; for they are dead, and their life is hid with Christ in God. (Col. 3:1, 3, 4.) The business that the saints, and that the ungodly have in the world, is clean contrary. Their business is for heaven, and yours is for earth; they are sowing to the Spirit, in hope of everlasting life, and you are sowing to the flesh, and shall reap corruption. (Gal. 6:6, 7.) They are making provision for another life, that never shall have end; and you are making provision for the flesh, to satisfy its desires. (Rom. 13:14.) And how is it possible for these to be united? What concord between light and darkness? Or Christ and Belial? Or righteousness with unrighteousness? (2 Cor. 6:14, 15.) "Can two walk together, except they be agreed?" (Amos 3:3.) We must better agree of our business in the world, and of our journey's end, before we can keep company with you. While you are for earth and we for heaven, it is not possible that we should go one way. While one is for the world, and another for God, they must needs differ: for God and the world are masters that are irreconcileable. If you will cleave to one, you must despise the other.

The work of the butcher and the soldier is to kill; and the work of the surgeon and physician is to cure. And do you think these will ever take one course? The soldier studies how to wound and kill: the surgeon studies how to close these wounds and heal them: and surely these must go contrary ways. Sirs, as long as your business is principally for the flesh and the world, and the business of the sanctified is against the flesh and world, and for the Spirit and the world to come, how is it possible that you should be agreed? You must bring heaven and earth together first; yea, heaven and hell together first, before you can have a Christian unity and agreement between the sanctified and the unsanctified.

5. There is no unity to be had, but in the Gospel. The apostle tells us, "there is one faith." (Eph. 4:5.) If an angel from heaven would preach another Gospel, he must be accursed. (Gal. 1:10, 11.) But the unsanctified do not truly and heartily entertain this Gospel. You think and say you truly believe it, when you do not. If you truly believed it, your lives would shew it. He that indeed believes an everlasting glory, will surely look after it, more than after the world or the flesh.

6. There is no Christian unity, but in the Christian nature. Contrary natures cannot close. Fire and water, the wolf and the lamb, the bear and the dog, will not well unite. The sanctified have a new, divine and heavenly nature. (John 3:6; 2 Pet. 1:4; 2 Cor. 5:17.) Their disposition is another way than it was before. But the unsanctified have the old corrupt fleshly nature still: one is as the fire, still bending upward; the other as the earth or stone, still bending downward to the earth: And how can these agree together?

7. There is no Christian unity to be had, where the affections run quite contrary ways. But so it is with the sanctified and the unsanctified. One loves God above all, and cannot live without holy communion with him, and retireth into him from the distractions of the world, and maketh him his rest, content, and solace: the other mentions the goodness of God, but findeth no such sweetness in him, nor desires after him. One treads a world underfoot as dirt, or valueth and useth it but as the help to heaven: and the other makes it his happiness, and sets his heart on it. One delighteth in holiness, and the other hateth it, or regardeth it not. One hateth sin as a serpent, or as death; and the other makes it his meat, and drink, and business. And how is it possible for men of such contrary affections to be agreed, and nature at such enmity to unite?

8. The sanctified and unsanctified are moved by contrary objects: one lives by faith on things that are out of sight, and strives for heaven as if he saw it, and strives against hell as if he saw it; for his "faith is the evidence of things not seen." (Heb. 11:1. 7.) "We live by faith, and not by sight. (2 Cor. 5:7; 2 Cor. 4:18.) But the unsanctified live upon things that are seen, and things believed little move them, because they are not heartily believed.

9. The holy and the unholy do live by contrary laws. One liveth by the law of God, and there asketh counsel what he must think, or say, or do, resolving to obey God, before his flesh, and all the world. The other will say, he will be ruled by God's laws, till his flesh and carnal interest contradict it, and then he will take his lusts for his law: his pride is a law to him, and the pleasures and profits of the world are a law to him; and the will of

great ones, and the customs of men are his law. And how is it possible for men to agree that walk by such contrary rules as these?

10. There is no true unity but in the covenant with Christ. As marriage uniteth man and wife, so every truly sanctified man hath delivered up himself to Christ in a peremptory absolute covenant, and hath quit all claim of interest in himself, and is wholly God's. But the unsanctified will not be brought to this, any further than the lips, and therefore they cannot be well united.

11. The true members of the church are "built on the foundation of the apostles and prophets." (Eph. 2:20, 21.) But the unsanctified regard them not, if they cross their minds.

12. There is no true Christian unity, but with the holy catholic church. The body is but one. (1 Cor. 12:12, 13; Eph. 4:4.) But the unsanctified are not of the holy catholic church, but only in the visible external communion of it.

13. There can be no true Christian unity with the saints, without a special love to the saints. For by this "we know that we are passed from death to life, because we love the brethren; he that loveth not his brother abideth in death." (1 John 3:14.) "By this must all men know that we are Christ's disciples." (John 13:35.) Love is the bond and cement of the church. He that doth not heartily love a godly, sanctified man, because he is such, hath no true unity with the church. But the ungodly love them not as such: they see no such beauty and loveliness in holiness. Though Scripture calls it God's image, they be not in love with God's image, but think it a conceit, or hypocritical pretence, or a wearisome thing. Why! poor carnal wretches, do you hate the godly, and yet would you have unity with them? Do you hate them, and yet cry out against divisions, when your hearts are thus divided from God and his servants? You must learn to love them with a special love, and Christ in them, before you can be united with them.

14. There is no unity to be had without a love to the body that you are united to. You must love the church, and long for its prosperity, and the success of the Gospel, and the downfal of wickedness. Thus do the saints; but thus do not the ungodly. Nay, many of them are glad when they hear of any evil befal the godly.

15. There is no unity without a singular respect to the special members that are ligaments and chief instruments of unity; even the officers of the church and most useful members. The overseers of the church must "be highly esteemed in love for their work sake." (1 Thess. 5:12.) Thus do the godly, but not the ungodly.

16. There must be an inward inclination to the communion of saints, before there can be any agreement and unity. All that are of the holy catholic church, must desire the communion of saints. Their "delight must be in them." (Psalm 16:3.) But the ungodly have no such delight in their communion.

17. If you will have unity and communion with the church, you must have a love to the holy ordinances, which are the means of communion; as to the word of God, heard and read, to prayer, sacraments, confession, &c.; but the ungodly either have a distaste of these, or but a common delight in the outside, and not in the spirit of the ordinance. And, therefore, they cannot agree with the church; when you loathe that which is our meat and drink, and we cannot feed at one table together, what an agreement can there be?

18. If you will agree, you must work in the same vineyard, and labour in the same employment, and walk the same way as the sanctified do: And that is in the way of holiness and righteousness, "giving all diligence to make your calling and election sure." (2 Pet. 1:10.) If you live to the flesh, and they live to the Spirit, (Rom. 8:5, 13,) What unity and agreement can there be?

19. There is no unity to be had, unless you will join in a defensive and offensive league, and in opposition to that which would tend to our destruction. What commonwealth will unite with them that defend their enemies and rebels? There is an enmity put in the beginning between the seed of the woman and of the serpent. (Gen. 3:15.) "Because we are not of the world, the world hate us." (John 15:19.) If you will be united to the church and people of Christ, you must be at enmity with sin, and hate it, and join for the destroying of it; and you must be soldiers in Christ's army, which the devil and his army fight against; and you must fight against the flesh, the world, and the devil, and not live in friendship with them. But this the unsanctified will not do.

20. And therefore because you will not be united to them in the state and kingdom of grace, you shall not be united with them in the state and kingdom of glory.

And thus I have made it plain to you, that none can have true union with the church of Christ, but only they that are sanctified by the Spirit.

Use 1. By this time you may see, if you are willing to see, who it is long of that the world is all in pieces by divisions, and who are the greatest hinderers of unity. Even unsanctified, ungodly men. And you may see how fit these men are to cry out against divisions, that are the principal causes of them: and how wisely they deal to cry up unity, and in the meantime resist the only ground and way of unity: As Joshua said to Achan, "Why hast thou troubled us? the Lord shall trouble thee this day;" (Jos. 7:25;) So I may say to all the ungodly, 'Why trouble you the church, and hinder unity? You shall one day have trouble yourselves for this.' They cry out against the ministry and others that fear God, as Ahab did to Elijah, "Art thou he that troubleth Israel?" But saith Elijah, "It is thou and thy father's house that trouble Israel, in that ye have forsaken the commandments of the Lord." (1 Kings 17:17, 18.) Sirs, I tell you, (and I may confidently tell you when I have proved it so fully,) that it is the ungodly that are the great dividers of the world. It is you that make the breach, and keep it open. We are willing to agree to any thing that is reasonable or possible; but there is no possibility of agreeing with the ungodly, unless they will turn. It would make any honest heart to ache, to see these wretches set all on fire, and then cry out against others as the authors of it. As Nero set Rome on fire, and then persecuted the Christians for it, as if it had been done by them. They pluck up the foundations, and hold most damnable, practical errors; and when they have done, they go about reviling other men as erroneous. I speak not in the excuse or extenuation of other men's errors: I have spoke my part against them also: but I tell you, it is the profane and ignorant rabble, and all the ungodly, whether gentlemen, scholars, or of what rank soever, that are the great dividers, and stand at the greatest distance from Christian unity. O what a happy church should we have, for all the sects that trouble us so much, if it were not for ungodliness that animateth some of those sects, and virtually containeth many more! Had we none but men fearing God to deal with, we should have no opposition to the essentials of religion; and we should still have the comfort of agreeing with them in all things necessary to salvation. They would carry on their differences in Christian meekness, charity and moderation; and at the worst our agreement would be greater than our disagreement. But when we have to deal with haters of holiness, or at least with men that are strangers to the sanctifying work of the Spirit, we have predominant pride, and selfishness, and covetousness to strive against: We have radicated infidelity, and enmity to God and holiness, giving life and strength to all their errors, and making them stubborn, and wilful, and scornful, against the clearest truths that can be shewed them. There is no dealing effectually with a carnal heart, for any but God himself. Unless we can create light in them, as well as reveal the truth to them, what good can we do them? What good doth the

sun to a man that is blind? They have understandings left, and therefore
they can err; but they have no heavenly light in them, and therefore they
cannot choose but err. They have wills, and therefore are capable of sin;
but they have no holy rectitude of them, and therefore sin they will with
obstinacy. When we dispute with the godly, that err through weakness,
we deal with men that have eyes in their heads, and life in their souls, and
some savour and experience of the matters of God. But when we dispute
with the ungodly, we deal with the blind, we talk to the dead, we offer the
bread of life to men that have no appetite or savour of it; yea, we speak
for God, to enemies of God; and for truth, to the natural enemies of such
truths; and the more obstinate enemies, because they know it not. Had we
nothing but mistakes to argue against, and had we but to do with men that
have the free use of their reason, we should do well enough with them. But
when we must persuade the deaf, the distracted, and the dead; when we
must dispute with pride, and passion, and enmity, and persuade a lion to
become a lamb, and a serpent to lay by his venom, no wonder if we find a
difficult task of it. Had we none but the godly to deal with, we should have
abundant advantage for success; we should deal with men that love the
truth, and are willing to use right means to discover it: they would pray
with us for truth, as well as dispute; they would with meekness search the
Scripture, and see whether these things be so or not: they would yield to
light when it appeareth to them, and not imprison it in unrighteousness.
And it would move us to more tender dealing with them, while we see and
love Christ in them, and when we remember that the men that we now dispute with, we must live with in heaven, and join with in the everlasting
praises of the Lord. I profess, sirs, I speak to you from sad experience, I
have been troubled with Antinomians, and Anabaptists, and other errors
in well-meaning men, as much as most: and many a day's work they have
made me in writing and disputing against them. But, alas! this is nothing
to the trouble that the profane, ungodly do put me to. I thank God I have
dealt with all these errors with so good success, that I live in peace by them;
and I know not of an Anabaptist, or Socinian, or Arminian, or Quaker, or
Separatist, or any such sect in the town where I live; except half a dozen
Papists that never heard me. But infidels, atheists, ungodly wretches, I am
pestered with still: one heresy called drunkenness, that denieth the use of
reason itself, doth still walk the streets in despite of all that I can say, or all
that the magistrates will do; and none of us all are able to confute them. In

one hour's time they will fetch more arguments from the alehouse, than all the reason in the town can effectually answer.

And as the ungodly are most desperately principled, of any heretics in the world, both for the quality and the radication of their errors; so there are far greater numbers of them, than of all other heresies set together. It may be we have one or two Anabaptists in a parish, and in some parishes none; in some few it may be twenty: but O that I could say, I had not twenty, and twenty, and twenty, and twice twenty more, unsanctified, ungodly persons in my parish, though I hope there are as many better, as in any parish I know. Alas, sirs, into how many parishes may you go, and find gross ignorance, profaneness, worldliness, contempt of God and heavenly things, to be their common air which they breathe in, and the natural complexion of the inhabitants, as blackness is to the Æthiopians. It is a blessed parish, that of three thousand inhabitants, hath not above two thousand natural heretics, even ungodly persons that are strangers to sanctification. And who then do you think is most likely to be the cause of our distractions and divisions?

Moreover, let me tell you, profaneness and ungodliness is not a single error or heresy; but it is the sum of all the heresies in the world. You will think this strange, when you see so many that join with us in a sound profession, and some of them zealous defenders of the truth; and many of them cry out against errors: but, alas! they believe not that which they think they do believe. They hold not that which they say they hold. There is much in their creed, that was never in their belief. Doubtless ungodliness is the nest of all the heresies in the world.

Will you give me leave to instance in some particulars. The greatest error in the world is atheism, when men deny the Godhead itself. And do not the most of the ungodly deny him in their hearts? If he be not just, he is not God; and they deny and hate his justice: If he be not holy, he is not God; and they deny in their hearts, and hate his holiness: If he be not true, he is not God; and they commonly believe that he is not true. Shew them where he hath said, that none but the converted, the sanctified, the regenerate, the heavenly, the self-denying shall be saved; and they will not believe that this will be made good, but hope it is false. If he be not wise, and be not the Governor of the world, he is not God. And these wretches quarrel with his holy laws, as if they could tell how to mend them themselves, and were wiser to make a law than God is; and by flat rebellion deny his government. So that we may truly say with David, (Psal. 14,) that these fools say in their hearts, that "There is no God;" or else they durst not say and do in his presence as they do.

Moreover, idolatry, which is the setting up of false gods, is a most abominable, damning sin. And every ungodly man is guilty of it. Covetousness is idolatry, (Ephes. 5:5,) and the sensual make their belly their God. (Phil. 3:19.) And pride and selfishness, which are the heart of the old man, are nothing else but making ourselves our idols. Every unsanctified man is his own idol; giving to himself the honour, and pleasure, and love that is due to God alone; and setting up his own will instead of God's.

Polytheism, which is the feigning of many gods, is a most damnable error: And how many gods have all that are ungodly! No man departeth from the one true God, but he makes to himself many false gods in his stead. His wealth, and his credit, and his throat, and his recreations, and the rulers that are capable of hurting him, are all as his gods, and to them he gives that which is due to God only.

Infidelity is one of the most damning errors in the world; when men believe not in Christ that bought them: but this is the case of all the unsanctified. An opinion they have that the Gospel is true; and Christ is the only Lord and Saviour; but infidelity is predominant in them, and therefore should denominate them; or else they should be saved, if they were true believers. Never did they give an hour's true entertainment to Christ in their hearts.

To set up a false Christ, is one of the most damning sins in the world. And what else do all the ungodly, that place their hopes for pardon and salvation, either in their own good works or carnal shifts, or at least, by false conceptions do make Christ not indeed to be Christ?

To have many saviours, is a damnable error. And how many do the ungodly make to themselves, while they depart from the Lord Christ?

To deny the Holy Ghost, is a damnable error. And what else do all the ungodly in the world, that will not be sanctified by him? This is the most palpable error that they are guilty of: They are baptized into the name of the Holy Ghost as their Sanctifier, and yet they will not be sanctified by him: nay, some of them make a mock of the Spirit, and of sanctification. And some of them will hearken to false, deceiving spirits, instead of the Holy Spirit of God.

Some heretics have denied some parts of the Scripture, and infidels deny it all. And what less do all ungodly men, that believe it not heartily, and will not obey it, but deny it in parts, and refuse subjection to it? They will not be so holy, not they, let the Scripture say what it will. Are not all the ungodly against the Scripture? Many a time have I heard them, when the times more encouraged them, deriding the Bible, and those that did but carry a Bible, or speak of the Scripture, or read it in their houses. Certainly, he that fights against the Scripture in his life, is more against it than he that only denies it with his tongue.

Moreover, the Pelagian heretics denied original sin, and justified man's nature: and so doth profaneness in a very great measure. Never were the ungodly truly humbled for their original sin, nor saw any such matter in themselves, as to make them abhor themselves: And what is this but actually to deny it?

The same Pelagians made light of grace, which is God's image upon the soul. But in this the ungodly go quite beyond them: they make a matter of nothing of holiness, but account it a fancy, or a needless thing; and many of them hate it, and if the times did but favour their malice, there were no living near them for any that fear God: In this they are devils in flesh; I cannot liken them to any heresy, but devilism, they go so far beyond the professors of them all.

One sect is against those that are their opposers, and another sect against their opposers; but ungodliness is against all that are godly of every party whatsoever; and is in open arms or secret enmity against the army of Christ, and against himself.

The Simonians, and Nicolaitans, and Gnostics of old, did hold that men might do any outward action, when there is no other way to escape suffering, as long as they keep their hearts to God. So think the ungodly, as appeareth by their practice: Before they will lose their estates and be brought to poverty, or before they will lie in prison, or be burnt at a stake, they will say any thing, or do any thing: they would worship a piece of bread as if it were God; they would turn to Papists or any that can do them a mischief, if it were the Turks.

Alas! the particular sects among us, do play a small game in comparison of the ungodly; and hold but petty errors to theirs: one sect is against one ordinance, and another sect is against another ordinance; but the ungodly are against all. The sectaries are against something in the manner or outside of the work, but the ungodly are against the spirit and life, and substance of the duty itself: one sect depraveth the doctrine of faith; and another the doctrine of repentance, and another the doctrine of obedience: but the ungodly deprave all the doctrine of holiness; yea, deny it, and not only deprave it: they sweep away all before them, and go by wholesale: they stand not to speak as other heretics, against this grace or that grace, but against all: it is godliness itself that the ungodly are against.

The sectaries oppose all parts of the catholic church, saving their own: but the ungodly are against the holy catholic church itself; as it is a church, and as it is holy, they are against it. The church is a society combined for holy obedience to Christ; and the ungodly are against that holy obedience.

The sectaries would have no communion of saints, but in their own way. But the ungodly are against the communion of saints in itself; for they are against the saints that hold this communion.

The Papists and Quakers are against our ministry, and rail at them, and labour to bring them into hatred. So do the worst sort of the ungodly, even of them that say they are Protestants, and of our religion. In their houses, and in the alehouses, in their ordinary discourse, they are cavilling against the ministers, or reproaching them: and some of them are more bitter haters and revilers of them, than almost any heretics that we meet with: yea, some of them are glad to hear the Quakers and Anabaptists reproach them, and secretly set them on: only they are ashamed to own these revilers, because they see them come off in the end with so much disgrace. But if they were but sure that Papists, or Quakers, or any sect that is against a godly ministry, had power in their hands to go through with their work, the multitude of the ungodly among us would soon join with them. How plainly did this appear in our late wars? When few ministers of noted diligence and piety, that desired to have lived at home in quietness, could be suffered to live among them; but the ungodly rise up against them as if they had been Turks or Jews, and drove them into garrisons to save their lives. The Separatists and Quakers, and other sects, dispute against the ministry with cavils and railings; but the ungodly would dispute them down with halters and hatchets, if the merciful Governor of the world did not tie their hands.

The Quakers, and many Anabaptists and Separatists, are against tithes, and all settled maintenance of the ministry. And do I need to tell you, that the ungodly, covetous worldlings are of the same mind? What need had ministers else to sue for their tithes? Were it not for fear of treble damages, the ministers in many parishes of England would not have bread to their mouths, nor clothes to their backs, before they got it by suit at law. How commonly do they think that all is won, and is currently their own, that they can but defraud the minister of? If it were not that they are under disgrace, the Quakers would soon have disciples enough upon this very account, because they are against tithes. And gladly do the ungodly covetous people hearken to that doctrine, and get their books, and would fain have that opinion take as orthodox. If the prince and parliament would but turn Quakers, and cry down tithes, yea, and ministry too, the miserable ungodly multitude would quickly be of that religion, and entertain their laws with ringing of bells, and shouts, and bonfires.

Another heresy there is, even the old sect of Anabaptists, that are against Christian magistracy! And another heresy, the Libertines, that would have the magistrates give men leave to sin. And are not all the profane of the same opinion! They dare not speak so freely indeed against the magistrates as against the ministry, unless when they are up in arms against him, but their very hearts detest that magistrate that takes part with godliness, and promotes religion, and puts down alehouses, and punisheth swearers, and profaners of the Lord's-day. They are commonly for the doctrine that Dell preached to the Parliament, that 'They should let Christ alone with reformation, and let him do his work himself:' or as another hath written, that 'He will never serve such a God that is not able to defend his own cause without the magistrate's sword.' The wretches might as well have said 'We will have no such God as cannot govern us himself without a magistrate; or cannot defend us against enemies without wars; or cannot preserve our estates without the charge and trouble of law-suits; or save our goods or lives, without punishing thieves or murderers; or that cannot teach the world, without ministers, or give us corn without ploughing and sowing; we will never serve such a God as cannot preserve our lives without meat and drink, and clothes; and lighten the world himself without a sun.' God can do all this! But must these dunghill worms impose it on him, and give him a law, and take down his creatures and institutions, and means, and bid him do all without them himself, or else he is no God? O wretched blasphemers! Why how much of this blasphemy are the ungodly guilty of, that hate the magistrate, or any other that executes God's laws, and would hinder them from sin, and drive them to the means that should make them better!

The Antinomians corrupt the doctrine of faith, and take it to be a believing that their sins are pardoned, that Christ hath even repented and believed in their stead; and he that hath this belief they think is safe, and that a man cannot thus believe too much or too soon. And this is just the common faith of the ungodly: they trust in Christ to save and pardon them, even without sanctification or conversion; and trust they will, let ministers say what they can: presumption is taken to be true believing, and by it they think to be saved. They believe that God will save them, and therefore they think they are true believers.

The Antinomians say, that no man should be discouraged from such a belief by any sin whatsoever. And this the ungodly hold and practise. The Antinomians hold that no man should stay for any evidences of grace in himself, before he thus believe that he is a child of God, and justified. And this the ungodly hold and practise. They believe and hope that they are justified and shall be saved, when they have not a word of proof for their hopes, nor any reason why they should be saved more than the rest of the world that will be condemned: only they believe it and hope it, and that they think shall serve the turn.

The Antinomians are against repenting and grieving for sin, and confessing it, as a means of pardon. And I am sure the ungodly are practically against it. Repent, and mourn, and turn from sin, they will not; nor confess any more but what they know not how to deny; but as much as they can they will hide it, excuse it, and defend it.

The Antinomians would not have one of their believers, if he fall into the grossest sins, to make the least question of his pardon and justified state for that. And so it is with the ungodly: they will confess, when they swear or are drunk, that they sin, (because they cannot deny it) but they will not believe that they are graceless and unpardoned; but all are sinners; and the best have their faults, and so have they; and this is the worst they can make of their sin.

The Pelagians say, that the will of man is so free, that he can turn and become a new creature at any time. And if this were not the opinion of the ungodly, how could they put off conversion, and say, It is time enough hereafter: but that it seems they think they can turn at any time, as if they had the Spirit and grace of God at their command.

And yet they hold the contrary to this. (And this is no wonder; for there is the very Babel of confusion in the soul of the unsanctified.) The Antinomians say, that man can do nothing to his own conversion, but is merely passive: If God have justified him before he was born, he shall be a justified person; and if God will give him grace, well and good; if not, he cannot help it. Just so say many of the ungodly: 'If we are elected we shall be saved; if not, let us do what we can, we cannot be saved: if God will not give us grace, we cannot have it; and if we perish, what remedy?' As if God

did deny his grace to any of you, but those that forfeit it by wilful sin! Or
as if your willing resisting it were no fault or forfeiture: Or as if God did
predestinate any besides the sanctified to salvation.

Abundance more such heresies I might reckon up, that are all comprised in ungodliness. Some infidels question the immortality of the soul:
and so do many of the ungodly: I have heard some of them flatly deny it,
and others of them do not well believe it.

Some infidels question whether there be any hell. And so do the ungodly
in their hearts, or else they dare never so boldly venture on it, and so mer-
rily live in the sudden danger of it.

Some infidels question the joys of heaven. And if the ungodly did not so
in their heart, they would not think a holy life too much ado to get it, nor
would they part with it for the pleasure of a filthy sin.

There is never an article of the Creed but some heretic or other doth
oppose it. And the ungodly are against them altogether, even while they
profess to believe them all.

There is never a one of the Ten Commandments, but ungodliness is
against it. There is never a petition in the Lord's-prayer, but ungodliness is
against it; for all that they are content to use the words. Instead of hallow-
ing the name of God, they dishonour it; and instead of living to the glory
of God, they seek themselves and their own honour. The kingdom of Christ
they are enemies to: in the church without them, they love not his government. In their hearts within, they will not endure it; and the coming of
his glorious kingdom they are afraid of. Instead of doing his will, they will
quarrel with it, and murmur at it, and disobey it, and do their own wills,
and would have God do their wills too, and have all others do them. Instead
of being content with daily bread to fit them for God's service, they drown
themselves in pleasure, or in worldly cares, to make provision to satisfy
their flesh. Instead of valuing and accepting the forgiveness of sin, as purchased by Christ, and offered in the Gospel, they have slight apprehensions
of so great a mercy, and refuse the conditions of it as too hard, and run
deeper into debt, and wilfully sin more. Instead of avoiding temptations,
and flying to Christ for deliverance from evil, they tempt themselves, and
run into temptations, and seek after them, and love the evil of sin, and are
loath to leave it and be delivered from it. So that they are against every
petition in the Lord's-prayer, though they use the words.

They are also against every ordinance of God, and lick up the vomit of
all sects that do oppose them. One sect is against the Lord's-day; and so are

the ungodly against the sanctifying of it, and spending it in holy worship, and delighting themselves thereon in God. Else what need so many acts to restrain them from sports and other profanation of it? And all will not do.

Another sect is against praying but by the book, and would have ministers restrained from praying in any other words than are commanded him. And the ungodly easily receive this opinion, and reproach all other prayers as extemporate and disorderly.

Another sect is against church-government by any but magistrates; these are called Erastians. And the ungodly are not only against it, but detest it, and reproach it. Let them be called to public repentance and confession for any public sin, and try whether they be not against this discipline. I know no outward duty that they are more against. They will hear us preach with some patience and quietness; but when we come to reprove them personally, and recover them from scandalous sins by necessary discipline, they storm and rage against us, and will not endure it.

Some Separatists are for the people's governing of the church by a major vote, and consequently ruling those that God doth call their rulers, and commandeth them to obey, (Heb. 13:17.) And so are the ungodly; they would rule their rulers, the ministers, and have them administer the ordinances of God according to their fancies, but they will not be ruled by them. Let the minister but require them to come to him to be instructed or catechised, and they will not be ruled by him, they are too old to be catechised: let him call them to any necessary profession or other duty, and they will do what they list. Let him but cross any of their conceits and customs, and they will sooner revile him than be ruled by him.

The Separatists will withdraw themselves from our churches and God's ordinances, if things be not suited to their mind. And so will many of the ungodly. Most parishes in England, that I hear of, where any kind of discipline is exercised, have more Separatists than communicants. The far greater part of many parishes forbear the communion of the church in the Lord's-supper, and have done many years together; even because they cannot be admitted without examination, or without some necessary or lawful profession, or because they cannot have the sacrament kneeling, or put into their hands, or the like. They will separate and be without the sacrament, or take it in a separate society, rather than they will be ruled by the pastors of the church in a gesture or undoubtedly lawful thing.

Another sect of late will not sing David's Psalms; and the ungodly will not do it heartily and reverently, but only with the voice.

Another sect, the Anabaptists, are against baptizing infants. And the ungodly do not holily and heartily devote themselves and their infants to God; they do not themselves renounce the world, the flesh, and the devil, and take God for their God, and Christ for their Saviour, to heal and rule them, and the Holy Ghost for their Sanctifier to make them holy: And how then can they do this for their children, which they refuse themselves? When they have offered their children to God in baptism, they bring them up to the flesh, and the world, and the devil, in their lives, and teach them to break the covenant which they made. So that they are far worse than Anabaptists.

Another late sect will not pray morning and evening in their families, nor crave God's blessing on their meat, nor teach their children and servants the duties of religion: and so it is with the ungodly. How many of you that hear me to day, have prayerless families; that let your people go about their labour as an ox to the yoke, without calling upon God! How few use to instruct and admonish their families, and help to prepare them for death and judgment! All that are about you may see that you are guilty of this heresy.

Another sect of late is risen up, that will not keep any constant times of prayer neither in family or in private, but only when they find themselves in a good mood, then they will pray. And so is it with many of the profane.

I am weary of mentioning these desperate errors: more of them might be mentioned, and the case made plain, that almost all the heresies in the world are met together in the ungodly and unsanctified.

Would you see the sum of all my charge, in order? It is this: 1. Many sects that trouble us much, yet do hold no errors but what may stand with Christianity and salvation. But the ungodly err in the essentials, and overthrow the very foundation of religion. Their errors will not consist with grace or salvation. They are damnable heresies. Yea, beside all that the sects aforesaid hold, they have many damning heresies of their own. These deadly heretics hold, that the world is rather to be sought than everlasting glory; that the pleasure of sin is to be chosen before the holiness of the saints; that their flesh is to be pleased before God; that it is better venture on their beloved sins, and keep them yet a little longer, than presently forsake them; that the way to heaven which God commandeth, and Christ and all his apostles went in, is Puritanism and preciseness, and godliness is more ado than needs; and that the body must have more care and diligence than the soul; and the trifles of this world be more looked after than the one thing necessary!

These, and abundance such damnable heresies do dwell in our cities and countries, in the minds of those that cry out against heresies. Ungodliness is the greatest heresy in all the world.

2. Other heretics have some of them but one or two errors, but the ungodly have all these together: they are the sink of all errors. As all God's graces make up the new creature in the sanctified; so all deadly errors and vices go to make up the body of ungodliness, when it is complete. Its name is Legion, for there are many of these evil spirits in it. The Anabaptist hath a scab, and the Separatist hath a wound; but the ungodly multitude have the leprosy and plague sores from top to toe.

Profaneness is a hodgepodge and gallimaufry of all the heresies of the world in one.

3. Many other heretics do err but in speculation, and only the brain is infected, and they do not at the heart digest their own mistakes. But the heresies of the profane ungodly people are practical, and have mastered the will: the poison is working in the heart and vital parts, so that it is far the more mortal for this.

4. Many sects at least do not practise their errors; but the ungodly live upon them: yea, their lives are worse than their opinions; they say bad, and do worse. You may see more heresy than you can hear from them.

5. Some erring persons have the substance of Christian truth mixed with their error, by which the power of the venom is abated, and they do good in the church as well as hurt. But the ungodly do not savingly, heartily, and practically, hold fast any the most fundamental truth.

6. Some sects are meek and temperate in their way; but the ungodly are carried on with fury and malice, against the whole body of the holy catholic church.

7. And some heretics are so thin and few, that where we have one of them to do hurt, we have a hundred or a thousand to contradict them. But the unsanctified and ungodly are the greater number, and think they should rule because they are the most; and the flock of Christ is a little flock. And so many thousands swarming all over the world, and making up the far greatest part of the world, is likely to do more against the truth and peace, than here and there a poor sectary in a corner.

8. And lastly, the errors of some others are easier cured; but the whole nature of the ungodly is turned as it were into error; it is rooted so at the

heart, that no power on earth is able to cure it, till God Almighty by insuperable light and life of grace, will do the cure.

And now I beseech you, judge impartially, who they be that are the deadly and dangerous heretics, and who are the hinderers of unity in the church. And how unfit these miserable people are to call for unity, and cry out against our many religions, who are heartily of no religion themselves, but against the life and practice of all. To hear an ungodly man go crying out of sects, of Separatists, of Anabaptists, and this and that, is as if we should hear a blackamoor scorn one for a spot on his face; or a murderer rebuke a man for an angry word; or a soldier that kills as many as he can, cry out of the surgeons for curing no more, or blame others for a foul word; or a common whore reproach another for a wanton word, or uncomely garments: or as if a madman should revile men for every slip he findeth in their speeches, and call them fools O that we knew how to cast out this master-devil of ungodliness! this Beelzebub the prince of devils! and then I should not fear the rest; no, not all the sects and errors in the world, that are found with true godliness.

Yet still remember these two cautions. 1. I do not excuse the errors of the best; and I lament that they have lamentably wronged the church, and in some respects they have the greatest aggravations. 2. And I still confess that some of the unsanctified are so civil and orthodox, as to be very useful in the church, and helpful against sects and heresies, because they are right in the brain as to speculation, and right in the tongue; and their error is kept buried deep in the heart, and therefore they err more to themselves than to others. I doubt not but many such are profitable preachers and defenders of the truth; and the church must be thankful to God for their gifts. And yet all that I have affirmed standeth good, that ungodliness is the transcendent heresy and schism.

Use 2. By what hath been said, you may easily perceive how little cause the Papists, or ceremonious, or any others, have to glory in such members of their churches as I have described. Can they expect a unity of the Spirit with these? If they glory that they have men and multitudes on their side, so may the Turks that have more than they; and so may the heathens that have more than either. And yet when a Papist hath deceived a poor licentious or ignorant man, or a proud or vicious silly woman, they glory in their convert. Never yet did I know any Protestant turn Papist, that was not an ungodly wretch before, and without the power of the religion which he professed. Do not say I speak censoriously, or uncharitably in this; for I think, upon consideration, all Papists will confess it: For they teach, that all that be not of their church are void of charity, and cannot so be saved; and that all must therefore come in to their church, because there is no charity or salvation without it. Though this be false, yet you see by it, that they confess that never any but graceless, unsanctified Protestants did turn to them; nor can they invite any to them but ungodly people. And whoever turneth Papist, doth thereby confess that he was ungodly before, and that he was not an honest, godly man; for in turning Papist, he professeth to go into that church out of which there is no salvation, and consequently no charity or saving grace. And if indeed you desire none but the ungodly to turn to you, take them if they will needs go, and try whether you can do any more good on them than we have done. I think we have little cause (but for their own sakes) to lament our loss of such as these; and that you have little cause to glory in your proselytes. And I have yet seen none that shew us any more holiness since their change, than they had before. A fair church you have, that is the common sty for all that will come to you; and that is glad of any to make up the number, that you may have that in quantity, that is wanting in quality.

Use 3. From hence also let Quakers and Papists, and all reproachers of our churches, take notice, how groundlessly they hit us in the teeth with the ungodly that live among us. 'These are your Protestants,' say they; 'these are your churches: these are the fruit of your ministry!' say the Quakers. No, these are the enemies of our ministry and doctrine; these are they that join with you, and such as you, to reproach us and revile us! These are the obstinate despisers of our ministry, that instead of learning of us do revile us; and instead of obeying our doctrine do make a mock at it. If they are any of them brought to a sound confession, and restrained from any vice, they may thank the doctrine which we preach for that (unless they do it only for fear of the laws). But their profaneness is it that we have endeavoured to cure them of, and cannot; for they are obstinate.

If Papists or Quakers accuse our doctrine as dead and weak, because it cannot cure all our hearers; what forgetful dotards are they, that observe not how they condemn themselves? Do the Quakers or Papists change us all to their opinions, by their books or preaching? Beyond sea they are fain to keep men in their church by fire and sword, for fear of losing them: and here, it is but here and there an ignorant, ungodly wretch, or a proud, raw novice, that turns to them.

You may therefore as well hit us in the teeth with yourselves, that revile us, and say, 'We are the fruit of your ministry,' as with the ungodly, and tell us that 'they are the fruit' of our ministry. For though they live among us, they are not of us. And we teach men no more to be ungodly than to be Quakers or Papists. If you say, that they are in our churches; I answer, Where discipline is exercised, the most of them are out, and the rest we weed up as fast as they so discover themselves, that we may do it without danger of pulling up the wheat with them. Many of us reject them by discipline; and all of us rebuke and disown them by doctrine. If Jews and heathens were among us, we could not preach more against them, than we do against the ungodly; nor could we labour harder to cure them. Tell us not therefore of them; they are none of ours, they disown us, and we disown them: they are our persecutors, as you are, that hate us when we have done our best for them, and love us least when we love them most; and cast back all our instruction in our faces, or cast it behind their backs and tread it under feet. They are those against whom we shake off the dust of our feet: they are not our disciples, but such as refuse to be Christ's own disciples.

Nay, I wonder that Papists and Quakers do not to their shame observe, that it is likely to be some evil spirit that sets them awork to rail against us, seeing all the drunkards, and whoremongers, and covetous wretches, and ungodly, malicious people in our parishes, be of their mind, and rail against us as they do: It is likely to be the same cause that hath the same effect. If it be the devil that sets the profane to revile us, judge who it is that sets these sects to speak the same, or like words against the same persons.

And you that are profane and ungodly, I pray you here take notice what a case you are in! You are so vile, that few besides yourselves will own you. We disown you: you are none of ours, because you will be none of Christ's. And the very Quakers, and other sects, disown you, and hit us in the teeth with you, as if you were our shame: All these bear witness against your ungodliness: and therefore if yet you will be ungodly, when Quakers are against you, and all are against you almost as well as we; if you will hear neither ministers nor sectaries, neither teachers nor railers, how many witnesses will rise up against you, and how speechless will you be!

Use 4. I have been all this while but about preparatives; and now I come to the work that I intended. Do not think that I have spoken all this of the ungodly, to hinder a union and Christian concord, but to prepare for it, by telling you the reason of our distance, and division, and what must be removed before we can be one. Truly, sirs, I come to you with peaceable intentions. I come upon a treaty with you, to see whether you will become one with us, and be reconciled or not. For the Lord's sake attend me considerately and impartially, for it is a weighty business that I have to propound to you, and a most excellent motion that I have to make. As you regard the God of unity that sends to you, and Christ the Prince of Peace, and the Spirit who is the principle of unity, and the church that is the seat of unity, and yourselves that may have the blessing of unity, hearken to the motion of peace and unity that I have to make to you from the Lord. Sirs, what think you! hath the world been long enough divided or not? Are we cut into shreds enough, and broken into pieces enough or not? Are our distances from one another great enough, and our spirits bitter enough or not? Is it not time, think you, to sound a retreat to our foolish wars? You call for unity: you talk for unity, and against sects and divisions: do you mean as you speak; and are you in good earnest, or are you not? Would you have us be all of one mind and way, or not? You talk against being of so many religions: is it the true desire of your hearts, that we should be all of one religion? If it be, hold fast to this. So far we are agreed. Let us lay this as a groundwork; We must be all of one church, one faith, one religion, if we will be saved.

Well then, it lies next before us, in order to inquire, What one religion and way we must be of; and what is our distance, and what course must be taken to make us one? Are you willing to lay by passion, and scorn, and hatred, and bitterness, and come to a treaty about the matter? O, sirs, if you were but all truly willing to search out the business, and to be ruled by God and reason, we should soon be agreed for all our differences. And how happy would this be for the troubled church; how happy for the offended, distracted world; how happy for your own souls! Well; what terms shall we agree upon? Somebody must begin the motion, sitting still will not heal us. I will make a motion that never a man of you, that hath the face of a Christian, can tell what justly to except against. Let us set the word of God before us, and take the best helps on both sides to understand it, and let this decide the case with us. What say you; will you stand to the word of God? Shall we appeal all to Christ, and try our differences by his revealed word? If this may carry it, we shall soon be agreed.

But if any of you have catched the popish perverseness, and say, 'The Scripture is dark, and a dead letter; every sect pleads Scripture for their way: this will not serve our turn; we must have a living judge;' I answer such a one as followeth: 1. Is the Scripture the law of God or not? If you say not, you may as well say you are infidels. If you confess it is, then it must have the use of a law. And, 2. Must not subjects understand a law to live by it, though they be not judges? And when estate and life depend on our obedience to the law; if this law be now so dark that the subjects cannot understand it, then it is no law, as not being capable of the use and ends of a law. And so if our salvation or damnation lie on our obedience to God's word and law, it is an intolerable reproach to God and it, to say it is such as we cannot understand. 3. Must we not be judged by this law? Undoubtedly we must. And then should we not measure our causes by it now? 4. May not arbitrators make use of a law to decide a controversy, before it come to the judge? Doubtless they may. 5. What judge would you have? There are but two in the world, that pretend to be the universal, infallible judge of controversies; and that is the Pope and a General Council. For a General Council, there is none in the world, nor likely to be to the end of the world. God forbid we should defer our peace till then! And its decrees are as dark, and much more uncertain than the word of God. And for the Pope, he is the head of a sect or party, and therefore not fit to be judge: you may well know he will judge on his own side. He must be judged by this word of God himself. He is too far off, of all conscience, for us to go or send to. Where Rome is, the most of you know not: a shorter journey may better dispatch our work. The Papists themselves tell us, that many popes have been murderers, adulterers, simonists, perjured persons, and some heretics and infidels. And must such as these be our only judges? They have erred often already, and therefore they may deceive us: and if you send for the Pope's sentence, you must take the messenger's word that he was there, and that it is true.

But yet if all this will not serve turn, I will make a motion, that none can gainsay that hath the face of a Christian. Let us first agree in all those points that Papists and Protestants, Calvinists and Lutherans, Arminians and Anabaptists, and Separatists, and all parties that desire to be called Christians, are agreed in! What, say you, is not this a reasonable motion! O happy you, and happy the places where you live, if you would but stand to it!

And let us consider of this motion, first in the general state of our difference, and then in the particular parts of it!

Truly, sirs, the main difference in this world is between the godly and the ungodly; and all other differences that are not parts of this, are nothing to this, being of lesser danger and easier toleration or cure. The whole world is divided into two armies: Christ is the Captain-general of one, and the saints only his true soldiers, and the seeming saints his seeming soldiers. The devil is the general of the other, and all the unregenerate or ungodly are his soldiers. An enmity is put, since the beginning, between the seed of the woman and of the serpent, (Gen. 3:15.) And there is no middle state, nor one man on earth that is not in one of these armies. I come not to reconcile the commanders, Christ and Satan, for they are irreconcileable; but to reconcile you to Christ, and draw you from a deceiver. I tell you, sirs, this great difference between the holy and the unholy, is the first that must be healed. We can go no farther with you, if you will not begin here at the heart of the difference. When this is done, you shall see, before I have done with you, that I will quickly tell you how we may do well, for all our other differences. You know if one of us believe that there is a God, and another that there is none, it were foolery for us to dispute how God must be worshipped, before we are agreed that there is a God. So here, when it is the nature of ungodliness to make men false to the very truths that they do profess, and heartily to be of no religion at all, it is in vain to dispute about circumstances and modes with such kind of men. Who would dispute whether infants should be baptized, with a man that knows not what baptism is? 'Even an accepting of God for our God, and Christ for our Lord and Saviour, and the Holy Ghost for our Sanctifier; and an absolute delivering up ourselves to the blessed Trinity in these relations, by a solemn covenant professed and sealed by water, renouncing the flesh, the world, and the devil.' O were but this much practically known, we should be all united in this one baptism. Still I say, unholiness is the great point of difference, and the dungeon of confusion, and puddle, where all the heresies of the world are blended and made into a body that is something worse than heresy. When you cry up unity, and cry down holiness, you are distracted, and know not what you say. You talk of joining us together, and you cast away the glue and solder. You talk of building the church in unity, and you cast away the lime and mortar, the pins and nails, and all that should fasten them. You complain that the garment of Christ is rent, and you throw away the needle and thread that should sew it up. You see our wounds and blood, and take on you to have pity on the church, and call for healing; but you hate and cast away the only salve. Do you not yet know the church's unity is a unity of the Spirit, and of Holiness? And that there is no way in the world for us and you to be united, unless you will be sanctified, and live in the Spirit, as you have done in the flesh?

Sirs, let us come nearer the matter: I know our towns and countries have two sorts of persons in them; some are converted, and some unconverted;

some holy, and some unholy; some live for heaven, and some are all for earth; some are ruled by the word of God, and some by their own flesh or wills. If ever these agree and be united, one party must come over to the other. Either the godly must become ungodly, or the ungodly must become saints and godly: Which must it be? Which do you think in your consciences is the way? Must we yield to you, or should you come away to us? (Pardon that I number myself with the sanctified; for I dare not deny the mercies of God, and the privileges of his house.) Let us come fairly to debate the case, and lay our reasons together, and I will here protest to you, if you can give us better reasons why we should forsake a godly life, I will turn to you; and if we can give you better reasons why you should embrace a holy life, will you here promise to turn to us? And let them carry it that have the better cause, and let us be resolved to go away united, and fall all together into that one way that shall be proved to be the best.

Well, let us come to a debate, and see whether we must come to you, or you to us.

1. If we ever agree and unite, you know it must be on terms that are possible. He that propoundeth impossibilities to be agreed on, is the enemy of agreement. But it is impossible for us to come to you, and so to unite with you. This I now prove. (1.) It is impossible to have any universal unity but in an universal head and centre, and that is only God, the Father, Son, and Holy Ghost. As I told you the army must unite in the general, the kingdom in the sovereign, the family in the master, the school in the schoolmaster. In order of nature, you must unite with God in the Redeemer by the sanctifying Spirit, before you can unite with us. But while you are unsanctified you are divided from God. Do you not feel your minds strange to him, your hearts draw back from him, and find by his strangeness to you that there is a division? It is impossible for us to be united to you, till Christ be united to you. For it is against nature, seeing he is the centre, and the head and fountain of life: And what good would it do you to be one with us, and not with him? God is against any unity without him: If you will not begin with him, he will take it but as a treasonable conspiracy, and will break it. We dare not go without him, lest he be angry and destroy us: Soldiers must not make either peace or war, nor so much as treat without the general. Do you not remember how Jehosaphat had like to have sped by a friendship and confederacy with Ahab?

(2.) Moreover the godly and ungodly are of contrary natures: I told you God hath put an enmity between them. You must change your nature or we ours, before we can unite. You may as well think else to unite fire and water, or to build in the air, or to incorporate fire and gunpowder; or to reconcile men and serpents; and marry the dog and the bear together. Sirs, these things are mere impossibilities. There is no agreement between Christ and Belial, righteousness and unrighteousness, light and darkness, death and life, the members of Christ, and the members of a harlot, or a drunkard, or such like. (2 Cor. 6:14.) We have contrary spirits, how then can we be one? One hath the spirit of holiness, and the other the spirit of profaneness; one is led by the Spirit of God, and the other by the flesh. We live not by one law: God's will revealed in his word is our law; and the will of the flesh, and the course of the world is your law. We live not on one sort of food, how then can we accord together? Christ and his heavenly truth, and Holy Spirit and ordinances, is the meat and drink of the saints; they cannot live without them. And the world and fleshly delights are your food; you cannot be without it. Your food would be our poison, your worldly cares, your drunkenness, and profaneness, would be a torment to an honest heart. They cannot live without some communion with God in faith and love, by prayer and meditation; and your heart is against it. They have not the same end as you have. Their work is all for heaven, and yours is all principally for earth. Their work and yours are contrary: they go one way, and you another: so that it is impossible to be united and agree, till one side change. And we cannot possibly turn to you; God holds us fast by his Love and Spirit, and will not let us go, nor suffer us ever to be willing to go. Do you not read Christ telling you, that it is impossible to deceive the elect? that is, so far as to turn them away from Christ. We are kept by the mighty power of God, through faith, to salvation. And who can break away from the upholding arms of Almighty power! Christ hath such hold of us, that he is resolved none shall take us out of his hands, (John 10:28,) so that we cannot come over again to you.

But you may come over to us if you will. God calls you, and Christ would welcome you, and the Holy Ghost would help you: The door is set open by the blood of Christ: the promise is to you and to your children, that you may and shall have Christ and life if you will come in, and accept the offer. The devil cannot hinder you against your wills, he holds you but in the fetters of your own wilfulness, by his mere deceits. Seeing, therefore, that you may come over to the sanctified, and they cannot possibly come to you, let any reasonable man be judge on what terms we should unite and agree.

2. Moreover, if we agree, it must be on terms of wisdom and honesty. A dishonest agreement is not to be desired, but abhorred. For you to leave your ungodliness, and turn to the love and fear of God, is an honest course of agreement; for it is but to leave dishonesty itself and become honest. I hope none of you dare charge the way of God and godliness with any dishonesty: God calls you to nothing but what is holy, and just, and good; and, therefore, honesty requireth you to yield.

But for the sanctified to become unsanctified; for the godly to become ungodly, to be one with you, this were the basest dishonesty in the world. We know your way to be of the devil and the flesh: and is it honest then to join with you in it? We have tried too long already in the days of our ignorance, and have found it dishonest and deceitful; and would you have us go against our own experience? We were once in the way that you are in, and were forced to renounce it, or else we had been undone body and soul for ever; and should we lick up the vomit which we were forced to cast out? We were once agreed with you, and God constrained us to break that agreement; and shall we renew it again? Alas, your way hath cost us dear; many a bitter repenting day, and many a sad thought, to the breaking of our hearts, and the very sense of God's displeasure; a taste of hell was cast into our consciences; many a groan, and tear, and prayer it cost us, before we could recover the hurt that we caught in the way of ungodliness; and yet we have not fully recovered it to this day. And would you have us stark mad, to forget so soon our former sorrows, and turn to a life that hath cost us so dear already? No, we have paid too dear for it, and smarted too much for it, to go that way any more: it brought us to the very brink of hell; and if we had but died in that condition, we had been damned at this hour: And would you be so unreasonable as to wish us to go back again? No, by that time you know as much of an unsanctified state as we do, you will run from it yourselves as fast as you can run; as the Israelites did from the cry of the company of Dathan and Abiram, "Lest the earth should swallow them up also." (Numb. 16:34.)

We are certain that the Lord, whom we serve, is the only God; and that he, and none but he should rule us; and that we have grievously wronged him, by disobeying him so long. And yet would you have us again forsake him? If we should lie in tears till we die, it were too little to satisfy his justice for one of the sins we have already committed; and if it had not been for the wonderful love and suffering of the Son of God, we had been lost for ever: And yet must we turn to this course again? God forbid. It was not so wise nor honest a course. "We ourselves," saith Paul, "were sometime foolish, disobedient, deceived, serving divers lusts and pleasures, living in malice and envy, hateful and hating one another." (You hear how he calls his former life.) "But after that the kindness and love of God our Saviour toward man appeared; not by works of righteousness which we have done, but according to his mercy he saved us, by the washing of regeneration and renewing of the Holy Ghost." (Titus 3:3, 4, 5.) And should Paul have turned a fool again, and be deceived and disobedient again, to agree with the rest of the deceived world? O sirs, we have seen that which you have not seen, and tasted that which you never tasted. Had you seen and tasted the love of God in Christ, and the delightful hopes of eternal life, and felt the comfort of his service, and the joys of the Holy Ghost, you would never wish us to come back again to agree with you in sin; but you would abhor yourselves the very thoughts of your former folly. Why, you may better persuade a man to repent that he was born, and to go into the womb again, than to persuade us to repent that we are newborn, and return to our former state of death. Death is not so sweet to us, nor hell, nor the wrath of God so lovely, nor sin, with all its pleasure, so desirable, that we should turn to them for peace with you. If we have escaped them once, and will not take that for a warning to come there no more, we deserve to pay for it.

Why, sirs, we have made a solemn covenant with God, in the face of the congregation, in our baptism, and oft renewed it in the Lord's-supper, and vowed that we would be his, and absolutely and unreservedly his. And would you wish us to break so solemn a covenant? What honesty is in such perfidiousness? We have renounced the flesh, the world, and the devil; and should we turn to them again for peace with you? O what a cursed peace were that! Let me tell you, that we have not found God so bad a master, as to forsake him for the sake of you or any creature. We have tried him, and found him better to us than all the world. He hath never given us cause to forsake him. And if we should now, after all the trials of his love, turn back to the way of sin and ungodliness, the devil himself would charge us with dishonesty. What! must the godly turn drunkards, and worldlings, and haters of godliness to have peace with you? Why, you may next persuade us even to turn devils, that we may be reconciled to you. The God that made us, hath forbid us upon pain of his hot displeasure, to walk in your ways. He saith to every one of us, as to Jeremiah, "Let them return unto thee, and return not thou unto them." (Jer. 15:19.) And should we obey God or men? Judge you whether. Why, sirs, are you so utterly unreasonable as to wish us, or any man living, to love you better than God, or to regard you more than God, or obey you before God? Or should we be so much worse than mad, as to yield to you if you did desire it? Why, what are you in comparison with the Almighty! O poor worms, that are even dying while you are speaking! that are but as bubbles ready to burst, when you are swelled to the highest in ungodly pride! That even while you are eating, and drinking, and making merry, are passing on apace to weeping and gnashing of teeth, and everlasting woes and lamentations! What should we regard such dust and dirt as you are, before the glorious God! It were far greater wisdom and honesty, for your children to set up a dog or a toad, and say, 'This is more to be loved and honoured than my father.' If a traitor against an earthly prince deserve to be hanged, drawn and quartered; certainly that man that would forsake God and his laws, to please such silly worms as you, did deserve to be hanged in the flames of hell, and to be tormented by infernal fiends, and ground to powder by the wrath of the Almighty! Well! if you have eyes that can see, you may see now past doubt, that we cannot turn to you that are ungodly, with any wisdom or honesty in the world, nor without the highest madness and dishonesty. But can you say so of your turning in to us? Is it contrary either to wisdom, or honesty, for you to turn unfeignedly to God, and to become a sanctified godly people? Methinks you should not have such a thought in your hearts: and, therefore, if we be not all of a mind, and go not all one way, it is most apparent that it is not long of us, but of you.

3. If we do unite and agree, it must be upon terms of safety. This much I hope you cannot deny us. You would not surely wish us to agree to our own destruction, and to make a bargain with you, that we may all join together in cutting our own throats? Do you think that this were a wise combination? How much less should we make an agreement to go the certain way to hell, and to join together in damning our own souls for ever? Sirs, if you dislike the way of holiness, do but find out any other way that will safely bring a man to heaven, and we will promise you to join in it. But unholiness will never do it. God hath told us as plain as can be spoken, "That except a man be born again, and be converted, he cannot enter into the kingdom of heaven:" (John 3:3, 5; Matt. 18:3:) "And that without holiness no man shall see the Lord:" "And that the righteous themselves are scarcely saved:" (1 Peter 4:18:) "And that if any man be in Christ, he is a new creature; old things are passed away, and all things become new:" (2 Cor. 5:17:) And that "if any man have not the Spirit of Christ, he is none of

his." (Rom. 8:9.) So that if God know who shall be saved, it is as certain as any thing in the world, that no unsanctified man can be saved. If leaping into the water be the way to drowning, or leaping into the fire be the way to burning, or leaping down from the top of a steeple be the way to break your necks, as sure is an unholy life the way to everlasting torment. And would you wish us to undo ourselves everlastingly for your friendship? What can you say to this now? If you say that your way is not so dangerous, it is but our precise uncharitable conceit: We have shewed you the Word of God for it; and forty times more we could easily shew you! And shall we believe you, or such as you, before God? You are liars, but God cannot lie. You see not what is done in another world; but God seeth it. You know not what is in heaven or hell; but God knoweth. And shall we not believe God that knoweth and disposeth of all, better than moles that never saw it, and ignorant souls that never knew it? God saith, that "fornicators, adulterers, drunkards, covetous persons, revilers, or the like, shall not inherit the kingdom of God." (1 Cor. 6:10, 11.) And that "they that are in the flesh cannot please God;" and that "if you live after the flesh ye shall die." (Rom. 8:5, 6, 7. 13.) And would you have us believe you, that there is no danger in a fleshly life? Sirs, we desire heartily to be united and agreed with you, but we are loath to buy it so dear, as the loss of God and heaven comes to. We are willing of concord with you, but we are loath to be damned with you: And do you blame us for this? And, alas, if you should tell us a thousand times, that you hope there is no such danger, or that you hope to escape as well as the godly, this is but poor security to us. Shall we be so mad, as to venture ourselves on such words as these, against the word of the Ruler of the world? What security can you give us, that we shall escape damnation if we turn ungodly? Are you able to save us from the wrath of God? Will you undertake to stand between us and his displeasure? What say you? If we will forsake a holy life, and live as careless worldlings do, and neglect God and our souls, and please the world and our flesh, will you undertake to answer for us in judgment? And will you venture to bear the punishment that we should bear? If you dare not undertake to save us harmless, why will you persuade us to do as you do? Nay, if you would undertake it, he were a madman that would trust you, and venture his salvation upon such undertakings; for we know you are not able to make them good. Alas! poor souls, how unable will you be to save yourselves, or to stay out of hell an hour longer, when devils have commission to carry you away! And shall we trust our souls upon your boasting words, when we know you are unable to help yourselves? Let us see first what you can do for yourselves or us, against the present hand of God. Can you keep off death, and rebuke diseases, and live here in health and wealth for ever, whether God will or no? How comes it to pass then that here is never a one of you near two hundred years of age? Let us see you chide back approaching death, and raise the dead bodies from their graves, and heal all the diseases that cut off mankind: If you cannot do these smaller matters, would you have us believe that you can save us from damnation? Why, sirs, must your neighbours lie some of them in poverty, and some in pain, some sick of one disease, and some of another, and you look on them and cannot cure them, or relieve them, and yet must we venture our souls upon your words! You cannot make an old man young again; and can you make the word of God prove false, or save those that God hath said shall perish, and bring unsanctified men to heaven whether God will or no? Well, sirs, let them that hate their souls, or care not whether they are saved or damned, forsake the Lord and a holy life, and join with you and see whether you can save them: but for my part I believe the word of God, and upon this word only I am resolved to build my hopes, and venture my soul, and all that little that I have in this world: trust you on what you please, this shall be my trust: and they that can find a surer ground to build upon, let them take their course.

But I must tell you, that if you would wish us all to cast away God and Christ, and heaven, to agree with you, you are monsters and not men; and if you are so cruel as to desire us to damn our souls for company, we must be so careful of ourselves as to abhor your motion, and rather to hate the dearest thing or person in the world, as they would draw us from Christ and everlasting life. (Luke 14:26.)

You see then what it is that standeth in our way, to hinder us from turning back to you. But what danger would you be in if you should turn to us? Would it hurt or hazard you to forsake your sensual, ungodly lives? Is there any danger in turning to God, and living a holy, heavenly life? What is the danger? Forsooth you may lose your estates or lives! A great matter indeed in comparison of eternal life: And must you not lose them shortly whether you will or not? And are they not in the power of God? And cannot he preserve them if he please? And if it be good for them, he is more likely to do it for his own, than for his enemies! But indeed he hath told you himself, that "he that will save his life shall lose it, and he that loseth his life for his sake, shall find it; even in life everlasting." (Matt. 16:25; 10:39.) And yet as the world now goeth in England, through the mercy of God, your lives are in no danger. It is but the scorn of ignorant, miserable men that you must endure. And will you stick at this, in the cause of God and your salvation? Nay, indeed you are in most dreadful danger every day, and night, and hour, till you forsake your former fleshly lives, and turn to Christ! You are all the while even within a step of death and hell, till you are converted and made a holy people; it is but one stroke of death to put an end to your lives and hopes, and you are gone for ever. So that you have nothing to lose, but a heaven to gain, if you join with the godly. There is no danger can come to you by turning, unless it be the loss of your sins; and that is a loss no more to be feared, than a man should fear to lose the plague, or leprosy that hath it.

Now I beseech you, sirs, as men of conscience or of reason, set both together, and equally consider how the case stands between us. If we join with the unholy, we run into hell, and lose God, and Christ, and grace, and salvation for evermore; but if you turn to the godly, you get out of danger, and make the most gainful match that ever was made by mortal men; and you can lose nothing but the sensual pleasures of sin, which are but exchanged for the joys of saints, as sickness is exchanged for health. And which now do you think in reason is the more fit, that you turn to the godly, or they to you? Truly, if you make so great a matter of leaving your sins, which are viler than your dung, that you will rather break with God and us, you must give us leave to make so great a matter of leaving Christ and his holy ways and people, that we will much rather break with you and all the wickedness in the world, and with our carnal selves, and that which is most dear to them: And I think we have good reason for it.

4. Moreover, this must be considered in our treaty, that if we agree, it is fit that our dearest friends be taken into the agreement: should we cast off them to agree with adversaries, and leave our old friends in hope of new? But if we come over to you, and turn unholy, we shall never have God's consent to the agreement, we must leave him out, and utterly lose him: when, alas, we cannot live, nor move, nor breathe, without him? We cannot have our daily bread, or one night's rest, but by his gift. And such a friend is not to be lost for you. And we shall lose the Lord Jesus and the Holy Ghost, and the communion of saints, and the peace of our own consciences. O what a peal would conscience ring us night and day! It would open hell to us: It would kindle the fire of God's wrath in our bosoms; and be scorching us as we lie down and as we rise up: and who would endure such a life as this for all the world? It is likely it is not thus with you; but that is because you know not what a case you are in, nor what a dreadful

thing ungodliness is; but we know it: and therefore what shift soever you make to keep your consciences asleep, I know not how I should quiet mine, if I were in your case, and knew but what I know of it.

But now if you will join with Christ and us, your true friends will be glad of it; you should not lose one friend in the world by it, unless you take the devil and his servants for your friends, that would destroy you. Judge then, whether you should come to us, or we to you.

5. Moreover, this must be considered in our treaty, that if we agree with you, we have some regard to our honour. And what honour is it to us to become the servants of sin and the devil, and be forsaken of God, and return to the slavery that lately we were delivered from? A hangman is ten thousand times more honourable than this.

But on the other side, if you will turn to Christ, you will come out of the greatest shame, and obtain the greatest honours that you are capable of: you will be the sons of God, and heirs of heaven, coheirs with Christ, fellow-citizens of the saints, and of the household of God; (John 1:12; Rom. 8:17; Eph. 2:19;) and be built up an habitation of God through the Spirit. (Eph. 2:22.)

6. Moreover, this is most considerable in our treaty, that if we agree, it must be upon the universal terms that all will agree upon; or else it can be no universal agreement. If a few should agree with you, this would not make a unity in the world. We must have terms that are fit for all to agree upon. And in good sadness, would you have all the world be such as you? Tell me, you that are covetous and proud, would you have all the world become proud and covetous to agree with you? Nay, if they should, when they are most like you, they would not agree with you: for the proud will envy the proud, and their pride will set them together by the ears: and the covetous would be greedily snatching the prey out of one another's jaws, and their mammon would be the matter of their strife. Tell me also, you that are drunkards or unclean, would you have all the world become drunkards and unclean for unity with you? You that are careless about your souls, and prayerless in your families, and forget the matters of everlasting life, would you have all the world set as light by God, and Christ, and heaven as you? Could the worst of you all have the face to make such a motion as this? What! would you have all holiness and heavenly-mindedness banished out of the world, because you have banished it from yourselves? Would you have all men shut their Bibles as much as you, and instruct their children and servants no more than you, and love God and serve him no more than you? Is it possible that such a heart as this can be in the breast of the worst

on earth? What! would you have all the world be drunkards, or fornicators, or haters of godliness, or at least unsanctified, because you are so? How quickly then would earth turn hell, and the flames of the wrath of God consume it! How certainly then would God forsake the world, as a man would be gone from toads and serpents! Can there be such cruelty in any but the devils, as to wish all the world to be damned with you for company, or to agree with you on such terms, that you may go hand in hand together to damnation? Or if you had such devilish hearts within you, as to desire such an agreement as this, can you think that all the godly would yield to it? No, let me tell you, not one of them in all the world will yield to it. If you set no more by the love of God, the blood of Christ, the presence and comforts of the Holy Ghost, and the hopes of glory, yet they do, and will do. If you will run into hell, you shall never get them thither with you for company.

But on the other side, there is nothing in the way of holiness, but what is fit for all men to agree upon. I know all will not; and therefore we expect not an agreement with all. But that is their unhappiness. There is no fit means of agreement but this.

7. Lastly, this also must be considered in our treaty; that we agree upon terms that are likely to hold, and not to be repented of hereafter. For what good will it do to agree to-day, and to break it or bewail it to-morrow? Why, alas, sirs, we know as sure as we breathe, that if we should agree with you in unholiness, we should quickly repent it, either by grace, or in hell-fire. Nay, we know that you will repent of these unholy ways and hearts yourselves, either by grace or judgment. Nay, there are even now some kind of purposes in many of you to repent. I have heard abundance of ungodly men profess that they hope to repent hereafter, and mend their lives, and leave their sins. And would you wish us to come and join with you in a way that you hope to forsake yourselves, and in a way that you propose hereafter to repent of? I know as surely as that the sun will set, that every ungodly soul among you, will shortly change their false opinions; and they that derided the servants of Christ, would wish then that they might be but door-keepers among them: you will wish and wish a thousand times that you had done as they did, and lived as holily as the best on earth: You will then wish, 'O that it were to do again! and that my life were again to be lived; and God would but try me on earth once more!' Those tongues that railed against religion, will a thousand times more reproach yourselves for those reproaches, and the neglect of this religion. You will then cry out 'Where was my wit and reason, when I made so mad a change, as

of God for the creature, Christ for sin, and heaven for hell!' Do you think, sirs, that it were any wisdom for us to agree with you now in that, for which you will fall out with yourselves for ever? And to go with you in that loose ungodly way which you will wish yourselves that you had never known?

Besides, we know that it is only the saints that we must live with for ever; and therefore you must become saints, if you would be united to us here. What! should we be so careful to agree with you awhile and be separated from you eternally, or do worse by suffering with you! But if you will unite with us in Christ and holiness, this will be a lastingunity; which you will never have occasion to repent of. The union between the Lord Jesus and his members, shall never be dissolved. Heartily join with his servants now in the ways of holiness, and you shall certainly join with them in the state of happiness, and in the joyful fruition and praises of the Lord.

Well, sirs, in this much of our treaty, I have laid the case plain and open before you, and shewed you that we cannot come over to you: it is not possible, nor honest, nor safe; we cannot forsake a holy life without forsaking God and our Redeemer, and our salvation, which no man that is a man indeed, should desire us to do; nor can we do it till we first forsake our understandings: But on your side the case is otherwise: you may turn to God and a holy life without any hurt or wrong to you at all; nay, it is the only way to your felicity, and if you do it not, you are undone for ever: so that the case is past all controversy before you, that there is no way in the world to unity, but by consent in piety. If half the commonwealth turn rebels, and so shall make a division in the body, the way to unite them is by the returning of the rebels to their allegiance, and not for the true and lawful subjects to turn all rebels and join with them. For without the head there cannot be a union. So that if the world be still divided and disagreed, it is not long of the godly, but of the ungodly: and if you would have an agreement, it is you that must yield, who cause the disagreement. You may do it, and must do it, or do worse; but the godly may not yield to you.

What say you now, would you have unity or division? Would you have peace or no peace? You complain that the world is of so many minds: would you have them all reconciled and of one mind? If you would, let us see it. The work sticks with you; on your hands it lieth, and it is you that must do it, if ever it be done. If you would have all ungodly, you deserve not to live on the earth. Shall we then without any more ado agree all upon a life of holiness? O than our towns and parishes would all join together in this agreement! And it must be this or none.

But perhaps some of you will say, 'What need you make so many words about a matter that nobody doth deny? We all know we should be holy and godly, and none should be ungodly; who doubts this? But the question is, What holiness and godliness is? Tell us therefore what you mean by it, and who those be that you take to be the godly, sanctified people?'

Answ. If we are all agreed of the necessity of holiness, then those that are not yet agreed to be holy themselves, do sin against their own consciences, and condemn themselves in the things which they allow, and wilfully divide themselves from Christ and from his church. And if any of you have been so long baptized into the name of the Holy Ghost as your sanctifier, and yet know not what sanctification is, and who are to be accounted sanctified and godly, you shew that you have perfidiously cast away and broke your covenant with God: and made but an ill use of your baptism, or any means and ordinances since. But if you know not who are godly or ungodly, I shall quickly tell you.

A godly man is one that being formerly in a state of sin and misery, both strange and backward to God and heaven, and a holy life, and prone to earthly, fleshly pleasures, is now by the powerful work of the word and Spirit of God, converted to unfeigned faith and repentance, broken-hearted for his former sin and misery, flying to Christ as the only hope and physician of his soul, and so is made a new creature, having his heart set upon God and everlasting life, and contemning all the pleasures of the flesh, and the things of this world, in comparison of his hopes and glory; hating all known sin, and not wilfully living in any; and loving the highest degree of holiness, and willing to use the means that God hath appointed to destroy the remnants of sin, and bring him nearer to perfection; this is a truly godly man. And he that is not such, is ungodly. He that yet remaineth in his natural depraved state, and is unacquainted with this great and holy change, that hath any sin that he had rather keep than leave, and any that he wilfully liveth in; and wilfully neglecteth known duties, as one that had rather be free from them than perform them, and had rather live a fleshly life than a spiritual and a holy life, and is more in love with the creature than with God; with his life on earth in flesh and sin, than a life in heaven with God and his saints in perfect holiness; this man is undoubtedly a wicked and ungodly man, how civilly or religiously soever he may seem to live in the world. And so I have in a few words told you, who they be that are godly, and who are the ungodly. The question now that we are treating about is, whether we shall all agree together to be godly? Do you not believe it to be best and necessary? If not, you are blind: if you do, let us agree on it without delay. You tell us with many great complaints of the many differences and divisions that are among us; but shall we agree so far as we are agreed? That is, shall we agree in heart and practice, so far as we are agreed in opinion and profession? O that you would make a solemn covenant, that you will but consent and go along with the godly so far as you confess you ought to do; and would but unite with us in faithfulness to the truths which you cannot deny. I think it will be best to call you to the trial in some particulars.

1. I hope we are all agreed that there is only one God that made us, and preserveth us, and redeemed us; and therefore that we are wholly his, and should resign ourselves, and all that we have, absolutely to him for his service. He is not worthy the name of a man that denieth this: And shall we all agree now in the practice of this much? Shall we wholly resign ourselves and all that we have to God, and labour to know what God would have us be and do, and that let us resolve upon, whatever the flesh or the world say to the contrary? Were but this much well resolved on, we were in a fair way to a full agreement.

2. We are all agreed in opinion or profession, that this God is our only happiness, and his favour is better than all the world, and that he is infinitely wise, and good, and powerful; and therefore that he must be loved above all things whatsoever, and must be most feared, and served, and trusted, and depended on.

And shall we but agree all in the practice of this much? O that you would but heartily consent to do it! Did we but join together in loving God above all, and fearing, and trusting, and serving him before all, we should quickly be of one heart and soul, and in a very fair way to a perfect agreement.

3. We are all agreed (that profess Christianity) that sin hath made us miserable, and brought us under the wrath and curse of God, and that the Lord Jesus Christ having redeemed us by his blood, is the only Physician and Remedy for our souls, and having manifested such infinite love in our redemption, and also purchased dominion over us, we are strongly bound to rejoice in his salvation, and fly to him for safety, and rest upon him, and live in the thankful admirations of his love, and in careful obedience to his gracious laws.

And shall we all agree in the practice of this much? Will you fly to Christ with broken, bleeding hearts, for safety from sin, and wrath, and hell, and set more by him than by all the world? Will you study with all saints to comprehend his love; (Ephes. 3:18, 19;) and admire him and his mercies, and devote yourselves to him, and be ruled by him? O that we were but all agreed in this much.

4. We are all agreed in opinion or profession, that the Holy Ghost is the Sanctifier of God's elect, or of all that shall be saved; and that except a man be born again by the Spirit, he cannot enter into the kingdom of heaven; and that without holiness none shall see God; and that no man is the son of God that hath not in him the Spirit of his Son. (1 Cor. 12:12, 13; Ephes. 4:5; John 3:5, 6; Heb. 12:14; Rom. 8:9; Gal. 4:4.)

Were we but all such now as we are agreed we must be, and would you but all consent to this sanctification and newness of life, the great difference were healed, and the work were done.

5. Moreover we are all agreed, or seem to be so, that the Holy Scripture is the word of God, and of infallible truth, and therefore must be believed and made the rule of our judgments and our lives.

Shall we all agree now in the practice of this? Will you appeal to the Scripture, and shall it be our rule? If the flesh persuade you to another course, and murmur at the strictness of God's word; if custom be against it, and the greater number be against it; if your profits, or pleasures, or worldly honours be against it, and your former opinions and practice have been against it, will you yet believe the Scripture before all, and be ruled by it above all the world? You are agreed I hope that God is to be obeyed rather than men, or than the flesh and the devil? Will you resolve that it shall be so? O if the word of God might be the rule, how quickly should we be agreed! For all the popish cavils at its difficulty, and men's divers expositions, yet how soon should we be agreed!

6. We are all agreed in opinion or profession, that there is a heaven for the sanctified, even an endless inconceivable glory with God, in the seeing of his face, and enjoying him in perfect love and joys; and that the seeking of this everlasting glory should be the main and principal business of our lives, which all things must give place to. He that will deny this can have no pretence to call himself a Christian.

O that we might but all agree in the practising of this! and that the principal love and desire of our souls were set upon the heavenly blessedness, and the chiefest of our care and labour might be laid out for the obtaining of it. Agree in this, and all will be agreed at last.

7. We are all agreed in our profession, that there is a hell, or state of endless torments, where all the finally unsanctified and ungodly must be for ever.

But why do we not agree in the diligent avoiding of such a dreadful misery, and using our best endeavours to escape it?

8. We are all agreed in profession, that the flesh is our enemy, and must be mortified. But will you agree in the practice of this mortification? We are agreed in profession, that the world is our enemy, and must be contemned, and that it is a vain and worthless thing compared with the glory that is to come: but yet men will not agree to renounce the world unfeignedly, and to be strangers to it, and part with all rather than with God and a good conscience; but while men speak contemptuously of the world, they seek it far more eagerly than heaven. We are agreed that the devil is our enemy, and yet men will not forsake his service.

9. We are all agreed in profession, that sin is a most hateful thing, hated of God, condemned by his word, and the only cause of the damnation of souls: and yet men love it, and live in it with delight. Shall we agree all to deal with sin as we speak of it? Will magistrates, and ministers, and people join together, to banish it out of town and country? Particularly we are agreed I hope, that whoredom, and wantonness, and gluttony, and drunkenness, and strife, and envying, and lying, and deceit, and cursing, and swearing, and railing, and backbiting, and speaking against a holy life, are all gross, hateful, damning sins, which every Christian must abhor. But why do you not agree in the hating, and forsaking, and beating down these sins? But town and country swarmeth with them as a carcase doth with maggots, or a stinking pond with frogs and toads: so that magistrates and ministers, punishments and persuasion, the laws of the land, and the laws of God, can do but little to rid the country of them; but the same men that confess all these to be great and grievous sins, will keep them and delight in them, as if it were in despite of God and man, or as if they bore a deadly grudge to their own immortal souls.

10. There is none of you that bears the face of a Christian, but must agree with us in profession, that "one thing is needful, and that we must seek first the kingdom of God and his righteousness, and labour most for the food that will not perish," (Luke 10:41, 42; Matt. 6:33; John 6:27,) and that "God should be loved with all our heart, and soul, and might," and that no man can love him too much, nor serve him too carefully, nor be too diligent in seeking of his salvation. Why then will you not all agree to do thus? But the

very same tongues that confess all this, will yet speak against the service of God, and call it Puritanism and preciseness, and say it is more ado than needs. Why, sirs, if you will say and unsay, there is no hold to be taken of your words, and therefore what agreement can be with you? Will you confess that all should take more care of their souls than of their bodies; and take more care for heaven than earth, and yet will you not agree to do it, but rather speak against them that do it, when you confess that it is best? Why, if you can agree no better with yourselves, how can you agree with us? If your own opinions and profession be at such odds with your wills and practices, no wonder if you be at odds with others.

More particularly, I hope you will all confess, that it is the duty of all that can, to hear the word of God, and frequently to read it, and labour to understand it, and to meditate in it day and night; and for parents daily to teach it their children at home and abroad, lying down and rising up, (Deut. 6:6–8; 11:18, 19; Psal. 1:2, 3,) and to pray in their families, and in private, even always or frequently to pray, and not to wax faint, but in all things to make known their requests to God, that all things might be sanctified to them by the word and prayer. All this is plain in the word of God. (Dan. 6:10, 11; Luke 18:1; 1 Thess. 5:17; Psal. 55:17; 1 Tim. 4:5; Phil. 4:6.)

But will you all agree with us in the practice of these things? Will all the families in town and country agree together, to pray morning and evening reverently to God, and to banish profaneness out of their doors, and to instruct their children and servants in the fear of God, and spend the Lord's-day in holy exercises, and help one another to prepare for death and judgment, and exhort one another daily, while it is called to-day, lest any be hardened by the deceitfulness of sin? (Heb. 3:13.)

To what purpose should I mention any more particulars, till we see whether you will unite and agree in these? All these are your own professions. I know you cannot deny any one of them, and yet we cannot persuade you to consent with us in the practice of what yourselves profess: no, nor scarcely to forbear the open opposing of it: Either resolve now that you will all agree with us in these things, which you confess the Lord hath made your duty, or else tell us plainly that you are the deadly enemies of unity and peace, that we may take you to be as you are, and trouble ourselves no more about you. If you are resolved against agreement and unity, tell us so, and save us the labour of any farther treaties with you. Talk no more childishly about our petty differences in ceremonies and forms of worship, about bishops and common-prayer-books, and holy-days, and such like, as long as you refuse agreement in the main. There is a difference between you that is an hundred times greater than these; some of you are for heaven, and some for earth; some of you live to the Spirit, and some to the flesh; some of you are hearing, reading, or meditating on the word of God, when others think it needless, and had rather have a pair of cards or dice in their hands: Some of you make God's law your rule, and some are ruled by the world and the flesh; some are drunkards, gluttons, wantons, worldlings; and some are sober, temperate, chaste and heavenly; some think almost any thing enough in the worship of God, and for the saving of their souls; and others think the best they can do too little; and when they have done most, lament that they do no more; some families use daily prayer, reading, and holy instructions; and others use daily swearing, railing, ribaldry, and perhaps deriding of holiness itself. In a word, some give up themselves to God and heaven, and others to the world, the flesh, and the devil; some are converted and become new creatures by the sanctifying work of the Holy Ghost; and others are yet in the state of nature, and never knew a true conversion.

This is the great difference of the world, sirs: till this be healed, it is in vain to talk of the healing of our petty differences. And therefore once more I tell you, if you will not be converted to a holy life, and unite with us on these terms, you are the enemies of peace and unity, and the great incendiaries of the world.

And now having proceeded thus far in the treaty with you, because I will either bring you to agreement, or leave you at least without excuse, I will here annex some further reasons to move you, if it may be to so happy a work.

1. Consider, I pray you, that if you will not agree with us in the things that you make profession of, and confess to be your duty, you are then treacherous and false to God, and to yourselves, and therefore not fit for any to make agreement with, till you change your minds. Do you know that God is best, and yet will you not love him better than the world? Do you know that heaven is the only happiness, and yet will you not seek it more than earth? Do you know that a holy life is best, and yet will you be unholy? Do you know sin is the worst and most dangerous thing in the world, and yet will you not let it go? Who will trust such men as you, that will go against their own knowledge and confessions? If you will be false to God, and false to your own souls, no wonder if you be false to us.

2. Moreover, all your pretended desires of unity and concord are base hypocrisy, as long as you refuse to unite with us in the way and state of holiness: To take on you that you are troubled at the divisions of the world, and to wish that we were all of one religion, and to talk against sects and opinions as you do, is mere self-condemning, and such gross dissembling, as exposeth you to shame. What! would you have us think you are against divisions, when you divide from God, and Christ, and the Holy Ghost; from the Scripture, from the holy catholic church, and from the communion of saints? Can you for shame say, that you are for unity and agreement, when you are dividing from us, and will not agree with us, unless we will be as mad as you, and damn our souls for company with you? To hear these ungodly men talk against sects and divisions in the church, is as if we heard a man that hath the leprosy, cry out against those that have the itch, or a murderer chide another for foul words.

3. And I must tell you, while you remain ungodly, you are the great heretics and Separatists that trouble the church of God, more than abundance of those that you reproach. I excuse not the least; but none of them are like you. As death is worse than sickness, as being that which all sickness tends to, and tie worst that it can do; so ungodliness is worse than sects, and particular errors or heresies, it being the worst that any error can do, to make a man ungodly. There are no such Separatists in the world as you. It is not only from a particular church or ordinance that you separate; but, as I said even now, you separate from God that made you, from Christ that bought you, from the Spirit that should sanctify you, from the word of God that must rule you or condemn you, from the body of Christ, and the holy communion of his people. The church would have you join with them in holy worship; and your godly neighbours would have you join with them in prayer and holy lives, and you will not, but separate from them all. They cannot have your help against the sins of the time and place you live in: they cannot have your company in the way to heaven; but when they go one way, you go another way. You are the great troublers of the world, and break the peace of church and state, and of all you have to do with. You trouble magistrates, and make work for lawyers; you trouble ministers, and frustrate their labours, and make their lives grievous to them, when it is much in your hands to make them joyous. You trouble all the godly that are about you, and you will find at last that you have most of all troubled your own souls. For shame therefore, before you speak any more against sects and separatists, or any other troublers of the church,

give over the ungodly separation which you continue in, and come in to the unity of the church yourselves, and live in that communion of saints which you say you do believe, and do not go on to trouble the church more than those that you speak against.

4. Consider also, whether you have not as much reason to live a diligent holy life, and seek God and your salvation with all your might, as any of your neighbours have. And, therefore, whether your own necessity doth not call aloud to you, to unite with them, and to do as they do. Your godly neighbours are meditating on the word of God, when you are thinking of the world, or on vanity: they are discoursing of the life to come, when you are talking of your worldly business, or pouring out a company of idle words. Ask your consciences now, whether you have not as much need to study the Scripture, and prepare for the life to come, as they? Your godly neighbours are at prayer, when you are sinning and drowned in the inordinate cares of the world, and have no heart to their employment. Let conscience speak, whether you have not as much need to pray as they. They abhor sin and are afraid of it, when you boldly venture on it. Let conscience tell you, whether you have not as much cause to be afraid of sin as they. Yea, and a hundred times more; for you are under the guilt and power of it. O wonderful madness of the ungodly world; that the example of the godly should not bring them to some consideration! A man that is converted and reconciled to God, and hath a pardon of all his sins, and is in a state of salvation, and walketh humbly and uprightly with God, doth yet think all too little that he can do; but fasteth, and prayeth, and watcheth against temptations, and humbleth his flesh, and followeth after God continually, and lamenteth after all that he is so bad, and can do no more. And his neighbour that liveth by him is an ignorant stupid sinner, unconverted, and under the guilt of his sin, and under the curse and wrath of God, having no assurance of salvation; nay, it is certain that he would be cast into hell the next hour if he die in that condition; and yet this man feels not any such need of prayer, and holy meditation, and conference, and so religious and strict a life. He that hath lost almost all the time of his life, and is not only quite behind hand in knowledge and abilities, but is an unsanctified miserable wretch, not sure to be out of hell an hour; this man perceiveth no such necessity of a holy life, nor why he should make so much ado. As if a rich man should be put to daily labour, and a man that hath nothing should think it needless: or as if a man that hath the tooth-ach, or a slight disease, should send for a physician; and he that hath the plague should sit

still and say, 'What needs this trouble?' Sirs, I beseech you look upon the holiest and most heavenly neighbours you have, and bethink you whether you have not more need to be diligent than they. Have not you immortal souls to lose as well as they? Are not you in danger of damnation as much, and a hundred times more than they? Should not God be your master as well as theirs? And his law your rule as well as theirs? And heaven be as dear to you as to them? Bethink yourselves when you hear them praying, or reading, or repeating sermons, and sanctifying the Lord's-day, and fearing to offend, 'Have not I as much need to do this as any of them? 'If then you have as much cause and need to live a godly life as others, join with them in it, and let all the town agree together, and none withdraw but he that can say, 'I have no need of it.'

5. And I pray you consider also, how easy it would make the way to heaven, if we would but all unite and agree to go together in it. This is it that discourageth the weak, and makes it so hard a matter to be saved, because there are so few that are godly: But if one or two poor people be resolved to seek first the kingdom of God and his righteousness, and to please God and save their souls, the rest do either look on and refuse to join with them, or else speak against them, and make them their ordinary scorn. And thus he that will be saved, must not only go to heaven without the company of the most of his neighbours, but must go through their opposition, and reproaches, and discouragements: and (the Lord be merciful to the miserable world!) most places that one shall come into, are more agreed against holiness and salvation than for it, and had rather that all the parish would agree together against a godly life (which is indeed against Christ, and heaven, and their own souls) than for it. And some places are so miserable, that you may hear them thank God that they have not one Puritan in their parish, or but few at most; meaning by Puritans, men that seek heaven above earth, and had rather leave their sins than be damned. And this dishearteneth many that have some mind to godliness, to see almost all the town and parish against it.

But now if you had all but so much wit and grace, as to meet together and make an agreement, that you will all be a holy people to the Lord, and you will all join together in a godly life, and you will all be the sworn professed enemies of the way to hell, and join together against your ignorance, and pride, and covetousness, and drunkenness, and swearing, and railing, and all profaneness and iniquity; and if you would all agree together to set up prayer, and reading, and holy exercises, in every house in town

and parish; and that you will all redeem the time for your souls, especially
that you will wholly spend the Lord's-day in the necessary delightful work
of God; then what abundance of your difficulties would be removed! And
how easy and pleasant would the way to heaven be! Then there would be
none to discourage poor ignorant souls, by deriding at a godly life; nor any
to entice them to wicked courses; nor any to tempt them by their ill examples; and the number of the godly would encourage men, as the fewness
of them now discourageth. This troubleth men in their passage to heaven
when we are ill-yoked together, and one draws backward as the other draws
forward: And if the husband be for God, the wife is for the world; or if the
wife be for heaven, the husband will needs go the way to hell: and if one
neighbour be godly, the two, if not ten or twenty next him will be ungodly:
and, as the Israelites' spies, they raise up false reports of the land, and of
the state of godliness, and of the persons themselves, to discourage others:
whereas if you would all agree together, you might march on comfortably
without all this ado.

O how sweet and pleasant a life it is, to see brethren dwell together in
such a holy unity as this. (Psal. 133:1.) Happy are they that dwell in such
towns and parishes as these, if there be any such in the world! Where
neighbours go all hand in hand together towards heaven, and take sweet
counsel together; and go to the house of God in company; and when others
meet in alehouses, and about fooleries and profaneness, they will meet
together to talk of their meeting in the presence of God, and the joy and
praises of the living God, and the communion with Christ, and with angels,
and with one another, which we shall then possess: when they will pray
together, and comfort one another with such words. (1 Thess. 4:18.) And
when others are talking idly, or of the world, they will be admonishing
and exhorting one another, and speaking words that are edifying to the
hearers, (Col. 3:16; Ephes. 4:29,) and opening their cases and experiences to
each other, and faithfully watching over one another, agreeing to tell one
another plainly and lovingly of their sins, and to take it thankfully of those
that do so, and endeavour presently to amend. What a sweet and blessed
life were this, if all our towns and parishes would agree in it! Who would
not rather live with bread and water in such a town as this, than be a lord
or prince among the ungodly! Well, sirs, it is much in your hands now to
make your own and your neighbours' lives thus sweet and comfortable, and
to make the way to heaven thus easy: Why then will you not agree and do it?

6. Moreover, such a holy unity and concord would be the highest honour to your towns and countries that in this world they can possibly receive. It is the highest glory of the kingdoms of the world, to become the kingdoms of the Lord and of his Christ. (Rev. 11:17.) You think it a great honour for your towns to be rich, and have fair buildings, and to have worldly privileges: but, alas, these are baubles in comparison of the other! O if it were but the happiness of this town and parish to be brought to such a holy agreement as I mentioned, that you would all join together in a godly life, and every family agree to worship God with holy reverence, and all set together against profaneness and all known sin, what an honour would it be to you of this place! How would your fame go through all the land! All countries would ring of Kidderminster, what a victory Christ had gotten there, and what an overthrow the devil and sin had there received! And what a blessed place and people it is, where they are all agreed to be holy and to be saved, and are all like the ancient primitive believers, that were of one heart and one soul. (Acts 4:32.) O how the world would ring of such a town, where there is not one family that is ungodly, that serveth the devil by worldliness, swearing, drunkenness, or any ungodly course; but all are united in Christ and holiness, and are likely to live together in heaven! Truly, neighbours, this would be a greater honour to you, and to the town, than if you were every man a lord or prince! In the eyes of God and all wise men, it would be the greatest honour in the world. And O what an excellent example would it be to all the towns and parishes in the land! When they see your holy unity and peace, or hear of a place that is so happily agreed, it may shame them out of their ungodliness, and kindle in them a strong desire to be like you, and agree together as you have done. O that you would but give them such an example, and try the issue!

7. And I desire every one singly to consider, that it is the unspeakable mercy of God, that he calleth you to this holy union with Christ, and communion of saints; and that he doth not thrust you away, and forbid you coming near, but will give you leave to be of the holy society, fellow-citizens with the saints, and of the household of God. God hath made his promise and offer so large, that you may have part in it as well as others, if you will not wilfully shut out yourselves. The feast is prepared; all things are ready, and you are every man and woman invited. Christ hath opened to you a door of admittance and access to God. And will you now refuse and undo yourselves? The sanctified are God's jewels. (Mal. 3:17.) His treasure and peculiar people; the beloved of his soul, and his delight; and the only

people in the world that shall be saved. This is true; for God hath spoken it: and you may be of this blessed number if you will. God hath not separated you from them, or shut you out by forbidding you to come among them. O do not you separate and shut out yourselves. You see your godly neighbours in possession of this privilege; and may not you have it if you will? May not you study the word of God, and call upon him in prayer, and set yourselves for heaven as well as they? Where doth the Scripture command them to it, any more than you? Or forbid you any more than them? The door is open, you may come in if you will. You have the same means, and call, and offer, and time, and leave to lead a holy life as they. And will you make so much of the difference yourselves as to be the only refusers? God hath done so much for you by the death of Christ, and so ordered the matter in the promises and offers of the Gospel, that none of you shall be able to say at last, 'I would fain have been of the blessed society, and fain have lived in the union and communion of saints, but I could not; God would not give me leave, and Christ and his church would not receive me and entertain me.' Not a man or a woman of you shall have this excuse; and therefore come in and join with the sanits, and thank God that you may.

8. And consider also, that if you will not agree with us in matters of holiness, we can never well make up the rest of our differences: our smaller controversies will never be well agreed, if you will not agree in the main. But if this were agreed, we should in season certainly heal the rest. It would make a man's heart ach to hear wretched sinners talk of our differences about bishops, and ceremonies, and common-prayer, and holy-days, and infant baptism, and the like, that are dead in their sins, and are yet disagreed from us in the very bent of heart and life. Alas, sirs, you have other matters than these first to talk of, and trouble yourselves with. A man that is ready to die of a consumption, should not be taking care to cure the warts or freckles in his face. We have greater matters wherein we differ from you, than kneeling at the sacrament, or observation of days, or other ceremonies, or doubtful opinions in matters of doctrine. Let us first be agreed all to serve one master, and seek one end, and be ruled by one law, and hate known sin, and live a holy life, and then we shall be ready to treat with you about a further agreement. But to talk of small matters, when we differ in the greatest matters in the world, as much as your souls are worth, and in matters which heaven or hell lieth on; this is but childish trifling, and whatever we may do for the peace of the church with such, yet to yourselves that will be small advantage.

Nay, I must tell you, that it is usually but the cunning of the devil, and the hypocrisy of your own hearts, that makes you turn your talk to these controversies, when the great breach is unhealed between Christ and you. It is commonly made a shift to delude and quiet a debauched conscience. Our poor people will not by any persuasion be drawn to a holy, heavenly life, but live in worldliness, and fleshliness, in swearing and drunkenness, and lying and deceit, and filthiness, and profaneness, and hate the minister or Christian that doth reprove them; and then forsooth they talk of common-prayer-book, and holy-days, and bishops, and kneeling at the sacrament, to make others, and perhaps their deluded hearts believe, that this is the controversy and difference. And so a wretched drunkard, or worldling, persuades himself that he is a religious man; as if the difference between him and the godly were but about these ceremonies or church-orders: when, alas, we differ in greater matters, as light and darkness, life and death, yea, next to the difference between heaven and hell.

And I must tell you, that you do but wrong the party or cause that you pretend to, when you will needs engage yourselves among them. What hath done more to the dishonour of the bishops, and common-prayer-book, and other late orders and ceremonies of the church, than to see and hear the rabble of drunkards, swearers, scorners at holiness, and such like, to plead for them, and be violent defenders of them? If you would devise how to shame these things, and bring them down, you can scarce contrive a more effectual way, than to set all the ungodly scandalous wretches to cry them up, and become their patrons; for it will make abundance of soberer people begin to question, whether it be likely to be good, that hath such defenders on one side, and adversaries on the other side.

And therefore, sirs, let us begin our closure and agreement in the main, if you would be ever the better for it, and have unity indeed. And if you say, 'What the nearer shall we be for agreement in the other things? Do not the godly still differ about church-government, and orders, and ceremonies?' I answer, 1. If we never should be agreed in these on earth, we might bear it the more quietly, because our very hearts and souls are united in the main, even in matters abundantly greater, and in all that salvation is laid upon; and, therefore, we have this comfort in the midst of our differences, that we shall all shortly come to heaven, and that perfection and the blessed face of God will unite and perfectly agree us in all things.

2. In the meantime we could hold a holy communion with them in the substance of God's worship; and we have a daily communion with them in the Spirit, and an endeared love to one another.

3. And the holiness of their natures will incline them to manage our remaining differences with meekness, humility, self-denial, moderation, and with great respect to the safety of the whole church, and the honour of God and of the Gospel.

4. And yet I must add, that with such there is a far greater advantage to heal the smallest difference that remains, than with any other. When we have one God to awe us, and one heaven to draw us, and one Christ for our head, and one Spirit and new nature to principle us and dispose us, and one law to rule us, and have all one ultimate end and interest, here is a great advantage for healing of any particular differences that may arise. If the liver, or spleen, or stomach, or brain, or lungs be unsound, the sores that are without will hardly be cured; yea, if there were none, these inward diseases may breed them; but when all is well within, the strength of nature, without a medicine, will do much to cure such small distempers that arise without. The life of faith, the love of God, the love of the brethren, and the church's peace and welfare, with the humility and self-denial that is in every Christian, will do a great deal to the healing of divisions among the godly. They will be content to meet together in love, and pray it out, and refer the matter to the Holy Scripture, and they have all some special illumination of the Spirit.

But perhaps you will say, 'Why are they not more fully agreed?' I answer, 1. Because there are such a multitude of ungodly persons among them, that hinder them from opportunities and advantages for agreement. And many of these ungodly ones are hypocrites, that take on them to be godly, and so are traitors in our bosoms, and hinder peace the more by seeming to be godly, when they are not. 2. Because of the remnant of sin that is yet in the sanctified, and because they are not yet perfect and in heaven. If they had no sin, they would have no divisions: and as their sin is healed as to the dominion of it, but not perfectly till they come to heaven; so their divisions are healed in the main, but not perfectly, till they are perfectly united to God in glory.

9. Consider also, I beseech you, what a joy it would be to Christ, and to the angels of heaven, and to all good men, if you would but all make such an agreement, and heartily join together in holiness! The whole fifteenth chapter of Luke is by divers parables to tell you this, what joy there is in

heaven itself, for the conversion of one sinner. O what would there be then, if towns and countries would agree in holiness! And I am certain it should be a joy to the princes and rulers of the earth; for such a unity will only hold, and be a blessing to their dominions. Plutarch makes it Agesilaus' reason, why the Spartans had no walls, because the people being all of one mind, had no need of walls. And Pliny tells us of a stone that will swim if it be whole, and sink if it be broken. And so will commonwealths that are broken from Christ, and void of the cement of the Spirit that should unite them.

And to the ministers of the Gospel, and all good Christians, such an unity as this would be an unspeakable joy. Somewhat I know of other men's hearts by mine own. Could I but prevail with this nation, yea with one town and parish to meet together, and heartily consent, agree, and resolve to join all together in a heavenly life, I should more rejoice in it than if I had the house full of gold and silver, yea, (as to mine own interest) than if I were lord of all the world. O what a joyful day were this, if I could this day bring you to this holy unity and agreement! How comfortably should I spend the remaining days of my pilgrimage among you, if you would but all be brought to this! Whereas I may now say as David, (Psalm 120:5,) for all the godly that are among you, "Woe is me, that I sojourn in Mesech, that I dwell in the tents of Kedar! My soul hath too long dwelt with him that hateth this holy peace; I am for peace; but when I speak, and persuade men to it, they are for war," and continuance in the dividing course of ungodliness. Alas, it grieveth us to see such divisions in all the churches and nations of the Christian world: and O that we did know how to heal them! But when we cannot heal the most ungodly separations and divisions of one town and parish, it discourageth us from hoping for any great measures of such large extent. Some attempts I have made, and more I would fain make, to further a union and peace among the churches through the land: and when I cannot procure the unity of this one town and parish, what hope can I have to look any further? Alas, what a shame is this to you, and what a grief to us, that we cannot bring one parish, one village that ever I knew of, in all England, to be all of a mind in those great, those weighty, needful things, where it is worse than a madness for men to be unresolved or disagreed! As Melanthus made a jest of a great man that went about to reconcile all Greece, and bring all the princes and states to peace, when he could not bring his wife and her servant maid to agreement in his own house. So with what hopes can we attempt any public peace, when we cannot bring one parish, one village, yea but very few families, to agree in that which they must agree in, or else the refusers will be certainly condemned! I beseech you, sirs, make glad the hearts of your teachers, and of all good men, by your agreement. You owe us this comfort; and you owe it to Christ, and the angels of heaven; deny us not our due, but without any more delay agree together to live as saints. What a joy it would be to your pastors, you are not easily able to believe. When Gregory Thaumaturgus came first to be bishop of Neocæsarea, he found but seventeen Christians in the city: and when he lay on his deathbed, he desired them to make inquiry how many infidels were unconverted; and they found but just seventeen infidels left, and all the rest were converted to Christianity. And though he rejoiced that he left but just as many unconverted infidels as he found converted Christians; yet he grieved withal, that he should leave those seventeen in the power of the devil. When I came to you, I found you all professed Christians; but O that I could say that I shall leave but seventeen unconverted when I am called from you, for all that! O that there were no more that are infidels or impious, under the name of Christians! But I and you are unworthy of so great a mercy.

10. And I pray you consider this in time, that all of you that now refuse this agreement in holiness, will wish, ere long, that you had heartily embraced it, and joined with the godly, and done as they. And why will you not be of the mind that you will be shortly of? And why will you be of that way and company that you will wish at last you had not been of? The prodigal in Luke 15 did think it a slavery to be kept up so strictly by his father's eye; he must have his portion in his own possession, and abroad he must be gone: but when smart had taught him another lesson, and misery had brought him to himself, then he is glad to be an hired servant, and casteth himself at his father's feet, in the confession of his unworthiness to be called a son, God grant that this may prove your case. But let me tell it you for a certain truth, there is not one of you that now is loath to become so holy, and join yourselves in the ways of God; but the time is at hand, when either grace or hell shall make you wish and wish again, that you might have but the poorest, lowest place in the society which you so despised. Mark what I say to you, sirs, in the name of God. If the Lord of heaven do not shortly make the most dull heart, the greatest derider of godliness among you, that heareth these words, to wish and wish a hundred times, that he had lived as holy and heavenly a life as the most strict of those that he had formerly derided, then call me a false prophet for ever, and spare not. When you feel the misery of unholy souls, and see the happiness of

the saints above you, then O that you had been but such as they, and lived as they, whatever it cost you! And as Balaam you will shortly say, "O that I might die the death of the righteous, and that my last end may be as his!" (Numb. 23:10.) There is never a one of you all but would fain be among the saints at judgment, and receive their sentence and reward; and therefore it is best for you to join with them now; or it will be too late to wish it then.

11. If all this will not serve the turn, but you will needs stand off, and separate yourselves from the servants of Christ, be it known to you, you shall ere long have separation enough, and be further from them than your hearts can wish. As you would not be united to them, and join with them in holiness, so you shall not be partakers with them of their happiness. One heaven will not hold you both; and there is but one to hold you; and therefore an everlasting separation shall be made: between them and you will a great gulf be set, so that they that would pass from you to them shall never be able. (Luke 16:26.) When they stand on the right hand, you shall be set upon the left; and when they hear "Come ye blessed," you shall hear "Go ye cursed;" and when they "go away into life eternal," you shall "go away into everlasting punishment." (Matt. 25:31, 32. 41. 46.) Then shall you see that "the man is blessed that walketh not in the counsel of the ungodly, nor standeth in the way of sinners, nor sitteth in the seat of the scornful; but his delight is in the law of the Lord, and in his law doth he meditate day and night—The ungodly are not so, but are like the chaff which the wind driveth away: therefore the ungodly shall not stand in the judgment, nor sinners in the congregation of the righteous: for the Lord knoweth the way of the righteous, but the way of the ungodly shall perish." (Psal. 50.) Then you will say to them that now you differ from, "Give us of your oil, for our lamps are gone out." Oh that we had part in your holiness and your hopes! But they will answer you, "Not so, lest there be not enough for us and you." We have little enough for ourselves, you should have done as we did; but then it will be too late, (Matt. 25:8-10.) It will then make the proudest heart to shake, to hear, "Depart from me, all ye that are workers of iniquity, I never knew you:" (Matt. 7:23:) You departed from me, and would not live in the communion of saints; and now Christ himself, of whom you boasted, and in whom you trusted, will not know you, but cause you to depart much farther than you desired, both from his saints and him. These are the true revelations of God, which may be laughed at and slighted now, but will certainly be made good on all that are not in time united to Christ and his church.

12. And let me tell you, to consummate your misery, when that day of everlasting separation comes, those servants of Christ whom you refused to join with in a holy life, will be so many witnesses against you to your condemnation: as Christ tells you, Matt. 25, he will say "Inasmuch as you did it not to one of these, you did it not to me." So, inasmuch as you refused the communion of saints, and perhaps derided them, you refused communion with Christ himself, and derided him. Then they must testify against you, 'We were willing to have had his company in the way of holiness, but he refused it.' And when you see them set so far above you, then your own consciences will say, 'We might have been of this blessed society, and would not; we might have done as they, and now sped as they; we were often entreated to it by our teachers; and full glad would the godly have been of our company in a holy life; but we obstinately refused all! Wretches that we are, we refused all! we thought it needless, our hearts were against it; we preferred our pleasures, and profits, and credit, and the customs of the world before it, and now how justly do we perish in our wilfulness, and must lie in yonder burning flames, and be separated as far as hell is from heaven, from those that we wilfully separated from on earth.'

Beloved hearers, I were not a believer, if I did not foresee this dreadful day; and I were not a man, if I did not desire that you might escape this misery; and therefore I could do no less than warn you, as you love yourselves, and would not be separated from them for ever, that you would presently be united to the godly, and live in the true communion of the saints; and withdraw yourselves from the ways of the ungodly, lest you be found among them, and perish with them. I have done my part in telling you the truth, and now must leave the success to God.

Use ult. But I must conclude with a word of advice to the godly: I have made a very large ambitious motion, for the conversion of all at once: but alas, it is far from my expectation that it should prevail. I am not so unacquainted with the power of sin, and the subtlety of the devil, and the wilfulness of blind unsanctified men, and the ordinary course of providence in this work, as to cherish any hopes that all the town and parish should consent. If many or any more do, I should be glad. But 'plurima quaeras, ut pauca feras:' an high motion, when reasonable, may be serviceable to lower hopes. By what I have here said, you may now see how little hope there is that ever the church should have any such peace on earth as we desire. If unholiness be the hindrance, and the greatest part of the world are so unholy, and so our unity is likely to rise no higher than our piety, you may see then how much unity to look for.

But for your own parts, be sure among yourselves to maintain the "unity of the Spirit in the bond of peace." "Love the brotherhood, even saints as saints." And because you are not the searchers of the heart, proceed according to the word of God. Let all that profess themselves a sanctified people, and live so that you cannot certainly disprove their profession, be used as saints by you, and leave the infallible judgment to God. It is only real saints that have the internal "unity of the Spirit, and saving communion; but it is professors of faith and holiness that must have external communion with us in ordinances, as they have a visible union of profession with the church. But if they profess not holiness, they ought not to have any Christian communion at all.

O Christians, keep close to Christ the centre of your unity, and the Scripture, which is the rule of it, and cherish the Spirit which is the vital cause; walk evenly and uprightly in a dark generation, and give no offence to those without, nor to the church of God. Know them that are over you in the Lord, and be at peace among yourselves, "and the God of peace shall be with you," (1 Thess. 5:12; Philip 4:8, 9.)

Object. 'But may not a profession of the same faith procure a sufficient unity among us, though all be not saints, and savingly regenerate? Let us first be of one religion, and then we may come to be sincere in the practice of that religion by degrees.'

Answ. 1. For the church's sake, we are thankful to God, when we see a common concord in profession, though most are false in and to the religion which they profess. Many ways God doth good to his church by unsound professors.

1. Their professing the same faith doth somewhat tie their hands from persecuting it. And of the two, we can better bear hypocrites than persecutors.

2. And it somewhat tieth their tongues from reproaching the faith, and arguing against it, and seducing others from it. And of the two, it would be more hurtful to the church to have these men open enemies to the truth, and bend their wits and tongues against it, and to have the multitude assaulting their neighbours with invectives and cavils against religion, than to have them falsely pretend to be religious.

3. And it is a great mercy to the church, hereby to have the benefit of these men's common parts and interests. When they profess the same

religion with us, though unsoundly, yet it engageth them to stand for the religion which they profess; and their illumination and conviction may lead them to do much service for the truth. By this means many hands are at work to build up the church of Christ. And by this means the lives of many faithful Christians are preserved, and their estates much spared. Many have skill in building, that are not true heirs of the house which they build. Many have excellent gifts for preaching and expounding Scripture, by which the church may be edified, and the truth defended against the adversaries, when yet the same men may themselves be destitute of the power of this truth. The church hath great cause to be thankful to God for the gifts of many an unsanctified man: had the church been denied the ministry and gifts of all men except saints, it would have been confined to a narrower room, and many a soul might have been unconverted that have been by the ministry called of unsanctified men. By some such did God work miracles themselves for the confirmation of the Christian faith. And in times of war, if the church had none but saints to fight for them, it could not stand without a continued miracle. And if we had not the daily help of others in civil and secular affairs, we should find by the miss of it, what a mercy we undervalued. Were every unregenerate man an open enemy to the church, we should live as partridges, and such other birds, that must hide themselves from every passenger.

4. Moreover, this profession of hypocrites doth much restrain them from many a sin, by which God would be much dishonoured, and the church more wronged, and the godly more grieved, and the open enemies more encouraged.

5. And also it is some honour to the Gospel in the eyes of men, to have a multitude of professors. Should Christ's visible church be as narrow as the mystical, and should none be professors of the faith, but those few that are sanctified believers, the paucity of Christians, and the narrowness of the church, would be a dishonour to Christ in the eyes of the world, and would hinder the conversion of many a soul.

All this I have said, that you may see that we do not despise a unity in profession, and that we are not of those that would have all hypocrites and common professors shut out: yea, that we take ourselves bound to be very thankful to God for the mercy which he vouchsafeth us, by the gifts, and favour, and help, and interest of many such professors. And such a unity of profession we shall endeavour to our power heartily to promote, as knowing that the church, as visible, consisteth of such professors.

2. But yet for all this, I must come closer to your objection, and tell you, that this unity of mere profession is comparatively so poor a kind of unity, that this will not, this must not satisfy us, and serve the turn, which I desire you to observe in these discoveries.

1. This unity in mere profession is properly no Christian unity, because you are not properly Christians. If this be all, it is but in the bark and shell that we are agreed: it is but a seeming agreement, from the teeth outward; but not a hearty agreement to be Christians. What! shall we all agree to say we are Christians, when with most it is not so? For all this agreement, you will still have one father, and we another. You will not be united with us in Christ the Head; you will not have the same Holy Spirit, who is the life of the new creature: you will be contrary to us in nature or disposition. You will not have the same intention and ultimate end with us, but you will aim at one thing, and we at another: you will not go the same way, nor walk by the same rule and law as we: It will be but a tying together the living and the dead. Bellarmin himself confesseth that the ungodly are but dead members. It is not life that uniteth a dead member to the living. You will be still either openly or secretly betraying the body to which you profess yourselves united, and taking part with its deadly enemies, the flesh, the world and the devil! Your very hearts and ours will still be contrary: you will love the sin that we hate and set ourselves against; and you will disrelish that holy, heavenly life, which must be our business and delight. Your affections will go one way, and ours another. You will live by sense, when we must live by faith; and you will be laying up a treasure on earth, when we are laying up a treasure in heaven: you will be asking counsel of flesh and blood, when we must advise with God and his holy word. You will look first to your bodies, when we must look first and principally to our souls. It will be your business to feed those sins, which it is our daily work to kill. You will make and apprehend it to be your interest to go contrary to us: and what agreement can there be, where there are contrary interests? Under all your outward profession, you will still retain a secret enmity and hatred to the life of holiness: and will not have that hearty love to the saints, as beseems all those that are members of Christ, and of the holy catholic church. So that when you have communion with the saints, it will be but an external and superficial communion in some common things; but you will have no communion with them in the same Head, and Spirit, and promise, and holy nature, and saving benefits of the Gospel. And shall this be called unity, that leaveth you at so sad a distance as this?

This is but such a union as a wooden-leg hath to the body; or as the vessels of honour and dishonour have by being in the same house together. In their highest professions, the Lord himself saith of unsanctified professors, that they "are none of Christ's," (Rom. 8:9,) and that "they cannot be his disciples," (Luke 14:33,) that they "are not Israel, though of Israel, nor are they children of God, nor the seed of promise;" (Rom. 9:6–8;) and when they plead their highest privileges, at last, Christ will tell them that he "knoweth them not." (Matt. 7:23; 25:12; Psal. 1:5, 6.) And if in mercy to the church, God cause the lion and the lamb to lie down together, yet will he not therefore mistake a lion for a lamb. So that you see what a poor kind of unity, and next to none it is, that mere profession maketh. And therefore this will not serve our turn.

2. Moreover, if we have no other unity, we are unlike to live in peace together. Though it be our duty to endeavour to have peace with all men, yet we can have but little hope of it. As long as there is so much difference and contrariety as I have mentioned; and as long as there is a secret enmity at the heart, it will be working into dissention, if God, for the sake of his church, restrain it not. The godly will be crossing your carnal interest, and hindering you in the sinful ways of your commodity, pleasure or vainglory! They will be calling you to self-denial, which you cannot endure; and putting you upon duties of holiness, righteousness and mercy, which your sinful flesh will utterly refuse. If you are scandalous, you will be called to confession, repentance, and reformation, or by church censures be cut off from them to your shame: and the magistrate also must trouble yon by the penalties of the law. The very examples of a strict and holy living, which are given you by the godly, will displease you, because they are so unlike to your lives, and therefore witness against your negligence and ungodliness. So that it is not possible that we should avoid offending you; for our very obedience to God will offend you, and our studying and following the holy Scripture will offend you, and our diligent labour to save our souls will offend you; and our hating and avoiding the poison of sin will offend you. And how then shall we live in peace with such? If you yoke a swine and a sheep together, one will be drawing to the washtub, when the other would be at grass; and one would be drawing to lie down in the mire, when the other would lie clean; one will be routing in the earth, and eating dung, which the other's nature is against. It is Christ, before me, that calleth the wicked by the name of swine, and the godly sheep: and if you will come no nearer us than this, we are likely to have but poor agreement.

And as our ways will displease you, so your galled, malicious hearts will manifest the offence, and will be girding, and maligning, if not slandering, deriding, or openly persecuting, as far as you have power, those that thus offend you. And what unity is this?

3. If reason persuade you not, do but ask experience itself, whether, in all ages, men that profess the same religion with zealous godly men, have not been their persecutors, and oftentimes more cruel than infidels themselves? The Arians, that call themselves Christians, were as cruel to the true believers as the heathens. The Papists profess the same Christianity as we, and take the whole Scripture as the word of God: and yet none of the heathenish persecutions do match or come near to their French massacres, and Spanish Inquisition, and the cruelty that in Ireland, England, and their part of the Christian world, they have exercised upon the sheep of Christ. The many ministers that were silenced in Germany, and some imprisoned, and many families undone, was by the Lutherans, against men that were Protestants as well as they. And they that cast out so many learned, holy ministers in England, and occasioned the expulsion of so many thousand persons fearing God, were professed Protestants as well as we. And that there may not be the appearance so much as of a difference in ceremonies to cover their proceedings, abundance of conformable men are troubled and undone as well as others, and they give out that 'none were worse than the conformable Puritans.' It was a holy observation of the Lord's-day, and opposition to the abuse of it by dancings; and it was hearing sermons, and instructing men's families, and praying together, that were the things inquired after, that occasioned our troubles. And (whoever was in the right or wrong) you all know that the late miserable wars among us, was between men that professed themselves to be of the same religion, not only as Christians, but as Protestant and Reformed (in the main). To this day you see among ourselves in towns and countries, that those that do not only dwell with us, and come to the same assemblies with us, and profess themselves of the same Protestant, Reformed Religion, have yet many of them a secret malignity against the godly, that will not be as loose and negligent as they, and will not as madly cast away their souls: And also even many greater hypocrites, that rank themselves with us in the same church order, and seem to own all ordinances of God, and government of the church, yet when this government crosseth them in their carnal ways, and these ordinances open the nakedness of their miscarriages, they prove stark enemies to the government, officers and ordinances themselves.

Indeed however we may abide together, (as the clean and unclean creatures in Noah's ark,) yet still at the heart there is so much enmity and distance, and in our ends and interests there are so much contrariety, that if the ministers and other followers of Christ, will faithfully discharge the duty that is required of them, they will certainly be persecuted by men of the same profession in religion; especially by the prouder and loftier sort of wicked men Because some will receive the same truth better from one than from another. I will give you my assertion in the words of a man, that you shall confess did speak impartially, and not out of any intemperance or singularity; who in a prosperous University, in peaceable times, being himself in favour, and of that judgment and of such learning as was likely to continue him in favour, did write thus concerning persecution: I mean Doctor Jackson, in his book of "Saving Faith," sect. 2, chap. iv, page 185, "The ministers of Christ may deny Christ, or manifest their ashamedness of his Gospel, as directly by not laying his law as closely to the great Herods of the world, as John Baptist did, (suppose the case be as notorious, and as well known to them,) as if they had been afraid to confess him, for fear of being put out of the synagogues, or said with those other Jews, We know that God spake with Moses, and gave authority to magistrates; but this man we know not whence he is, nor do we care for his counsels. Yet were John Baptist's kind of preaching used in many kingdoms, though by such as profess the same religion with the potentates, they should offend with their boldness, I think it would prove matter of martyrdom in the end. That any age, since the Christian religion was first propagated, hath wanted store of martyrs, is more to be attributed to the negligence, ignorance, and hypocrisy, or want of courage in Christ's ambassadors, or appointed pastors, than unto the sincerity, mildness or fidelity of the flock; especially of the belwethers or chief ringleaders. Or, if Satan had not abated the edge of primitive zeal and resolution, by that dishonourable peace concluded between Christianity and Gentilism, after the settling of the Goths and Vandals in these parts of Christendom; had he not utterly benumbed mankind by locking up their spiritual senses in midnight darkness, fettering their souls in superstition, since the time he himself was let loose: Rome Christian had seen more martyrs, even of such as did not much dissent from her in most opinions held within six hundred years of Christ, in one year, than Rome heathen at any time had known in ten. Even in churches best reformed, it would be much easier, I think, to find store of just matter of martyrdom, than of men fit to make martyrs. And he that hath lived any long time in these quiet mansions, and seats of muses, secure from Mars his broils, or external violence, hath great cause either to magnify the tender mercies of his gracious God, or suspect himself for an hypocrite, if he have not suffered some degrees of martyrdom: but unto such as have been exercised therein, it bringeth forth the quiet fruit of righteousness."

Thus you see this learned doctor, though in favour with the rulers of the age he lived in, did think that a man that would not be an hypocrite, but faithfully discharge his duty, was likely to suffer martyrdom from those of the same profession with himself, and that it must be by very great mercy from God, or by hypocrisy and unfaithfulness in us, if any minister do escape the hands of the wicked that are of his own profession. So that you may see that mere profession will make but a poor agreement or union among us: sin will be sin still, and the flesh will rage still after its prey in unmortified professors; and the word of God will still disgrace them and condemn them, and consequently trouble them and exasperate them; so that if you come no nearer to us than a profession of the Christian Protestant religion, you will still be soldiers in the army of the devil, and be still flying in the faces of true believers, whenever they do but cross you in your sins.

3. Consider also, what a poor benefit comparatively it is to yourselves, to be joined with the saints by a bare profession, and no more. Will it make you happy to see their faces, or to live among them? So do the brute beasts, and so do their persecutors. Will it make you happy to be called by the name of Christians? No more than it maketh a picture rational to be called by the name of a man. And what if by your parts and moral virtues, you are some way helpful to the church? So is the wooden leg to the body, which is yet not a member, but a crutch.

4. Yea, methinks it should rather double your sorrows, that you are so miserable among the happy. You live with them that have part in Christ, when you have none in him. You join with those that have the Spirit of God, and a holy disposition and conversation, when you have none: you kneel by them whose spirits are importunate with God in prayer, when your hearts are dead: you sit by them that are quickened and sanctified by the word, which to you is but a dead and empty sound. You are famished among them that are feasting upon Christ, and upon the precious promises of eternal life. You are but as carcases among the living: their company maketh not you alive; but your noisome conversation is grievous unto them, unless it be some of you that are embalmed and beflowered with some common

graces, for the sakes of those that else would be more troubled with you. And is this so great a comfort to you, to be dead among the living, and to be heirs of hell in the midst of them that are heirs of heaven? Methinks (till you are sanctified) it should be a daily honour to you, to look them in the faces, and think that they have Christ and grace, and you have none; and to hear in the holy assemblies the mention of their happiness, and the name of that God, that Christ, that heaven, where they must live forever, and in which their blessedness consisteth, when you must be turned out into everlasting misery.

That you may not think I am singular in all this, I will add here some human testimony for confirmation of it. Zonoras, Comment. in Epist. Canon. Can. 45. ex Basil. M. Epist. 2. ad Amphiloch. gives us this as one of the canons of the Greek church received from Basil, "If any one receiving the name of Christianity, shall be a reproach to Christ (that is, saith Zonoras, by a wicked life), his name or appellation is no profit at all to him." And even in the Roman canon law, this is one canon taken out of Augustine, "Parvulus qui baptizatur, si ad annos rationales veniens. non crediderit, nec ab illicitis abstinuerit, nihil ei prodest quod parvulus accepit." (Decret. part 3. disl. 3. p. 1241.) that is, A baptized infant, if when he comes to years of discretion, doth not believe, nor abstain from things unlawful, it profiteth him nothing which he received in his infancy. If it were needful after the canons both of the Greek and Latin church, to give you the like words from particular Fathers, I could soon perform it.

5. You are so far from being happy by your visible church-state and outward profession, and communion with the church, that you have the greater sin, and will have the sorer punishment, because among such examples, such means, and calls, and mercies, you yet resist the grace of Christ, and are void of that holiness which your tongues profess. The poor Indians hear not that which you daily or weekly hear; nor have the opportunities in public and private that you have had. If they lie in ignorance and unbelief, they can say, it is because they never read or heard the Scripture, nor ever had a man to tell them of the blessed tidings of redemption, or open to them the way to life: But so cannot you say for yourselves. They were the less excusable, if they had seen but one of your days, or joined but once in those holy assemblies which you profane. The mouth of Christ himself hath told us concerning the rejecters of his ministers and his Gospel, that it shall be easier for Sodom in the day of judgment than for them. (Matt. 10:15.) You will find a hotter place in hell, that pass thither from those seats,

from this assembly, from such a neighbourhood, and such a nation, than if you had passed thither from among the Turks or Indians.

6. Moreover, there is in some respects, less hope of your salvation, that have long lived unconverted in the outward communion of the church, than of other men. As a sick man is in a more desperate case that hath long used the best and only means, and all in vain, than he that never used any. I confess you have the advantage of being still under the means; and that is your hope (as long as it lasteth), but then you have the dreadful symptom of frustrating these means; and that is your terror, above those that yet remain without.

7. Moreover, if you agree with us but in profession and outward communion, you will be thereby more capable of doing us the greater mischief. I know God doth benefit his church by many of the unsanctified, as I said before. But many others of them are the greatest plagues to it. One enemy in our own armies, or in our councils, may do more against us, than ten thousand open enemies abroad. False-hearted bishops, pastors, yea, and magistrates, that have the name and not the nature of Christians, are they that have betrayed the church, and broken it in pieces, and made the cause of Christ a stepping-stone to their worldly ends. It was a Doeg that betrayed David and Abimelech. It was a Judas that betrayed Christ himself. You are now our daily hearers, and live some of you civilly among us, and take yourselves confidently for Christians and saints as well as others, and secretly scorn those that would rob you of that honour, as appropriating it unto themselves, and say as Zedekiah to Micaiah when he struck him, "Which way went the Spirit of the Lord from me to speak unto thee?" (1 Kings 22:24.) But if the times should turn, and you had but your will, at least if you were but forced or driven by authority, we should soon find many of you to be blood-thirsty enemies, that now are so confident that you are Christians and true servants of God. A little money would hire those Judases to betray Christ, and his cause and church, that now are our familiars, and put their hands into the same dish with the true disciples. While they are among us, they are not of us; and therefore when temptations come, they will be gone from us. It is well if half this assembly that are now hearing me, would stick to godliness, if godliness were but the persecuted, scorned way of the times: yea, if they would not forsake even the name itself of Christian, and forsake these assemblies and outward worship, if the rulers were against it, and did but persecute it, so that it must cost them any thing dear to hold it.

8. Moreover, these hollow-hearted Christians, that agree with us but in the outside and the name, are capable of dishonouring Christ and the Gospel, much more than if they were open enemies. If a professed heathen or infidel live wickedly, this cannot be cast upon the Gospel or the Christian name, nor can Christ and his servants be hit in his teeth with it, or reproached by it: but when those that take on them to be Christians, and join with Christians in their public worship, shall live like heathens, or worse than some of them, what greater wrong can be done to Christ? Will he not one day take such wretches by the throat, and say, 'If thou must have thy pride, and drunkenness, and covetousness; if thou must needs swear, and curse, and rail, or live an ungodly, fleshly life, thou shouldest have kept thee out of my church, and not have called thyself a Christian, and taken an easier place in hell: Must thou bring thy wickedness into my house, and among my servants, to dishonour me? Must I and my servants be reproached with thy crimes?'

And this is one great cause why Christ hath appointed discipline in his church to admonish and reform, or reject the scandalous: And this is the reason, among many others, why faithful Christians (though they would make no unjust divisions and separations) would yet have the church of Christ kept clean, by use of holy discipline, as he hath appointed; because it is from such false-hearted professors usually, that the name of Christ is reproached in the world: These are they for the most part that make Turks and Jews, and all other enemies, say, that Christians are as bad as others, because those that are as bad as others, do take on them to be Christians. When drunkards, and fornicators, and covetous persons, and profane, do come to the congregation, and say they are Christians, when in heart and deed they are not, what wonder then if infidels and enemies of the church reproach us and say, 'You see what Christians are.' How could a Papist do the Protestants a cunninger and surer mischief, than to take on him a Protestant, and then commit fornication or other horrid lewdness, or join with some abominable sect, to make men think that the Protestants are such as these! And how can you do Christ a greater wrong than to carry the dung of the world into his church; and to cover all the crimes of infidels, with the name and garb of Christianity, that it may be said, 'All these are the crimes of Christians!' And therefore it is that Christ and his faithful ministers, though they would have as many as is possible to be saved, yet are not so forward to take in all, as others be: for Christ needeth not servants, but it is they that need him; and he had rather have a few that will honour him by mortified holy lives, than a multitude that will but cause his Name and Gospel to be reproached. It is certain from church history, that the holy life of some one or few persons (as Gregory Thaumaturgus, Macarius, and many the like) hath drawn in multitudes, and converted countries to the faith: when the wickedness of whole towns and countries of professed Christians, hath caused many to fall off, and caused the enemy to insult.

We will not for all this break our rule, nor presume to search the hearts of men any further than they appear in outward evidence. We will still take all professors of Christianity as Christians, that null not their own profession. Basil was advised by Athanasius himself, to receive the Arians themselves into communion, if they did but disown their former errors, and subscribe to the Nicene Creed, and seek the communion of the churches. And he practised this, though many were offended at it. But yet he must needs say, that it is better for the church to have a few that are holy, and answer the nature of their holy calling, than to have multitudes that will but prove our shame, and make the infidel world believe that Christianity is not what it is. Yea, and these are they most commonly too (though they may proceed to a higher profession) that are carried about with every wind of doctrine, and that turn to heresies, and cause and continue the divisions of the church: for they that are such, serve not the Lord Jesus, when they profess to serve him. (Rom. 16:17.) When heresies do arise, it is such chaff as this that is carried away, that the approved Christians indeed may be made manifest. (1 Cor. 11:19.) Abundance of proud unsanctified persons do us as much good in the church as fire in our thatch, or as mutinous soldiers that are but the enemy's agents in the army, to set all the soldiers together by the ears, or discover their councils, or blow up their magazines. And would you have us contented with such a kind of agreement and communion with you as this, which you and we are like to be so little the better for, if not the worse?

9. Furthermore, it is not this mere agreement in profession, that will satisfy Christ himself, and, therefore, it must not satisfy us. It is not in this that he attaineth the principal ends of his redemption, nor seeth the travail of his soul. Alas, the blood of Christ is lost to you, and all the ordinances and means are lost, and all the labour of ministers is but lost to you, as to any pardon of sin, or life, or heaven, that ever you shall have by them, if you go on further. And would you have us be contented with such an agreement as this?

10. Lastly, Consider that if we agree no further than in an outward profession of the Christian faith, alas it will be but a short agreement. We may be together here awhile in the church, as fishes good and bad in one net; but when it is drawn to the shore, a separation will be made. Here you may sit and kneel among us awhile, and go away with the name of Christians: but alas, it is but a little while till this agreement will be broken, and a dreadful everlasting separation must be made. Dreadful to the unsanctified, but joyful to the saints. And what great good will it do to you or us, to be tied together a little while, bywords and shows, and then to be everlastingly separated, as far as light from darkness, heaven from hell, and the greatest joys from the greatest sorrows. O blame us not if we motion to you, and beg of you a far nearer union and agreement than this!

I think I have now sufficiently proved, that if we will be indeed of one religion, and ever come to a right agreement, it is the unity of the sanctifying Spirit that must do it. It must be a union and agreement in true conversion and holiness of life, and nothing lower will serve the turn. If God do us any good by the profession, gifts, or interest of hypocrites and unsanctified professors, we will thank him for it, and take it as a mercy; but it is a higher design that must be in our hearts; and woe be to them that come no nearer the holy catholic church, and the unity of the Spirit, and the communion of saints, than by an outward profession and participation of sacraments, and such like outward ordinances of communion!

Quest. 'But suppose we should be united in the Spirit, and agree in holiness, do you think this would heal the divisions of the church? Do you not see that the most godly are all in pieces, as well as others? Is it not such that have been the principal cause of our late divisions? You promised to shew us how we might do well, for all our other differences, if we were but agreed in holiness; will you now shew us what advantage that would be?'

Answ. To be agreed in holiness, and to be heartily one in the essentials of Christianity, is an exceeding advantage to us in all our disagreements about lesser things: As

1. Were we but once united in the main, and sanctified by the uniting Spirit of Christ, our principal differences were healed already. We should no longer be of different minds, whether sin or holiness be best; or whether earth or heaven should be chosen for our portion; nor whether God, or the flesh, or the world, should be obeyed. You little think what abundance of differences are at once reconciled in the very hour of a sinner's conversion. Before that hour, we differed in judgment from all wise men, from all the

saints of God, from all the holy prophets, apostles, and martyrs, as well as from all the godly about us; and from all men of right reason, and faith, and experience; yea, we differed from the Holy Ghost, from Christ, from God himself; yea, from none so much as him. Wicked wretches! you differ from the godly because they agree with God; but you differ more from God than from them. When you despise a holy life, are his thoughts like your thoughts? When you revile his servants, and scorn his yoke and burden as too heavy, are you then of the mind of Christ? O no; your darkness and his light are far more distant than you are able to conceive. Were you but once reconciled to God, by converting, sanctifying light, you would at once be reconciled to his servants; for in the matters of chief concernment to the soul, they are all of his mind; for he is their instructor. And then what a deal of healing would that be! O what abundance of differences are ended upon the day of true conversion! And withal, what abundance of differences would be new made! For now you agree with the devil, and with your fleshly desires, and with distracted, wicked men, and all this agreement would then be broke: for this friendship with the world is enmity to God, (James 4:4.) and such divisions as these Christ tells us that he came to send. (Luke 12:51.) But you would presently be agreed with God, with the holy Scriptures, with all the apostles and servants of the Lord, and with all men of spiritual wisdom and experience in the world, in the great and principal matters of your lives. And it is a multitude of particulars that is contained in this agreement that is made when a sinner is truly sanctified.

2. If once you were united in the spirit, and agreed in a holy life, you would differ in nothing that could keep you out of heaven. And if we have some small differences on earth, as long as they are such as cannot hinder our salvation, they may be the more easily borne. Paul and Barnabas had a little falling out; but O how sweetly are they now reconciled! Jerom and Chrysostom, Epiphanius and John of Jerusalem, Theophilus and Chrysostom were at odds; Luther and Zuinglius had their disagreements; but O how happily are they now agreed! Our imperfection of knowledge causeth us here to err and differ in part: but if we are all united in Christ, and agreed in the main, how quickly shall we see that blessed light that will reconcile all our controversies! Marvel not to find some contests among the most learned and most godly, unless you will marvel that earth is not heaven; or that in that body we see not the face of God, which is the all-disclosing reconciling light. If we were all here together in the dark, and were of many opinions about the things before us; if one did but come in among

us with a candle, it might end all our differences in a moment. When we are
newly out of this obscuring flesh, and this dark, deceitful, earthly world,
O what an inconceivable reconcillation will be made by that blessed light.
There is no contending or quarelling: for there are none of those errors
or passions that should occasion it. As imperfect holiness produceth an
answerable imperfect unity, so perfect holiness will perfectly unite. And is
not this then the only way to unity, which will help us here to what is here
attainable, and secure us of eternal perfect concord in the world that we
are passing to? O see that you be once agreed in the things that are necessary to salvation, and then the hour is near at hand that will end all your
differences, and agree you in the rest.

3. If once you be but agreed in holiness, you will have no difference
left that shall destroy any grace in you, that is necessary to salvation. The
power of Divine faith, and love, and hope, and fear, and zeal, will still be
safe. Your diseases will not destroy your vital faculties. And if the head, the
heart, and principal parts be sound, you may the better bear a small distemper. The disagreements of the ungodly from God, from Scripture, and
the saints, are mortal to them, and prove them under the power of darkness and of Satan, that leads them captive at his will. (2 Tim. 2:26; Ephes.
2:2–3; Acts 26:18.) But the differences of the sanctified are but as the different complexions or statures of children, or at worst but as their falling out, which will not cause the father to turn them out of his family; so
that as long as faith, and love, and hope, and other graces are kept sound,
we shall certainly do well for all our differences. And this is the benefit of
agreeing in holiness.

4. Moreover, if once we were all agreed in the Spirit, and in holiness of
heart and life, we should escape all the heresies, or errors that effectually
subvert the essentials of the Christian faith. Mistaken we might be; but
heretics we could not be. I stick not upon the bare word, whether small
errors may be called heresy; but taking heresy as commonly it is taken, a
sanctified person cannot (at least habitually) be a heretic. For should a man
so hold a point inconsistent with any one essential point of the Christian
faith (at least habitually and practically hold it), it is as impossible that this
man should be then a Christian, as that contradictories should be true. And
therefore certainly, whoever is a true Christian, is free from such heresies. And therefore, as if you are sure a man so holds a heresy, you have no
reason to believe his shows of holiness; so where you see a great appearance of real holiness, you must long deliberate and have good evidence,

before you judge that man a heretic: for they cannot be heretics, though they may have many errors, (as 'in sensu composito' all confess.)

5. Moreover, if we but all agreed in true holiness, we should be freed from most of those scandalous sins which are the common occasion of our reproaches and divisions. It is sin that is the great trouble of the church, and of the world. (John 7:25.) This breeds our quarrels. This setteth all into a flame. When a drunkard, or an unclean person, or a slanderer, or a railer, or any scandalous person is reproved, or openly admonished, or for impenitency rejected, then the devil and sin bestir themselves, and rage against the church and officers, and ordinances of God. It is sin within that animateth the malignant to be contentious: and it is to defend and take part with sin, that they fall out with God, and his word and servants. Now holiness is contrary to this sin that troubleth us. Mortification of sin is part of sanctification. If therefore we were agreed in holiness, it were as ready a way to procure our peace, as quenching the fire in your thatch, is the ready way to save your house. I know there are too many scandals given by the best. But it is commonly by the weaker, worse sort of the best. And it is not a common thing with them neither. And none of them make a trade of sinning, nor have any unmortified reigning sin. If a Noah, a Lot, a David, be once scandalous in all his life, this is not the case of all the godly; and it is not like the case of the ungodly that are either often, or impenitent in it. And therefore though it may disturb the church; yet not so much as the frequent and impenitent scandals of the ungodly. O could we but all agree against this make-bate, this great disturber and troubler of the world, what peace might we enjoy!

6. And also, if once we could agree in holiness, the matter and occasion of offences, separations, and contentions would cease. What caused the Donatists' separation of old, but the scandals in the church; and the receiving of such, upon repentance, into communion or ministry? And so the Novatian schism also was occasioned. And though the Donatists and Novatians were to blame to be against the ordination or reception of such penitents; yet the prevention of the sin would have been the prevention of the breach. What hath caused so many to turn Separatists in England, but seeing so many ungodly persons in our churches and communion? You that are most offended at schisms and private churches, are the common occasions of it yourselves. If such ungodly persons were not in our assemblies, few godly persons would separate from them. Though I do not justify them, yet I must needs condemn you as the cause. Were it not for you, we

should be more of a mind among ourselves. But when your rotten ulcers and corrupted lives have raised a stink in our assemblies, this causeth our division: The Separatists stop their noses and are gone, and will come here no more; and the rest of us think that for your sakes, and the peace of the church, we should stay as long as we well can, like patient surgeons, that will not forsake their patient because of a rotten, stinking sore, as long as there is any hope of cure, or of saving the body, by cutting off the rotten member. And thus while some are more patient and charitable towards you, and some are more impatient of your sin, or else afraid of God's displeasure for having communion with you, here comes our divisions among ourselves, for your sakes. And therefore if we were but agreed in holiness, all this were ended. There would then be no habituated drunkard, or worldling, or railer, or swearer, or other ungodly persons in our churches; and then who would scruple communion with them? And so what should hinder but we might all be one? And yet will you not agree in this?

7. Yea, if we were united in the Spirit of holiness, the very dividing, unpeaceable disposition of men would itself be healed, and so we should have peace. For an uncharitable, dividing disposition is part of the old man, and of that unholiness which we must forsake. And charity and meekness, and a peaceable healing temper, is holiness itself. And therefore this must needs do much to heal and reconcile us. Read but James 3 throughout, and it will satisfy you of this, if you will be satisfied. Those that pretend to be wiser than the rest of the godly, and to have more illumination, "If yet they have bitter envying and strife in their hearts, they glory in vain, and lie against the truth: for this wisdom descendeth not from above, but is earthly, sensual and devilish. He that is truly wise and endued with knowledge in the church, must shew out of a good conversation his works with meekness of wisdom. For the wisdom that is from above, is first pure, then peaceable, gentle, easy to be entreated, full of mercy and good fruits, without partiality, and without hypocrisy. But where envying and strife is, there is confusion, and every evil work." (James 3:13–17.) See here what a spirit sanctification doth contain, and whether this be not the only healing way. It is first indeed pure; but next it is "peaceable, gentle and easy to be entreated." They that cause divisions and offences contrary to the doctrine which is taught, do not serve the Lord Jesus, whatever they may pretend or think. Peace and holiness must be followed together. (Heb. 12:14.) Yea, "peace with all men," if it be possible, and in our power, (Rom. 12:18,) so

that by changing the unpeaceable disposition, and drying up the fountain of our strifes, an agreement in the Spirit would reconcile us.

8. Moreover, if we would all agree in the Spirit of holiness, it would destroy that carnal selfish disposition, and that end which is the dividing interest, and take away the bone of our contentions. It is selfishness that causeth the great divisions in church and state, and sets the world together in wars and quarrels: every unsanctified man is selfish; his self and selfish interest is more to him than God and his interest. And such men as these will never live with any man in peace, any longer than they may have their will and way. They will not agree with neighbours if self be but touched by any. They will hate the magistrate whenever he would punish them. They will hate the pastors of the church if they faithfully discharge their offices in reproving them, and calling them to repentance, and such confession is as necessary to their cure. If it were father or mother, a selfish person cannot bear it, if they go against his selfish interest. There is no living at peace with selfish men, if you do but cross them in their credit or profit, or sensual delights; and this we must do, unless we will incur the displeasure of our Lord. We are cast upon an impossibility of living in peace with wicked men. For God hath commanded us to "rebuke them plainly, and not to suffer sin upon them." And if we disobey God to please men, it will cost us dearer than their favour can repay. But if we obey God and do our duty, we are as sure to be hated and reproached with the most, as that the earth is under our feet. Give a wicked, selfish sinner as plain Scripture and reason as can be given, and you shall not stir him from his selfish interest: if you punish him, or reprove him openly, or exercise church censures on him, or any way touch his carnal, selfish interest, and when you have done, go about to satisfy him with reason, you may as well almost go reason a hungry dog from his carrion, or reason a wolf into the nature of a lamb, or reason a mastiff to be friends with a bear. Many a trial I have made; and many a time I have stopped their mouths, and satisfied them in reason, that they ought to deny themselves, and confess and forsake their sins, and yield to God (or made them confess so much at least); but their selfish minds were no more satisfied, for all that, than if I had never spoken to them. Scripture is no Scripture, and reason is no reason to them; and God shall be no God to them, if self do but contradict it; and that is, whenever he contradicteth self. They can no more believe, and like, and love that doctrine or duty, or counsel, or course of life, that crosseth self, and calls them to any great self-denial, than a child can love to be corrected. So that

self being so certain a peace-breaker and disturber of the world, and yet being the reigning principle in all that are unsanctified, you may easily see that this is the hindrance of our unity and concord; and that sanctification must needs be the principal remedy. For sanctification is the destruction of selfishness, and teacheth men self-denial, and centreth all men in one interest, which is God. Among the unsanctified, there are as many ends and intetests as men: for every one of them hath a self to please: and then what unity can there be? But the sanctified are all united in God, as their common principle, end and all; and therefore must needs be reconciled.

9. Moreover, if we could but all agree in the Spirit of holiness, we should then overcome that pride and self-conceitedness, that breaks our peace, and raiseth errors, and puts us into dissentions. What makes us all so hardly to agree, and to be of so many minds and ways, but that every man naturally is proud and self-conceited, and wise in his own eyes, and confident of every fancy of his own? All his own reasons seem strong to him; and God's own reasons do seem unreasonable to him: and can we ever agree with such men as these, that think themselves wiser than God and Scripture, and dare prefer the very folly of their own muddy brains, before the word and wisdom of their Maker? Give these men as plain Scripture and reason as you will, they have more wit (as they think) than to believe you; and what they want in reason, they have in pride and self-conceit; and therefore your wisdom is folly to them. But now when the Spirit of holiness comes, it takes them down, and abaseth and humbleth the proud and self-conceited, and makes them ashamed of the folly and weakness of their own understandings, so that a man may speak to them now as to men of reason, and have a hearing and consideration of his words. A humble godly man is low in his own eyes; and therefore suspicious of his own understanding in doubtful things; and therefore is more flexible and yielding to the truth; when others are so stiffened by pride that they are more ready to deride the wisest that shall contradict them: If therefore we could but all agree in holy meekness and humility, what readier way could there be in the world to draw to an end all our differences and divisions!

10. Moreover, if we could but agree in holiness, it would free us from that uncharitableness that causeth our disagreement in other things; and it would possess us with a special endeared love one to another: and who knoweth not that love is a uniting, healing thing? Sanctification principally consisteth in love to God and man, and this the unsanctified principally want. It is want of love that makes men surmise the worst of one another,

and make the worst of all that they say and do, and draw matter of contention from that which never gave them cause. Love would put a better sense upon men's words and deeds, or at least would bear them far more easily. But instead of love, there is a natural enmity in all that are unsanctified to all the servants and the ways of God. And can we ever be agreed with our natural enemies? Why malice will so pervert their understandings, that all that we say or do will be misconstrued; and as a man that looks through a red glass thinks all things to be red that he looks upon; so these men through the distemper of their malicious minds, will find matter of quarrelling with all that we can say or do. Illwill never saith well. Our very obedience to the law of God, and seeking to save our own souls, will be matter of quarrel, and taken to be our crime. If we will not run into hell-fire with them, and think there is no danger, when we know the contrary, it will be a fault sufficient for their malice to reproach us with; so that if we should agree with ungodly men, in all our opinions of religion; yet if we will not damn our souls, and make no bones of displeasing the great and dreadful God, there is no peace to be had with them. They have no peace with God, and they have no solid peace with themselves; (for God hath professed "that there is no peace to the wicked," Isa. 48:22;) and how then can we expect that they should have peace with us? But sanctification doth beget that effectual love, that is as healing to a divided church, or to disagreeing persons, as the most precious balsam or wound-salve is to bodily wounds. Love will not let you rest in wrath, but will keep you under smart and disquietness, till you are either at peace, or have done your part to procure it. Husband and wife, parents and children, brethren and sisters, do seldom fall into greater dissentions than strangers: And when they do fall out they are more easily reconciled. The Spirit of grace doth possess unfeigned Christians, with as dear a love to one another, as is between the nearest relations. For by our new birth the saints are brethren in Christ. If you saw an army fighting, or a company of people quarrelling and scolding at one another, do you think there could be a readier way to make them all friends, and end their quarrels, than to possess them all with a dear and tender love to one another? If it were in my power to cause all contenders to love those that they contend with as themselves, do you think I should not soon agree them? Why, you know, if you know any thing in Christianity, that sanctification causeth men to love their neighbours as themselves, and to "love one another with a pure heart fervently." (1 Pet. 1:22.) "For by this we know that we are passed from death to life, because we love the brethren: he that loveth not his brother abideth in death." (John 3:14.) And therefore it is a case exceeding plain, that the readiest way in the world to reconcile our lesser differences, is, to be united in the Spirit, and to agree upon a holy life.

11. Moreover, were we all united in the Spirit, we should have all one God, one master of our faith, and one lawgiver and judge of all our controversies: And this would be an exceeding help to unity. The principal cause of divisions in the world, are the multitude of rulers, and masters and judges. For with unsanctified men, their own conceits and carnal interest are their counsellor and judge. The rulers of the world, that have the power of the sword, and can do them good or hurt in their estates, are the masters of their religion more than God. They will follow this man or that man, that best pleaseth their fancies and fleshly desires; and so will never be of one mind. But sanctification takes down all other masters of our faith, save Christ and those that declare his will. Let flesh and blood say what it will, let all the world say what they will, if God say the contrary, his word shall stand and be a law to them. And can there be a readier way to unity, than to bring us all into one school, and subject us all to one Lord and Master, and to bring us all to refer our differences to one most wise infallible Judge? Though we do not yet understand his will in all things, yet when we understand it in the main, and are resolved to search after the knowledge of the rest, it is a great preparative to our agreement, when we all look but to one for the deciding of our controversies. Whereas the unsanctified have as many judges and guides, as persons; for every man is a guide and judge to himself.

12. Moreover, were we but once agreed in holiness, we should all have one light for the ending of our differences; and that light would be the true infallible light. For we should all have the same holy word of God, as the extrinsic light, which is most true, as coming from the Lord of truth: and we should all have the Spirit of truth within, to teach us the meaning of that word without, and to help our understandings, and assist us in the application, and destroy the corruptions that blind us and hinder us from perceiving the truth: whereas the unsanctified are all in the dark; and what wonder, if there they disagree, and are of many minds! They be not guided by the word and Spirit, and they are strangers to the light that must reconcile us, if ever we be reconciled. It is true, too true, that the godly are illuminated but in part, and therefore as yet they differ in part. But yet this imperfect illumination doth more to a true and safe agreement, than all

the world can do besides. If you would stop your ears against the flesh, and yield to all the teachings of the word and Spirit, we should be sooner agreed.

13. And if we were once united in the Spirit and holiness, we should all have the use and benefit of all the reconciling, healing means and ordinances of God; which would be an exceeding great advantage to us. The unsanctified have but the outside, the sound, and shell of ordinances; but it is the sanctified that have the light, and life, and fruit of them. Every chapter that you read, and every sermon that you hear, will do somewhat towards the healing of our breaches: it will further our knowledge and our love. The communion of the saints in all holy duties, especially at the Lord's-supper, when they partake of one Christ, will inflame their love, and humble them for their divisions, and solder and glue their hearts together, as being all one bread and one body: and so they will be all as of one heart and soul. (Acts 4:32; 1 Cor. 10:16, 17; Acts 2:42–44. 46.) When we hear of the tender love of Christ to his weakest members, how can we choose but love them if we be his disciples! When we hear how much, and how freely he hath forgiven us, how can we choose but forgive them! (Matt. 18:35.) When we have communion with them in holy worship, as servants of the same Lord, as members of the same body, how can we choose but have the affections of fellow-members! (1 Cor. 12:26.) When we join with them in prayer, or holy conference, and perceive the fragrant odour of their graces, and the holy breathings of their souls after God, we cannot choose but love Christ in them. As the new commandment so frequently pressed in the Gospel, is the law of love, (John 15:12. 17,) and the new nature of the saints is a disposition of love, for this they are taught of God effectually; (1 Thess. 4:9;) so the ordinances do all of them exercise that love, and engage us to it. We must leave our gift at the altar, and go first and be reconciled to our brother, if we remember that he hath any thing against us. (Matt. 5:23, 24.) We must pray for forgiveness, but on condition that we do forgive. Differences and divisions that make a breach in Christian charity, are so insufferable among the saints, that they long for healing, and smart as the wounded body doth, till the time of healing; and are pained as a bone out of joint, till it be set again. And as they cannot bear it themselves, (when they are themselves,) so the church cannot bear it, but is engaged to watch over them, and set them in joint again; so that God hath hedged in his servants into one holy society, that they should not straggle from him, or from each other, and hath set pastors over them for this very end, to guide them and keep them in holy unity. (Ephes. 4:11–14.) Now all these uniting, healing ordinances are

effectual upon the sanctified; for their hearts are open to them, and their new nature is suited to the new commandment and work: but to others they are in a manner as food or physic to the dead: they hate the power of them; they break the holy enclosure of discipline and proudly rebel against their guides: and say, "Let us break their bands, and cast away their cords from us:" (Psal 2:3:) 'What, must we be ruled by such and such?' It is but the outside of sacraments, praises, and prayers that they are acquainted with; and these have no such healing force: so that in this you see the great advantage that we should have for full agreement, if we were but once agreed in the main, and united by the sanctifying Spirit.

14. Moreover, if once we were united in the Spirit, and in holiness, we should manage all our differences in a holy manner, and be awakened and disposed to seek after healing in a healing way. It would put us upon inquiring after peace, and studying the meetest terms of peace, till we had found out the way in which we should accord. The spirit of love and holiness would provoke us to begin and seek for peace with those that will not seek to us, and that seem averse to it; and to follow after peace when it flyeth from us, (Heb. 12:14,) and even to lie down at the feet of men, and deny our honour and worldly interest, if it might procure brotherly love and peace. Whereas a proud unsanctified heart will scorn to stoop, especially to those that are below them, or have wronged them, and will scorn to ask forgiveness of those that they have wronged! When you have shewed them the plainest word of God for it, and persuaded them to it with undeniable reasons, you lose your labour, and may almost as well persuade the fire to be cold. If you will stoop and humble yourself to him, and ask him forgiveness, and give him the honour, or change your mind, and be of his opinion, and say as he saith, and do as he would have you, perhaps you may have some peace with the most ungodly man. But the servants of Christ have a spirit of meekness and humility, and self-denial; and therefore if there be fallings out among them, they can humble themselves and seek for reconciliation. If there be difference in judgment about any weighty matters, they will go or send to one another as brethren, and confer about it in love and meekness, and search the Scripture, and seek after truth, and compare their evidences, and pray together for that light and love that must reconcile them: If they fall out, they can say to one another, 'We are brethren, and must not live at a distance, nor suffer any wounds in our affections, or any breach of charity to remain: The sun must not go down upon our wrath: Come, let us go together in private, and beg of God that he would

repair our love, and reconcile us, and prevent such breaches for the time to come.' And thus they can pray themselves friends again. I am persuaded that one quarter of an hour's fervent prayer would do more to quiet our distempered minds, and reconcile us, if thus we would get together in private, than many hours' debates without it. Now the spirit of holiness is a spirit of prayer; and therefore disposeth the servants of Christ, as meekly and lovingly to search for truth, so earnestly to pray themselves into agreement.

15. Moreover, were we once united in the Spirit, we should be under the promise of Divine assistance, which the unsanctified have no part in. When we pray for light, and peace, and concord, we have a promise to be heard and helped, at least, in the time and measure as shall be fittest; we have a promise of the Spirit to be our Teacher, and to lead us into truth: we have promises for the maintaining and repairing of our healing graces, and our communion graces; our love to Christ and one another; our patience and meekness, and the rest. And this must needs be a great advantage to unity and agreement. For God is partly engaged for it.

16. And if we were united in the Spirit, and agreed in the main, the great truths which we are agreed in would very much direct us, to find out the rest which yet we differ in. For these have an influence into all the rest, and the rest are all connected to these, and also linked and knit together, that we may find out many by the help of one. All holy truths do befriend each other, but especially the great and master points which the rest depend upon, and flow from: There is no way to a right agreement in other points, but by agreeing first in these fundamental rudiments.

17. Also if we were once agreed in holiness, we should have that continually within us and before us, that would much take us off from vain contendings, and from an overzealous minding of smaller things. We should have so much to do with God in holy duties, and so much to do with our own hearts in searching them, and watching them, and exciting them, and mending them, reproving and correcting them, supporting and comforting them by the application of the promises, that we should have less time for quarrelling, and less mind of it than the unsanctified have. We should have so many great and practical truths to digest and live upon, that lesser and unnecessary matters, which are the common causes of contention, would find less room: or at least, we should allow each truth its due proportion of our study, and talk, and zeal; and so the lesser would have comparatively so small a share, and be so exceeding seldom and remissly meddled with, that there would be the less danger of contentions.

18. Yea, if once we were united in the Spirit, the very forethought of an everlasting union in heaven, would have a continual influence upon our hearts, for the healing of our breaches. We should be thinking with ourselves, 'Shall we not shortly be all of one mind and heart! and all be perfected with the blessed vision, and reconciling light of the face of God! There will then be no dissention or division, or unbrotherly censures, or separations. And should we now live so unlike our future life! Shall we now be so unlike to what we must be for ever! Shall we now cherish those heart-burnings and dissentions, that must not enter with us into heaven, but be cast off among the rest of our miseries, and shut out with the rest of our enemies, and hated for ever by God and us? Must we there be closed in perfect love, and be all employed in the same holy praise of God and our Redeemer; and does it beseem us now to be censuring, contending, and separating from each other?' Thus the belief of the life to come will be a more effectual means with the godly for agreement, than any that unsanctified men can use.

19. Moreover, they that have the spirit of holiness, have a dear and special love to truth as well as unto peace. And therefore they have a great advantage for the receiving of it in all debates; and consequently they are fairer for a just agreement. They are friends with the most searching, spiritual truths: but the ungodly have an enmity to all that truth that would shew them their sin, and misery, and duty, and make them holy, and lead them up from the creature unto God. And as the proverb is, 'He that would not know, cannot understand.' When you deal with a wicked, graceless heart, you do not set reason against reason, (for if that, were all, we should soon have done,) but you set reason will, and passion, and appetite and fleshly interest: and when you have convinced them, you are little the nearer prevailing with them. You may as well think to satisfy a hungry belly with reasons, or to tame a wild beast with reasons, as to humble the proud, and bring the sensual person to self-denial, by all your reasons. For they love not the truth, because they love not the duty that it would persuade them to, and because they love the sin that it would take from them. There are two forts of Satan in a wicked man, that none but God can batter, so as to win them: that is, a proud and ignorant mind, and a hard and sensual heart. Many a year have I been battering them by the word of God, from this place, and yet with many can do no good. But the sanctified heart that loveth the truth will meet it, and welcome it, and thankfully entertain it. Love maketh a diligent hearer, and a good scholar, and

giveth us hope that informations and debates may be successful. A godly man is so far from hating truth, and flying from it, that he would give all the riches of the world to purchase it: he prays, and reads, and studieth for it; and therefore hath great advantage to attain it.

20. Moreover, if we were all agreed in holiness, and united in the Spirit of Christ, we should love the truth in a practical manner, and we should know that every truth of God hath its proper work to do upon the soul; and therefore we should love the end of each truth better than the truth itself. And therefore we could not pretend the truth against the ends of truth. And therefore we should see the security of those ends in all our debates and controversies. We should not make havock of the church of Christ, nor easily be guilty of divisions, nor quench our love of God and of our brethren, under pretence of standing for the truth; which unsanctified men will easily do. Truth is for holiness, and love as its proper end. Ungodly men will tread down love and holiness, or at least disadvantage it, and hinder it in the world, for the exalting of their own conceits, under the name of truth. They will cure the church by cutting it in pieces, or by cutting the throat of it, and are presently dismembering for every sore: but with the godly it is not so.

21. Moreover, the sanctified have a great advantage for agreement, in that they have hearts that are subject to the truth, and will be true to it when they understand it. Did they but know the right way, they would presently walk in it. Nothing is so dear to them that should not be forsaken for it, or sacrificed to it. But the wicked are false to the truths which they are acquainted with. They hold it or imprison it in unrighteousness, (Rom. 1:18,) and therefore is wrath revealed against them. "They like not to retain God in their knowledge;" and therefore God doth often give them up to a reprobate mind. (Rom. 1:28.) "They receive not the truth in the love of it, that they might be saved:" no wonder therefore if "God give them up to strong delusions to believe a lie, that all they might be damned that believed not the truth, but had pleasure in unrighteousness." (2 Thess. 2:10–12.) "When they know the judgment of God, that they that do such things are worthy of death; yet they do them, and have pleasure in them that do them." (Rom. 1:32.) We may well think that God will sooner reveal his truth to them that will obey it, than to them that will but bury it in the dunghill of a corrupted heart. And that he will rather hold the candle to his servants that will work by it, than to loiterers that will but play by it; or thieves or fornicators, that had rather it were put out; or to enemies that would do mischief by it, and

will throw away the candlesticks, (the ministers,) and put the candle into the thatch. Is there not many an ungodly person that hears me this day, that is convinced in his conscience that a holy life is best, and yet will not follow it and obey his conscience? Are there not convictions at the bottom, that the diligent, heavenly Christian, whom thou reproachest, is in a safer condition than thyself; and yet thou wilt not imitate such. Can you expect that God should acquaint such with his truth, that are so false to it?

22. If we were but all agreed in true holiness, we should have the great advantage of a tender conscience, together with an illuminated mind. For spiritual wisdom, with tenderness of conscience, is a great part of sanctification. And it is a great advantage in controversies and debates, to be wise and tender-conscienced: for wisdom makes men able to discern, and a tender conscience will make them afraid of mistaking and contradicting the truth; and will keep them from rashness, and unadvisedness, and levity; so that such an one dare not venture so easily upon new conceits, and will be more suspicious of himself, and of any thing wherein himself is much concerned: especially if he see great probabilities against it, or the judgment of the universal church, or of many wise and godly men against it, and see that it is likely to have ill effects; in all such cases a godly man will be tender-conscienced, and therefore cautelous. But is it so with the ungodly? No: but clean contrary. None so bold as the blind. Solomon's words describe them exactly; "The fool rageth and is confident." (Prov. 14:16.) If he be in an error, or entangled in any evil cause or way, you know not what to say to him for his recovery. The less he knows, the more he despiseth knowledge, and sets his face against his teachers, as if they were but fools to him, and scorns to be ruled by such as they, whom God hath made his rulers. Will you go to dispute or debate the case with one of these? Why be sure of it, they will put you down and have the day. It would do a man good to dispute with a wise, and learned, or sober, rational man, and to be overcome by reason and by truth: but no man will have so sure a conquest against you, as he that hath the least of sense or reason. He will go away and boast that you could not convince him: as if a madman should boast that the physicians could not all of them cure him. An obstreperous, proud, self-conceited fellow, will never yield to the clearest reason, nor ever be put down. We have a proverb, that 'There's no gaping against an oven, especially if it be hot.' If he have passion as well as ignorance, and a tongue, he will have the best. He that speaks nonsense saith nothing while he seems to speak. These men have the faculty of saying nothing an hour

or two together, in abundance of words. And there is no confuting a man that saith nothing. Nonsense is unanswerable, if there be but enough of it. Who would dispute against a pair of bagpipes, or against a company of boys that hoot at him! If you will make a match at barking or biting, a cur will be too hard for you: And if you will try your skill or strength at kicking, a horse will be too hard for you. And if you will contend with multitude of words, or by rage and confidence, a fool will be too hard for you (as you may see by Solomon's descriptions, and by daily experience). But if you will dispute by equal, sober reasoning, it is only a wiser man by evidence of truth that can overcome you: and to be thus overcome is better than to conquer: for you have the better if truth overcome you; and you have the worse if you overcome the truth.

So that you may easily perceive what an exceeding hindrance to unity and peace, it is to have to do with ungodly persons, that are blind, and proud, and brazen-faced, and of seared consciences, that fear not God, and therefore dare say any thing, as if they could out-face the truth, and the God of truth. But the sanctified have illuminated minds, and therefore are the more capable of further information; and they have tender consciences, and therefore dare not be unadvised and contentious, and strive against the light; and therefore have great advantage for agreement.

23. And if all these advantages should not yet so far prevail, as to bring us up to a full agreement, yet if we be but united in the Spirit and a holy life, we should be the more easily able to bear with one another under all our lesser differences, until the time of full agreement come. We should hold our differences (as brethren their diversity of statures and complexions, or at least as common human frailties) with love and compassion, and not with hatred and divisions. We should lovingly consult together upon rules or terms on which we might manage our unavoidable differences, to the least disadvantage to the cause of Christ, and to the common truths that we all maintain, and to the work of God for other men's conversion, and to the least advantage to sin and Satan, and the malice of ungodly men. And I think this is a fair agreement for imperfect persons, short of heaven; to have unity in the Spirit, and agreement in things of greatest weight, and to bear with one another in smaller matters, and manage our differences with meekness and peace.

24. Lastly, If all this be not enough, there is yet more for our encouragement. 1. If we are but once united in the Spirit, and agree in a holy heart and life, we have the infallible promise of God, that we shall shortly all

arrive in heaven, at the place and state of full perfection, where all our differences will be ended, and we shall be perfectly agreed in mind and will, being one in him that is the only centre of universal peace and concord. And it is a great comfort to us in our darkness and differences, that we are in the sure and ready way to perfect light and harmony of mind. 2. Yea, and till we come thither, we are still on the mending hand; and if we do but thrive in holiness, we shall certainly thrive in concord and peace. And it is a comfort to a sick man, not only to be certain of a full recovery, but to feel himself daily on the mending hand. 3. And in the meantime God himself will bear with all our differences, though not so far as to approve or cherish them, yet so far as to own us for his children, though we are too often falling out with one another; and so far as to pity our frailty and infirmity, and to pardon us, and deal as a father with us. And if our quarrels cause him to use the rod, it is but to keep us in quietness afterwards; that as we had the taste of the sour fruits of our contentions, so we may after have the quiet fruits of righteousness.

And thus I have given you in four-and-twenty particular discoveries, a sufficient proof, that a unity in the Spirit, and an agreement in holiness, hath abundant advantages for our further agreement in lower things; and such as all other men are destitute of; and therefore that there is no way possible for a just, a safe, a durable agreement, but that we all agree in a holy life, and be united in the sanctifying Spirit of Christ.

But perhaps you will object, If all this be so, whence comes it to pass that there are so many differences still among those that you call the sanctified? Do we not see that they are more contentious and divided into parties, and make more stir about religion than any others?

Answ. 1. The differences among the godly, are nothing for number, or greatness, or weight, in comparison of yours. I have shewed you in my discourse of the Catholic Church, twenty great and weighty points, in which they all agree together, and in which the ungodly agree not with them. What if they agree not, whether church-government should be exercised by the elders only, the flock consenting; or by all the flock, the pastors guiding? Or whether one among the pastors should be of a superior degree, or of a superior order, or whether they should only be of the same degree and order, though chosen to preside and moderate for the time? What if one think that it is necessary to read the public prayers out of a book; and another think it is necessary to pray without book; and a third more truly thinks it is in itself indifferent, whether it be within book or without?

With other such like differences as these, which will keep no man out of heaven. Are these like our differences with ungodly men? Our differences with you are, Whether heaven or earth is chiefly to be loved and sought after? Whether grace and holiness, or sin and carelessness be the better? Whether it be the more sweet and desirable life, to be heavenly-minded, and live in the love and service of God, and to be much in holy communion with him, and meditating upon his law, and upon the life to come; or on the contrary, to live to the world and to the flesh? Whether it be better to obey the word of God, and his ministers that speak in his name; or to obey our fleshly desires, and the proud conceits of ignorant minds? In a word, our difference with the ungodly, though they will not confess it and speak out, is plainly this, Whether heaven or earth be better? And whether God be God and shall be our God? And whether Christ be Christ, and shall be our Christ? And whether the Holy Ghost shall be our Sanctifier? Or whether we shall live after the flesh and rule ourselves, against the will and word of God, and so in effect, whether God be God, and man be man? And whether we should live as men or as beasts? And so whether we should choose salvation or damnation? If you could but understand yourselves, and the depth of your deceitful hearts, you would see that here lieth the difference. For though some of the unsanctified have a fair and plausible deportment, and will speak handsomely of the Christian religion, because they have had an ingenuous Christian education; yet all this is indeed but little more than formal compliment, so far are they from a heavenly mind and a heart that is truly set on God, as their careless lives, and carnal, unsavory conference sheweth, if not their scorns at a state of holiness. So that our differences are nothing in comparison of the difference with you.

2. Moreover, the servants of God do mind the matters of religion more seriously than others do; and therefore their differences are brought to light, and made more observable to the world. Their very heart is set upon these heavenly things, and therefore they cannot make light of the smallest truth of God; and this may be some occasion of their difference: whereas the ungodly differ not about religion, because they have heartily no religion to differ about: they trouble not themselves about these matters, because they do not much regard them. And is this a unity and peace to be desired? I had rather have the discord of the saints, than such a concord of the wicked. They are so careful about their duty that they are afraid of missing it in the least particular; and this (with their imperfect light) is the reason of their disputings about these matters. But you that are careless of your duty, can

easily agree upon a way of sin, or take any thing that comes next to hand. They honour the worship of God so much, that they would not have any thing out of order; but you set so little by it, that you will be of the religion that the king is of, let it be what it will be: and it is easy to agree in such an ungodly, careless course. Astronomers have many controversies about the positions and motions of the heavens: and all philosophers have many controversies about the matter of their sciences: when ignorant men have none of their controversies, because they understand not, and therefore regard not the things that the learned differ about. And will you think ever the better of ignorance, or ever the worse of learning for this? The controversies of lawyers, of historians, chronologers, geographers, physicians, and such like, do never trouble the brains of the ignorant: but for all that, I had rather be in controversy with the learned, than without such controversy with you. If you scatter a handful of gold or diamonds in the street, perhaps men will scramble for them, and fall out about them, when swine will trample on them and quietly despise them, because they do not know their worth: will you therefore think that swine are happier than men? The living are vexed with strifes and controversies, about almost all the matters in the world, when the dead carcases in the grave lie still in peace, and are not troubled with any of these differences. And will you say therefore that the dead corpse is happier than the living? Sirs, the case is very plain, if you will see, that thus it is as to the matter in hand. It is a death in sin, and compliance with the times and carnal interest, and a disesteem of spiritual, holy things, that is the cause of the agreement of the wicked. But the godly know the worth of the things that you set light by, and therefore make a greater matter of them than you, and therefore no wonder if they have more debates and controversies about them.

3. And this also is another reason of the difference. It is the interest of Satan to divide the servants of Christ, but to keep his own in unity and peace: and therefore he will do what he can to accomplish it. He knows that a kingdom divided cannot stand: and therefore he will do his worst to divide Christ's kingdom, and to keep his own from being divided. By a deceitful peace it is that he keeps his servants to him. And by casting among them the matter of contentions and divisions, he hopeth to get Christ's followers from him. So that the devil himself is the promoter of your unity and concord, but the destroyer of ours; and therefore no wonder if you have fewer differences.

4. Besides, the way that ungodly men go in, is so suited to the common corruption of nature, that it is no wonder if they be all agreed. All the world can agree to eat, and drink, and sleep; and therefore all the sensual sinners in the world may easily agree upon an overloving of meat, and drink, and sleep; and so of riches, and honours, and pleasures. And as it is easy, so it is not much desirable, no more than if you should all agree to cast yourselves headlong into the sea: When every house is infected with the plague, there is an agreement among them: but had you not rather be one of those that disagree from them? But to agree in a holy heavenly life, is contrary to corrupted nature; and therefore no marvel if it be more difficult. When a physician hath an hundred patients in hand, he may easily get them all to agree to eat and drink that which they desire; but if he require them to forbear the things that they most love, because they will hurt them, the understanding sort will agree to him, but so will not the rest. In a rotten house, the fall of one bearer may occasion the fall of all the house, because their weight inclines them downward: but if you take up one stone and cast it upward, all the rest of the stones in the heap will not fly upward with it. It is easier to draw others with us down hill, than up the hill.

5. And it is considerable that the differences among the servants of Christ, are not always from themselves, but from the ungodly enemies that contrive their dissentions, and set them together by the ears, that they may fish in troubled waters, and the better attain their wicked ends. It is the envious man that soweth these tares while we are asleep, and casteth in this wildfire among us.

6. Moreover, one of the greatest causes of the troublesome breaches and divisions in the church, is because there are so many unsanctified persons among us, that seem to be of us, and to be truly godly, when it is not so. You think it is the godly that have these divisions, when the most and worst of all our divisions proceed from the ungodly that have an unsound and unrenewed heart, under the cloak of piety and zeal: for if they were truly gracious persons, they durst not do as many of them do. 1. They durst not so rashly and easily venture on novelties as they do, without deliberation, and reading, and hearing what can be said on the other side. 2. They durst not so easily make a division in the church of Christ. 3. Nor so easily cast a stumbling-block before the weak; and matter of reproach to our Christian profession before the wicked. 4. Nor durst they so easily reproach, and condemn, and cast off the unanimous faithful ministers of Christ. 5. Nor durst they so easily censure the universal church in former ages, as many of them

do. 6. Nor durst they sacrifice the success, and honour of the Gospel, and the common acknowledged truths, and the saving of men's souls thereby, to their private opinions, and ends. 7. Nor durst they make so great a breach in charity, nor so arrogantly condemn or slight their brethren, whose piety and soberness they cannot deny. These with many other evidences, do let us know, that ungodly men crept in among us, are the causes of most of our most dangerous divisions. And will you lay the blame of this upon religion, which the devil and the secret enemies of religion do perform? It is your dishonour and not ours: for these men are of your party, though they seem to be of us. Satan knows well enough, that if he have not some of his followers to be spies in Christ's army, and to raise mutinies there and betray the rest, he is likely to be the more unsuccessful in his attempts. Was Judas more a dishonour to Christ, or to the devil? He was among the followers of Christ indeed; but he told them beforehand of him, that he was a devil; and he never betrayed Christ till Satan had entered into him.

7. Lastly, The saints themselves are sanctified but in part, and many in a low degree; and being imperfect in holiness, must needs be as imperfect in holy unity and peace. It is not their holiness that causeth their contentions, but the remnants of their sin. And therefore it is but small credit to the way of sinners. Were we but perfectly rid of the vices that you cherish, and perfectly separated from the ways that you so much delight in, and had we no remnants of your disease and sinful nature in us, we should then have perfect unity and peace. Do you think that it is long of our religion, that we disagree: No: if we were but perfectly religions we should be perfectly agreed. It is because we are holy in no greater a measure, and not because we are holy at all. It is not because of the way of godliness that we have chosen; but because we walk no faster, and no more carefully in that way. It is our too oft stepping out of it, and not our walking in it, that breaketh our peace with God and man, and our own consciences. Search all the Scripture, and see where you can find, that ever God encouraged his servants to divisions. No: but on the contrary, he oft and earnestly cries them down, and warneth all his followers to avoid them, and the causers and fomenters of them. There was never master so much for unity as Christ, and never was there a law, or a religion that did so much condemn divisions, and command brotherly love, and peace, and concord, and forbearing and forgiving one another, as the Christian law and religion doth. And will you yet say that our divisions are long of our religion, or of Christ the author of it? You may as wisely say, that eating is the cause of weakness, because

that some are weak for all their meat. But you will find that none can live without it. Or you may say as wisely, that physicians are the causes of the diseases of the world, because they do not cure them all. I tell you, there is none in all the world that have done so much for unity and peace, as Christ hath done. No: all the world set together have not done half so much for it as he. He hath preached peace and unity, forgiving and forbearing, and loving one another, yea, loving our enemies; and he hath gone before us in the perfect practice of what he taught. He hath offered himself a sacrifice to the justice of his Father, that by his blood he might reconcile us unto God. He is the great peace-maker between God and man, between Jews and Gentiles, taking away the enmity, and becoming himself the head of our unity; and giving us one spirit, one faith, one baptism, that we might be one in him who is one with the Father. So that to charge the Centre of unity with our divisions, and the Prince of peace himself with our discords, or his holy word or ways with our disagreements, as all one as to charge the sun with darkness, and to say that our lawgivers and laws are the causes of theft, and murder, and adultery, which condemn them to death that are approved guilty of them. The cause of all our disagreements and divisions is, because we are no more holy than we are, and because we are no more religious. So that I may leave it now as a proved truth, that we must unite in the Spirit, and agree in holiness of heart and life, if ever we will have true unity and agreement.

And now, sirs, you have seen the only way of unity opened to you: it is plain and past all doubt before you. If yet you will divide from God and his servants, and if yet you will be numbered with the stragglers or quarrellers, do not say but peace was opened and offered to you. Do not say, you could have peace, but that you would not. Do not say any more hereafter, that there were so many religions and so many ways that you could not tell which to join with! never more pretend the differences of the godly as a cloak for your ungodliness. I have opened the nakedness of such pretences. You shall not be able, when your lives are scanned, to look God in the face with such an unreasonable impudent pretence. Your consciences and the world shall then be witnesses of your shame; that while you cried out of sects and heresies, and were offended at the divisions of the church, it was yourselves that were the cause of it: It was you, and such as you that were the great dividers; and that obstinately proceeded in your divisions, when the way of peace was opened to you; and would not be united in the Spirit to Christ, and would not agree in holiness with his church, when you were acquainted that there was no other way to peace. Would you but have joined in a firm and everlasting covenant to God the Father, Son, and Holy Ghost, as your only Creator, Redeemer, and Sanctifier, as members of the holy catholic church, and have lived in the communion of the saints, you should have received the forgiveness of sins, the resurrection of the just, and everlasting life: but in refusing, and obstinately refusing these, you refused all your hopes of blessedness, and wilfully cast yourselves on the wrath of God; and therefore must endure it for ever.

The last advice that I have to give, upon the ground of this doctrine, is, To all that are united in the Spirit, and agreed upon a holy life. I mean to say but little to you now; but briefly to tender you these two requests.

1. I beseech you Christians but to live as Christians, in that holy unity as your principles and profession do engage you to. Hath true Christianity and holiness such abundance of advantages against division, and yet will you be guilty of it? Against all these bonds and healing principles and helps, will you be dividers? Doth it not grieve you, and even break your hearts, to hear ungodly persons say that professors are of so many minds and parties, that they know not which of them to follow; and that we had never concord since you bore the sway? O do not seek by your contentious ways, to persuade people that holiness is a dividing thing, and that religion doth but tend to set the world together by the ears. Is it not a precious mercy to us of this place, that we have among us but one church, and one religion, and have not church against church, and Christian against Christian? I charge you from the Lord, that you be thankful for this benefit; and that you look upon divided places, and compare their case with yours, that if ever dividers come amongst you, the sense of your felicity in this blessed unity may cause you to reject them; and that you do not suffer any Delilah to rob you of your strength and glory. Were you but once here in pieces among yourselves, what a scorn would you be to all the ungodly! What sport would it be to them, to hear you disputing against one another, and reproaching and condemning one another, and as bitterly as the wicked do reproach you all? Do you not pity those places where divisions have made religion to be a scorn, and the tender love and unity of the saints is turned into uncharitable censures and separations? Take warning then that you come not to the like. If you should, you would be as inexcusable as any people in the world, because you tried and tasted so much of the sweetness and benefits of unity as you have done; shew men by your lives, that holiness is the

most certain way to unity, as ever you desire either to propagate holiness, or to have any evidence of it in yourselves.

2. Judge by this undoubted truth, of any doctrine that shall be offered you, and of the ways of men and of yourselves.

1. Suspect that doctrine that tendeth to divisions in the church. If it be not for unity, it is not of God. (Rom. 16:17.) Christ came to heal and reconcile, and is the Prince of Peace; and, therefore, sendeth not his servants on a contrary errand. He will justify your dividing from the unbelieving world; but he hateth dividing among his servants. He that is for church-division, is not (in that) for Christ or you.

2. Whatever holiness they may pretend to, adhere not to those men, and think not too highly of them that are for divisions among the churches, or servants of the Lord. You will see them repent, or come to shame and confusion the last. You fly from Christ, if you fly from unity.

3. Think not that you have any more of the Spirit or of holiness, than you have of love to the unity of the saints. It is the spirit of Satan and not of Christ, that leadeth you to church-divisions: it is a counterfeit holiness that maketh you not desirous of unity with all the saints. If you be not first pure and then peaceable, your wisdom is not from above. As you would all take that man to be an enemy to holiness, that is an enemy to chastity, temperance, or common honesty; so have you reason to think of him that is an enemy to the church's unity and peace. Shew that you have the Spirit by the unity of the Spirit; and shew that you are holy by loving the union and communion of the saints.

> Him that is weak in the faith receive ye, but
> not to doubtful disputations.
>
> —Romans 14:1

I have already proved to you in the foregoing discourse, 1. That the true unity of the church of Christ is a unity of the Spirit, and that the unsanctified are the causes of our divisions. 2. That a unity in mere profession, is but a low and miserable unity, which will not satisfy nor serve the turn. 3. That a unity in the Spirit of holiness, is a great advantage for the healing of all our lesser differences, or that we may do well for all those differences, if we are truly sanctified. I come now to the fourth and last part of my discourse, which is to shew you, that 'it is not the will of God that the unity of his church should consist in things indifferent, or in the smaller matters, or in points of doubtful disputation.' To which end I have chosen this text, in which Paul doth purposely and plainly lay down this point, in order to the reconciling of a difference that was then among the Romans; I shall not now stand to discuss whether the weak that Paul here speaks of, were some Christians tainted with a Pythagorean conceit, and guilty of some excessive austerities (which some have thought, 1. because here is no mention of circumcision: 2. and because they are said to eat herbs only); or whether it were some converts of the Jews, that scrupled the forsaking of their ancient ceremonies, which is the common and more likely exposition. 1. The person here spoken of is "Him that is weak in the faith," that is, who is yet so ignorant in the doctrine of faith, as not to know that these ceremonies are abolished, or these matters are no part of duty, which he placeth duty in; and, consequently, who is so weak in con-science as that he dare not omit the observation of these days and cere-monies. The points in which the weakness of these persons are said to be manifested, are, 1. In their abstaining from flesh, and eating herbs. 2. In their observation of certain days as holy.

2. The thing commanded is, that these persons for all their weakness be received, that is, 1. Into brotherly internal charity. 2. Into Christian exter-nal communion. For it seems, that by the reason of this their weakness, there grew divisions in the church. The weak were so self-conceited, as to censure the strong, because they did not observe their ceremonies. And the strong were too contemptuous of the weak, and made light of them as a superstitious people, unfit for their communion: Paul chides them both; the weak for censuring the strong, and the strong for contemning the weak; and commandeth that for the future, the weak forbear his judging, and the strong receive the weak whom they contemned, and so that they join in inward love, and external communion.

3. And he addeth this caution, for the manner of their reception and behaviour, that it must not be "to doubtful disputations" either to the cen-suring of one another, or to unseasonable, uncharitable contendings and disputes about these smaller things. Three things Paul seemeth to suppose in the matter of their controversy. 1. That they were matter of some indif-ferency. 2. That they were small, and of lowest consideration in religion. 3. That to the weak they were so dark and doubtful, as to be the matter of disputes. But for all these, he would have no breach in their charity or communion.

One doubt we must not overpass: and that is, how this will stand with what he saith in the Epistle to the Galatians. Here he saith, "Let not him that eateth, despise him that eateth not: One man esteemeth one day above another; another esteemeth every day alike: Let every man be fully persuaded in his own mind:" But there he saith, "Ye observe days and months, and times, and years; I am afraid of you, lest I have bestowed upon you labour in vain." (Gal. 4:10, 11.) And of circumcision, "Behold, I Paul say unto you, if ye be circumcised, Christ shall profit you nothing; for I testify again to every man that is circumcised, that he is a debtor to do the whole law." (Gal. 5:2, 3.) For the understanding of this you must observe, 1. That there is a great difference between circumcision and the ceremonies here spoken of. 2. And between the outward act of circumcision, and the sacrament of circumcision as appointed by God. 3. And there is a great difference between the using it as necessary to justification, and the using the outward part only for some lawful end. 4. And between the time when the Gospel was but newly revealed, and the time when it was oft and fully declared to the world. 5. And between those that are ignorant for want of full information, and those that are obstinate after long instruction. 6. And between those that scruple the omission of such ceremonies themselves; and those that would obtrude them as necessary upon others. Observing these distinctions, you may see the difficulty plainly resolved, as followeth. 1. In this text, Rom. 14, Paul speaketh not of circumcision, but of meats and days only. For circumcision engaged men further to Moses's law, than these single ceremonies. 2. When Paul saith he was afraid of the Galatians, because of their observation of days and weeks, and months, he means because they still adhered to the abrogated law, after so long and plain instruction. 3. And though he circumcised Timothy, (Acts 16:3,) and yet speak against it, (Gal. 5:2, 3,) the difference of the cases is exceeding great. For, 1. It was but the outward circumcision of the flesh that he used with Timothy (as with one that did not intend by it any engagement to Moses, or necessity of it to justification.) But it was the entire sacrament of circumcision which was pretended to continue necessary, by the false teachers, and which he exhorted the Galatians to refuse. And circumcision as a sacrament doth signify two principal things. 1. An engagement to, and profession of faith in the Promised seed, as promised and future. 2. An engagement to Moses's law (for this use it had after the law was given.) Now when Christ was come, that man that would still be circumcised into, and profess to expect a Messiah yet to come, and that would engage himself to that law, which contained the types of a future Messiah, and was but a schoolmaster to lead to Christ, I say that person that was thus circumcised (as all were that received it according to the institution) did plainly deny that Christ was come, and therefore Christ could profit them nothing. But yet a man that used but the outward sign to avoid an impediment to the Gospel (as Paul did in the case of Timothy), or if it were erroneously, as a mere custom, as the Abassines now do, might yet be saved by Christ nevertheless. 2. And when Paul used it, it was as an indifferent thing; but he condemned it as supposed necessary. 3. When he used it, it was in the beginning of the publication of the Gospel, that (as Austin speaks) he might give the ceremonies an honourable burial: but when he condemned it, it was after the full publication of the abolition of the law, against those that would have raked it out of the grave again. 4. He bore with it in the weak; but he condemned it in the wilful 5 He bore with it in those that scrupled the forsaking it as they were Jews; but he condemned it in those that would have laid this yoke as necessary on the Gentiles.

Object. 'But it seems here that Paul is against the necessary observation of the Lord's-day, when he is for esteeming all days alike.'

Answ. If you understand the subject of the debate, you will understand his speech. It is only Jewish holy-days that was the matter in question, and therefore of these only he is to be understood. As for the Lord's-day, it is plain in the New Testament, that Christ did not only rise upon it, and appear to his disciples on it, and send down the Holy Ghost upon it; but that the disciples presently after Christ's resurrection, began their religious assemblies on it, and so continued them, by the guidance of the Holy Ghost; and so settled that day for the use of the holy assemblies of the church, calling it the Lord's-day. (John 20:19, 26; Acts 2:1; 20:7; 1 Cor. 16:2; Rev. 1:10.) And it is past all doubt in the history of the church, that since the apostles' days till now, the church hath constantly kept this day as thus established, by the name of the Lord's-day; which the fathers called the Christian sabbath, as they applied the name of an altar to the table, and of a sacrifice to the supper of the Lord; so that he that will reject the observation of the Lord's-day, must take on him to be wiser than the Holy Ghost in the apostles, and than all the catholic church of Christ, from the beginning, till these contentious persons did arise.

The text being thus explained, the doctrine before-mentioned is plain in it before us, viz.

Doctrine. 'It is the will of God that the unity of the church should not be laid upon indifferent, small, and doubtful points; but that true believers, who differ in such things, should notwithstanding have inward charity and outward communion with one another, not censuring, nor despising, nor dividing from each other upon this account.

In handling this point, I shall briefly shew you, 1. What I mean by things indifferent. 2. What I mean by smaller matters. 3. What by doubtful things or disputations: and then I shall give you the reasons of it, and then apply it.

1. For the explication. 1. By things indifferent I do not mean things, 'hic et nunc,' indifferent in the use; but things that are not ordinarily in themselves either commanded as duties, or forbidden as sins, but left as lawful or indifferent by the Scriptures, unless as some accident or circumstance may make them to be good or evil.

2. By smaller matters, it is none of my intent to persuade you, that any thing that is but an appurtenance to faith or piety is absolutely small: but they are small in comparison of the far greater things, and so small that many are saved without them, and they are not of flat necessity to salvation; and the greater matters must be preferred before them.

3. By things doubtful, I do not mean such as are not certainly revealed in the Scripture, nor yet such as perverse heretical men do raise doubts about when they are plain in themselves: but I mean such points as are revealed certainly, but more darkly than the greater points, and therefore cannot be so clearly known; so that the sum is this, 1. Indifferent things must not be taken to be necessary, or sinful, but to be indifferent. 2. Lower and lesser points must not be taken to be greater or weightier than they are. 3. Points of less certainty that are more darkly revealed, must not be taken to be more clear and certain to us than they are. 4. And it is not on such darker, smaller matters that God hath laid our salvation; or that the church's unity and peace dependeth.

II. For the fuller demonstration of this, let these reasons be observed: 1. If our unity were laid on these smaller matters, the multitude of them is such, that we should never agree in all. The essentials of Christianity are so few, that all men may well be expected to learn, and know, and entertain them. But the smaller points are so many, that there is no hope of an universal agreement in them all. You know in the body of man or beast, the great master veins that are the stock of all the rest, are but a few; but follow them farther, and you shall have so many divisions, and sub-divisions, till you find them to be many hundreds or thousands. So is it with the arteries, and with the nerves. The body of a tree is but one, and the first division perhaps is but in two or three parts; but follow it to the very ends of the branches, and you may find many thousands. So is it in divinity: and therefore if none should be in unity with the church, but those that understand every branch of Christian verity, what hope of union could there be?

2. Moreover, the smaller points are far less discernible than the greater be; and therefore there is the less hope that ever the church should have unity in these. The great arms of a tree are easily discerned, when the extremities of the branches are very small. The trunks of the master veins are great and easily seen, but the points and capillary veins are so small, as hardly to be perceived. So God in mercy hath made very plain those few essential points of faith that salvation lieth on; but if you follow on these generals to all the particulars and appurtenances, you shall find them run so small as well as so many, as that it is impossible that unity should consist in these.

3. Furthermore, if our unity were laid on these, religion would be for none but the learned, and (as the ancients ordinarily argue against the heathens that cavilled at the plainness of the Scripture) God should then be partial, and should make a way to heaven that poor men cannot go. For the poor cannot possibly attain to so much learning, and spend so much of their lives in study, as may bring them to the knowledge of all these lower, difficult points.

4. Yea, if our unity or salvation lay on these, it is certain it would shut us all out, both from unity and salvation; so that there would no two be at unity in all the world, and no one be saved. For all men on earth are ignorant in many lesser truths, even such as are revealed to us in the Scripture, and we should endeavour to understand. What man dare affirm that he understandeth every word of the Holy Scripture? Did the Pope himself think that he had attained to this infallibility, he would ere this have written us an infallible commentary. If the best must say with Paul himself, "we know but in part," then surely those smaller, doubtful things, which all the truly sanctified know not, are not the matter of the unity of the church.

5. I have shewed in my Discourse of the Catholic Church, that to shut out all, from the church and our communion, that differ from us in such lower things, is utterly against the design of Christ, and the tenor of the Gospel, and very dishonourable to him and to his church: God hath more mercy than to shut out the weak; and will you dishonour him so far as to persuade the world that he hath no such mercy? The design of the Gospel is

grace and love! How tender was Christ, even of his little ones that believe in him! how compassionate is he to them in their infirmities! And would you go about to persuade the world that he hath so little of this compassion, as that he will admit none to heaven, or to the communion of his church, but those that attain to knowledge and agreement in all these lesser, doubtful controversies, and indifferent things? The church is small enough already; but if you would cut off all, that do not agree in every circumstance, you would make it small indeed. This is no better than, under pretence of faith and unity, to unchurch the church, and damn yourselves, and all the world.

6. The arguments in the text are very forcible; "For God hath received him." (ver. 3.) As if he should say, 'Dare you despise or cast out him that God receiveth?' "Who art thou that judgest another man's servant?" (ver. 4.) "Why dost thou judge thy brother? or why dost thou set at naught thy brother? We shall all stand before the judgment seat of Christ." (ver. 10.) The church doth not censure men for small or doubtful things; nor must we condemn those that God doth not condemn.

7. The laying such stress on smaller things, doth multiply controversies, and fill the minds of men with scruples, and ensnare their consciences, and engage men in parties against each other to the certain breach of charity, and ruin of the peace of the church, and of their souls. The fire of contention will never go out for want of fuel, if unnecessary things be made necessary, and small things pretended be great, and uncertain things pretended to be certain. Abundance of vice will be daily set and kept at work, upon this borrowed stock.

8. And what a world of precious time will be wasted by this means, while men are studying and reading to maintain their own opinions; and when they must waste their hours when they are together, in conferences and wrangling disputations, to the discomposing of their own and others' minds, and certain troubling the church of God! O what use have we for those precious hours, for surer, greater, and more needful things!

9. The things that our salvation, and the church's peace, are indeed laid upon, are so great, so necessary, so pleasant, and so profitable, that it leaveth us the more without excuse, to waste our time in things unnecessary. We have our great Creator to know and honour; we have the mystery of redemption to search into and admire; we have the nature, and life, and death, and resurrection, and ascension, and glorification, and intercession of Christ, to study and believe; and all the love and wisdom of God, the mercy, and the holiness and justice, that was revealed in him; we

have judgment to prepare for; and all the graces of the Spirit of Christ to be received, or cherished, increased and exercised in our souls. We have a hell to escape, and a heaven to obtain, and the foreseen glory of it to feed upon, for the strengthening and delighting of our souls; we have many particular duties of holiness and righteousness to attend to: and in the midst of all this great employment, should we make more work and trouble to ourselves, and that about unnecessary things?

10. These unnecessary or lower things, when once they are advanced above their rank, do undermine and wrong the greater matters, which they pretended to befriend. They divert the thoughts and speeches from them, and take up the affections, and will not be contented with their due proportion; but are, as the proverb is, 'Like a beggar on horseback, that will never light.' If men be set upon ceremonies, or private opinions of their own, they are upon it in all companies; and you shall sometimes have almost nothing else from them. And that is not all; but the interest of their unnecessary, or lower points, is ordinarily set up against the interest of that body of Christian verities which we are all agreed in; so that they can be contented that Christianity lose much advantage in the greater points, that their cause may be advantaged. If this were not so, we should not have had ceremonies and formalities cast out such abundance of excellent preachers heretofore: nor private opinions have set so many against the labours of faithful ministers, as, to our grief and shame, we have lately seen: and the mischief is, that unnecessary things made necessary, do so involve the imposer's interest with their own, that they think they are necessitated to drive them on, and see their impositions obeyed, or else their wisdom or authority is despised.

11. And thus they directly lead men to persecution, and occasion those that must needs have their wills, to lord it over God's heritage, (1 Pet. 5:3,) when the desire of being the church's god, hath prevailed so far with any of its members, as to set them upon a course of law-giving and domineering, and bringing others into a conformity to their wills; they look upon all men as sinners that disobey them, and think that their power will warrant them to force obedience to their commands, or else to deprive the church of her pastors. Many a congregation have I known change preachers for ceremonies; when as if God's will and word in necessary things to men's salvation, had been preferred to the will and word of the bishops, about things called indifferent by themselves, the case had been altered; and they would rather have let the ignorant have been without a ceremony than a

sermon. It is the unhappy fate of almost all that are set upon unnecessary things, that they cannot endure that others should have the liberty of differing front them. It is not enough to them to enjoy the freedom of their own consciences, about meats, or holy-days, or gestures or vestures, or other formalities, unless all others be compelled to do as they do. When they are but moved to comply with others, though plain Scripture and the practice of the primitive catholic church be alleged for it, yet it moveth them little or nothing. But if others will not comply with them, they cry out against them as enemies to unity and peace; and say, It is not fit to suffer men to be of so many minds and ways; that is, it is fit all should be compelled to do as they would have them.

12. And another mischief that followeth the making unnecessary things to be necessary, is, that it openeth a gap to so many more of the same kind, that no man knows how to stop it, nor when we have ceremonies and inventions enough: But upon the same ground that these are brought in to-day, the next Pope or Bishop thinks he may bring another to-morrow; and so we can never tell when we have all, nor when will be an end.

13. And in the multitude of things unnecessary, we shall be in danger of losing the things that are necessary, they will be so buried or obscured in the crowd: the substance will scarcely be perceived for the ceremony.

14. And methinks it is such height of pride for mortal men to arrogate such a power, and to desire and endeavour such a thing, that I wonder how they dare attempt it. I mean to make universal or unnecessary laws for the church, in the matters of faith or worship. Can a man that hath one spark of humility left in him, desire that his will may be a law to all others, in doubtful or indifferent things? And proceed so far as to desire, that none may have liberty in the church that are not of his opinion, or will not be ruled by him, in things indifferent, or of no necessity! Surely a man of any humility would think with himself, 'Am not I also imperfect in knowledge? And may I not be mistaken? What is my judgment that it should be a law to the church, and that I should be so highly conceited and confident of it, as to turn out godly ministers or people from the church or worship of God, for not conforming themselves to my opinion in things of such a low and indifferent nature!' He that would be the law-giver to the church, and suffer none but those of his own opinion in such points, would be the lord of the church, which can know the voice of none but Christ, and owneth no other Lord but him.

15. And the sin is the greater, because they have so little interest or pretence to lead them to these usurpations: They must have their will, though it get them nothing. Who made them law-givers to the church of Christ? Cannot they allow Christ this part of the Sovereignty, to make laws for his church? And cannot they be content with a ministerial power, to proclaim and promote the laws of Christ, and according to these to guide his church?

16. And hereby men are drawn to a human kind of religion: and they do more properly believe, obey, and worship these imposers than Jesus Christ; when they must fetch the very matter of their religion, not from the Bible, but the canons or decrees of men, their conscience, obedience, and reward will be according thereunto.

17. And hereby the adversaries of the church have occasion to insult over us, and think our differences to be more than indeed they are. When the unity of the church is laid upon things indifferent or of smaller moment, there will presently be disagreements, and these will be the enemy's matter of reproach. It is this that makes the Papists tell us of our differences among ourselves, because we have made them seem something to them, when they are next to nothing. 'O,' say they, 'where is your church of England now?' Why! what is the matter? Is the church of England dead? Or is any thing taken down that was essential to the church of England? Was a prelacy ruling by a lay-chancellor over many hundred parishes, chosen and governing without the body of the clergy, essential to the church of England? I am confident the most of the sober, godly ministers in England, are for the apostolical, primitive Episcopacy still. Was the book of canons, or the book of common-prayer, or the ceremonies essential to the church of England? Surely they were not; and if so, it is living still. But if any say, that these were essential to it, we may thank them for the death of it, that made it of such a human, mortal frame, which any prince might spurn down at his pleasure. Surely the church or churches of Christ in England, are of a more heavenly, durable frame, that may be persecuted, but hardly destroyed, while the men are living, of whom it doth consist.

Hence also it is, that the Papists tell us, that we have changed all our worship. And wherein? Why we have not the same baptism that we had; nor the same administration of the Lord's-supper, nor the same public prayer, nor the same way of marrying, churching, burying, &c. And what is the difference? Is it that we say not at every time the very same words? Why so you may as well say, that Paul was mutable, because he wrote not the same words in every one of his Epistles, nor spoke not the same words in all his prayers, no not in public. And so both you and we are mutable, because we preach not the same words every day in our sermons. God hath bid us pray; but he hath prescribed us no necessary form of words, but the Lord's-prayer. If the difference be, that we use not the common-prayer-book; doth that make a different sort of worship? Is it not the same sort of worship if we say the same words, or words to the same sense, either on the book or off it? If once men lay the nature of worship, and the unity of the church upon things unnecessary, then what changes will seem to be in our worship, when indeed there are none? Then the Papists may tell us of our divisions in worship, because one man sitteth at the singing of psalms and another stands; and one readeth with spectacles and another without; and one weareth a cap, and another weareth none; and one preacheth on one text, and another upon another. But be it known to all the Papists in the world, that our religion is not changed at all: our worship is the same whether within book or without. Our prayers are the same for matter with those in the common-prayer-book. And if I should one day use the common-prayer-book, and another day forbear it, I should not change the worship of God. To pray is part of his worship: but whether it be on a book or off it, is no part at all, but only a mode or circumstance, which may be altered as occasion serveth. I doubt not but a book is fittest for some; but not for all. And do they think, that we know not what adding, and chopping, and changing they have made with their mass-book? Who is it then that hath changed their worship? Is it like the same book that it was before the changes made by Gregory the Great? It was so ordinary a thing to change the manner and forms of worship, that private bishops did it without any synods: whence else had the world the forms that are now in use? Tell us how many of those in the 'Biblioth. Patrum' were made by apostles, or general council, if you can. When Basil the Great had set up a new way of singing to God, and made some other changes in worship, the clergy of Neocesarea were offended with him for the novelty, and told him, that none of that was used in Gregory's days: To whom he answers, that neither was their own litany known in Gregory's days, (who yet had lived not one hundred and forty years before, and was the famous founder of their church by miracles.) Basil, Epist. 63. And Basil added to the clergy of Neocesarea. 'But how can you tell that these things were not in use in Gregory's days, when you have kept nothing unchanged which he was used to?' And that you may see his mind in this; he adds, 'But I pardon all these things, (though God will examine all:) only let the principal things be kept safe.' If we had changed the sacraments, as the Papists have done, viz. a commemorative sacrifice into a real sacrifice of Christ himself; the sacramental body and blood of Christ into the real body and blood; the administration of it in both kinds, into one kind alone, defrauding the people of the cup; the communion into a private mass, the people only looking on the priest, when he receiveth alone himself, &c. I say, had we made such changes as these, they might have called us changelings indeed, and have told us of novelties in the worship of God.

18. Moreover, this laying so much upon lower and unnecessary things, doth impoverish the soul, and make it low, and empty, and formal, according to the matter that it hath to work upon. As the great unquestionable truths of God, are they that sanctify and elevate the soul, and leave their image on it; so will contending about private opinions, or laying out our zeal in ceremonies and shadows, depress the soul and famish it, and turn our religion into a shadow. We find, by sad experience, that people are so prone to turn all religion into mere words, and shows, and customary formalities, that when we have done our best, we cannot cure them of this mortal sin: "God is a Spirit, and will have such worshippers as worship him in spirit and in truth." (John 4:23.) We have little need to cherish this disease of hypocrisy and seeming histrionical outside religiousness, when we see so many perish by it, after all that we can do for their deliverance.

19. And this making a religion of unnecessary things, or laying the church's unity thereon, is a dangerous snare to delude the ignorant and ungodly, and make them believe that they are godly people, and in the way to heaven, as well as others. I use not this, or any argument, against the profitable use of any forms, in order to the understanding of the matter; nor against the due circumstantiating of the worship of God. But if profitable forms, and God's own ordinances, are somewhat liable to this abuse, we cannot devise how to increase the danger, and quite enthral these miserable souls more certainly, than by multiplying unnecessary formalities, and placing religion and unity in them. For they that are most ignorant, and empty of the love and fear of God, and the bitterest enemies to a heavenly life, will presently set in with these formalities, and make themselves a religion of these; and then they will take themselves to be as godly as the best. You shall never make them believe that they are ungodly. They think the difference lieth but in the way and manner of serving God: you serve him one way and they another; but yet they serve him as well as you: yea, they will overdo in these indifferent things, that they may make

up that which is wanting in true godliness; and then they will think that they are better and righter than you. Thus did the heathens cry out against the ancient Christians, with a 'tollete impios,' away with the ungodly; and killed them, and cast them to wild beasts to be torn by them, because they would not worship their idols. And so many ungodly wretches now, that will not be persuaded to a holy life, will yet cry down others as impious, because they observe not all the ceremonies which they observe. When we have used all the means we can to bring them to the study of the Scripture, and to meditate in the law of the Lord, and to holy conference, and fervent prayer; to hatred of sin, the contempt of the world, the mortifying of the flesh, to the love of God above all, to a thankful admiration of the love of Christ, and the great mystery of redemption, to the believing, delightful forethoughts of everlasting life, and preparation for it, &c.; I say, when we have done all to bring them to this which is godliness indeed, we lose our labour, and leave them as we find them. They cannot away with so precise a life: but yet a religion they will have instead of it, to deceive their souls, and quiet them in the way to hell. For instance, I must speak it with grief of heart, that I meet with no small number among us that know not who Christ is; some say he is God and not man. Some say, he is man and not God; some say he was made both God and man at once; some say, he is neither God nor man, but a spirit; some say, he is not God, but the Son of God, and hath the power of God given him: Abundance say, that he is God only and not man, now he is in heaven, though he was both on earth: And very many know not what Christianity is, nor wherein the Christian religion doth consist. And yet all these persons, that are heathens rather than Christians, are the most zealous keepers of Christmas, (as it is called,) and the bitterest condemners of those that do not; and so do make themselves believe that they are Christians as well as others. The same persons that know not who Christ is, nor what it is to be a Christian, are so much for kneeling at the taking of the Lord's-supper, that they dare not be so irreverent as to sit or stand; but will rather never receive at all: (nor are they fit till they change in a greater matter than the gesture:) and yet, poor souls, they think themselves to be very religious, and more reverent than others, and that here lieth the difference between them. It would grieve the heart of a considerate man, to see a multitude of miserable sinners to live in wickedness, in cursing, swearing, drunkenness, filthiness, neglect of God and a holy life, drowned in worldlymindedness, and as regardless of the life to come, as if they thought they should die like the beasts; and even hating those that will not be ungodly as well as they; and yet as hot for ceremonies, and holy-days, and kneeling at the sacrament, and the common-prayer-book, as if they were more devout than others; and it seems they have made themselves believe in good earnest, that they are true Christians and godly men, because in the depth of their ungodliness they can make a stir against those that will not be of their mind, and use these ceremonies as well as they.

If any of you say, that I am now speaking against your opinions or ceremonies themselves, as if I could not give you leave to use them, you will but shew yourselves mistaken hearers, and false reporters. No, it is the laying too much stress on these matters, and making indifferent things seem necessary, as if God's worship, or the unity of the church lay on them, which I speak against: And therefore I must needs say, that both sides may be guilty of this sin: principally the imposers of them, that would have all men forced to do as they do; and next them there may be too much guilt in those that make indifferent things seem evil, or lesser evils to be much greater than they are, and so would make a religion of avoiding what others make it their religion to observe. And whether your religion lie in being for or against these points (in such as the apostle speaks of in my text) is no great difference: for the religion of both will prove but a mere shadow; yea, an over hot opposing of such middle things, doth teach those that are for them to believe that they are matters of very great moment, or else they think you would not make so great a matter of them. And then when you have taught them by your fierce opposition to make a great matter of them; and custom and their party hath taught them to think their way is best; both these set together delude their souls, and make them think that because of their formalities, they are godly men, in the depths of their ignorance, ungodliness and misery.

20. Lastly, observe how we sin against the sad experience of the church in all ages, by laying our religion or unity upon these smaller or unnecessary things. What hath distracted the church so much as contendings about their ceremonies and orders, and precedency and superiority! Heresies I know have done their part (especially the Arians); but smaller matters have had too great a hand in it; what plentiful evidence could I give you of this! The lamentable divisions of the Christian world about Easter-day, which the first General Council was fain to meet about and decide, is too sad an instance. But alas, the present age itself hath given us too sad and plenteous proofs of it. By a heap of ceremonies, and unnecessary things,

the Roman church hath almost drowned both the doctrine, worship and discipline of Christ, and miserably torn the church in pieces, and so continues to do. And what work this mistake hath made in England, I have no mind to tell you, while our smart and sufferings tell you of it more plainly than it is fit for me to do. Indifferent things have shut out that which was better than indifferent. Consider well these twenty reasons, and then judge whether the religion or unity of the church should be placed in unnecessary things. The imposing of them I shall speak of by itself.

Use. From the text and doctrine explained and confirmed, we may see these following consectaries arise.

1. Hence we see the tender mercy of God to them that are sincere in the faith, though weak. If their understandings be dark, and their judgments in lesser things mistaken, and their consciences therein erroneous; yet if they be but true believers, and right in the main, and willing to know the mind of God, and to obey it, God would not have them excluded from the communion of the saints, but rather received with charity and compassion; and would have the stronger bear with their infirmities. (Rom. 15:1.) He will not himself reject them; and therefore he would not have them rejected or despised by his servants.

Use 2. Hence also we may see, that God will bear more, and so must his church, with smaller errors, than with the uncharitable or dividing management of those errors. Though men should err about meats, or days, or such like matters, we must yet receive them and love them as believers: but yet if they will hereupon despise, or censure one another to the breach of charity, and trouble of the church, this must be sharply rebuked, as Paul here doth.

Use 3. Hence also you may learn, how far men should desire and enjoy a liberty in matters of religion, and how far the magistrate should interpose with force, and how far not. A liberty to live in sin, or to subvert the Gospel, and the souls of others, the magistrate should give to none: but a toleration in things of a lower nature, that hazardeth not mens' souls, nor the unity of the church, should be granted to the weak. Can we be bound with charity to receive them, and yet to provoke the magistrate to punish them, and deal more severely with them than we! This may not be desired.

Use 4. Hence also you may see what an enemy Popery is to the unity of the church, and how impossible it is that the church should have unity upon their terms; when they have composed a religion of so many ceremonies, and unnecessary things, and new devised articles; and sacraments;

and none must be a catholic Christian with them that will not be of this religion, and vow or practise all their novelties. So far are they from practising the doctrine of my text, that they set themselves in opposition to it, and place their religion and the unity of their church in such things as Paul here requireth us not so much as to judge one another in; or in worse than these. A catholic unity is impossible on their terms.

Use 5. To conclude, I advise all that are unfeigned friends to the unity of the church, to practise the wholesome doctrine of this text. If you have zeal, there is sin enough in yourselves and others to lay it out upon: Bear not with infidelity, sensuality, impenitency, or any ungodly course. If men be not so much as weak believers, and seem not saints at least of the lower form, receive not these into your communion; but leave them under your common, compassionate charity. If you can prove that God receiveth them not, then do not you receive them. But as you are Christians, take heed of cutting off or despising the members of Christ; and of giving a bill of divorce to any soul that is truly espoused to him: you have drunkards, and railers, and notorious ungodly ones enough to exercise all your zeal, if you join both head and heart and hand against them: and can you find in your hearts to fall upon one another for indifferent things, or smaller matters, which the unity of the church doth not consist in? I speak to both sides impartially; and I beseech you so understand me. What if thy weak brother pray upon a book, darest thou therefore despise him? And what if thy brother pray without a book, darest thou therefore judge him? Nay, darest thou desire that none but such should have liberty to preach or worship in the church? What if thy weak brother dare not receive the sacrament, unless he kneel in the act of receiving it? Darest thou therefore despise him? And what if thy brother on the other side, do rather take it in another gesture, because he is sure that Christ and his apostles sinned not in so doing, and because he finds that our kneeling is contrary to the practice of the ancient church, (yea, 'ad hominem,' I may say,) contrary to General Councils, yea, to the last canon of the first General Council itself, which even the canonists say that no provincial council, or bishops, can repeal (with many other reasons; dare you therefore judge him, because he date not imitate you rather than Christ and his apostles, and the primitive church for many hundred years? If any imagine that I go against this necessary toleration myself, because all here receive the sacrament sitting; I answer, let them prove that ever I refused one person merely because they would take it kneeling, if they can. If you say, Why then are not all admitted to take it kneeling? I answer, soft and fair; there are greater matters than kneeling in the way. Do but first let go your vicious courses, and agree with us in a holy life, and turn unfeignedly to God, and live in the church-order that he hath plainly commanded; and then, if I cannot give you satisfaction, you shall have liberty to take it in the gesture that you desire, so be it you will grant me my liberty as I grant you yours.

One instance more: To-morrow is the day called Christmas-day, and many days called holy-days do follow it; if you will but read and mark this chapter, Rom. 14, I am persuaded it may prevent a great deal of sin, that many of you on both sides may be guilty of. Is it not a wonder that after so large and plain a decision by the Holy Ghost, as here you find, there should yet be any controversy among us about this case? Do you take the word of God for your rule or not? If you do, why then doth it not rule you, and end the difference? Do you not read the apostle's words, "One man esteemeth one day above another; another esteemeth every day alike: Let every man be fully persuaded in his own mind." (verse 14.) If you were Papists that would say the Scripture is obscure, and therefore you must have a General Council, you could scarcely devise how a council should speak more plain than this. But nothing will serve some men, but their own wills. Dare you on the one side, despise your weak brother now for esteeming these days above the rest? Why, perhaps it is to God that he esteemeth, and the ancient custom of the church, and practice of many godly persons, do persuade him that is right: and dare you on the other side condemn or reproach them that make not this difference of days as you do? If we are contented that you have your liberty (which truly I would not deprive you of, if it were in my power), cannot you be contented that we have ours? There are three opinions about these holy-days. 1. Some think the observance of them a necessary religions duty. 2. Some think the very outward observance to be an intolerable sin. 3. Some know that both these extremes are erroneous, and therefore they take the thing in itself to be indifferent, but as circumstances or accidents may make it good or evil: and these are in the right. They that are in the middle can bear with others, but the other cannot bear with them, nor with each other. There is no proof that ever I saw, that the church observed any of these days, for many hundred years after Christ. For the Clement, the Dionysius, the Cyprian, that are cited for it, are known to be spurious. And it is unlikely that none of these would have been mentioned as well as the Lord's-day, if they had been then observed, when there was so much ado about the time of Easter-day. Yea, it is certain that for many hundred years after Christ, it was not agreed on, which was the day of Christ's nativity; some thought it was on January 6, and therefore called it the Epiphany, or Appearance: and of old, both the birth-day and circumcision of Christ were supposed to be on the same day; that is, on the sixth of January, Cassianus witnesseth that the Egyptians were of that mind; Collat. 1. 10. c. 11. And Epiphanius witnesseth the same of the Greek, and Asian, and Syrian churches. Epiphanius himself and Nazianzen, and many others, were of this mind, that it was on January sixth, and that thence it was called the Epiphany. And Chrysostom in Hom. in Natal. Dom. tells us, that it was but ten years before he wrote it, that the Romans had persuaded the church of Constantinople to change the day to December 25. And yet the countries about Jerusalem held to the sixth of January, as Causabon hath shewed, Exercit. 2. cap. 4, p. 170, 171, and cap. 11. p. 186, 187. Yea, indeed the day of Christ's nativity is yet unknown, as if God had kept us ignorant of purpose. Many very learned men, as Broughton, Helvicus, Scaliger, Beroaldus, think that the day was about autumn, in the beginning of October. Calvisius, Paræus, and many more are for other times than December 25, and Jac. Cappellus, and many others, still go to the old way for January 6. And Th. Lydias, out of Clem. Alexandr. is for May 20. Scultetus, Clopenburgius, and many others, do shew, that indeed the time is utterly uncertain. And no wonder if the day be uncertain when the very year is so uncertain, that there is no probability of ever coming to a full agreement about it among the learned in chronology, till the last coming of Christ agree them! Our late most learned chronologer, Bishop Usher, was confident that we were about four years too late in our common account, as in his Annals may be seen. And what man can reveal the things that God hath purposely concealed? For my part, I dare not judge men for keeping or not keeping such days as these. But if any will make it a necessary thing to the universal church, I must resist the usurpation as Paul, that had circumcised Timothy, did cry down circumcision when some would have obtruded it as a necessary thing. And for this I have an argument that sustaineth my religion itself; even the sufficiency of the Holy Scripture. If this be not the law of God, then farewell Christianity. If it be his law, it is sufficient in its kind, and to its ends; which is, 1. To determine of all things that were then fit to be determined of: 2. And to determine of all that the universal church in all times after must be bound to. There is no universal lawgiver but Christ. If this day be of necessity, it was so then as well as now, and it is so to one country as well as another: for there is the same reason for it in one age and place as in another. And, therefore, if Scripture be not a sufficient rule for universal duties of religion, then we are utterly at a loss; and as Popery will come first in, so infidelity is likely to come next. I doubt not but 'pro re nata,' upon emergent occasions, church-governors may appoint religious anniversary solemnities. For the occasion of these being, 1. To some one place or province only: 2. And not existent in Scripture-times; it did not belong to the universal law to determine of them. But in cases that equally belong to the universal church, and where the reason and occasion was existent in the apostles' days as well as now, if there we have not their determination, no others can come after them and make it universally necessary. And indeed neither General Councils nor apostolic tradition, can be pleaded for the necessity. And sure I am, that the one day in seven, even the Lord's-day, of his own appointment, which the universal church hath constantly observed, is a festival for the commemoration of the whole work of redemption, and therefore of the birth of Christ, though especially of the resurrection: and therefore we are not without a day for this use.

I speak not all this to condemn any that use these days, but to excuse those that use them not, and by telling you a few of those many reasons which they have to give for themselves, to persuade you both to lay by the opinion of necessity, and to forbear condemning those that differ from you, and be content that they have their liberty, as we are freely content that you have yours; and lay not the unity and peace of the church upon such things as these, when the Holy Ghost hath so plainly decided the case. And I could heartily wish that the Lord's own day were not most wilfully neglected by many that are most forward for other holy-days. It is a fearful self-delusion of ungodly people, that no means can bring them to a new, a holy, and heavenly life; and yet they will make themselves believe that they are religious, by pleading for forms, and days, and ceremonies. Alas! poor soul, if thy eyes were but opened, thou wouldest see that thou hast other kind of matters first to look after! It would grieve one to hear a man contending for kneeling, and holy-days, and prayer-books, that is in a state of unregeneracy, and a stranger to sanctification, and under the dominion of his sins, and under the curse and wrath of God. Get first a new and holy nature; make sure of the pardon of sin, and of peace with God, and then the discourse of lower matters will be more seasonable and more savoury.

Is it not a shameful self-condemning, to keep holy-days for the dead saints, and to hate and rail against the living? Do you know what kind of men those were that are called saints, and holy-days were kept in remembrance of them? They were such as those that now are hated by the world, and took the course in a holy and diligent care of their salvation, as these do, and therefore were hated by the world, as the godly now are; and when wicked men had put them to death, the godly that survived would keep a day in remembrance of their martyrdom, to encourage others to constancy for Christ. And also because the unruly multitude were so set upon their pleasure, that they kept the idols' festivals for their sport sake; therefore some pastors of the church did think it better to let them have festivals for the saints to take their pleasure in, to turn them off from the idols' festivals. So Gregory Nyssen tells us of Gregory Thaumaturgus in his Oration of his Life, that he made holy-days for his neighbours of Neocesarea, when the Roman fury had martyred many; and he used this as a pious wile, to draw the licentious vulgar from the idols' festivals, by letting them play on the martyrs' days, till they could be drawn up to a holy observation of them. Whether the course were right or wrong, by this you may see the original of such days. And Gregory the Great of Rome would, for this very end, have all the heathens' festivals turned into Christian festivals. But if any of you will hate a saint, and refuse the communion of saints, and will not imitate them in holiness, and yet will keep holy-days for them that are dead, Christ himself hath given you your doom, Matt. 23:29-33, which I desire you to read.

Well, sirs, I have said enough, if enough will serve, to prove that the unity of the church must not be laid on things indifferent, nor upon low and doubtful points; but it must be a unity in the spirit of sanctification. It is the few, the great, the certain, and the necessary points, that we must all agree in if ever we will agree, and compassionately tolerate the differences that are tolerable.

If after all this, there be any so proud, and selfish, and ungodly, and unmerciful, that they will set up their own conceits and wills against the plain commands of God, the long and sad experience of the world, and against the peace of their brethren, and the unity of the church, and will have no agreement unless all others will be conformed to their wills, I shall say no more to such, but that these are not the sons of peace, nor the living compassionate members of the church, but self-idolizers, that God is engaged to pull down: and it is not by such as these that the church must be healed and repaired; but it is by them that are sensible of their own infirmities, and compassionate to others, that are of a Christian catholic spirit, and have catholic principles and affections, and see such a beauty in the image of Christ, that they can heartily love a gracious person, notwithstanding his many tolerable infirmities, and think themselves more unworthy to be tolerated by others, than such as I have described to be tolerated by them.

—Preached December 24, 1657